T0315109

LEARNING BEHIND BARS

Learning behind Bars

How IRA Prisoners Shaped the Peace Process in Ireland

DIETER REINISCH

UNIVERSITY OF TORONTO PRESS
Toronto Buffalo London

© University of Toronto Press 2022
Toronto Buffalo London
utorontopress.com

ISBN 978-1-4875-4582-6 (cloth)
ISBN 978-1-4875-4583-3 (EPUB)
ISBN 978-1-4875-4589-5 (PDF)

Library and Archives Canada Cataloguing in Publication

Title: Learning behind bars : how IRA prisoners shaped
the peace process in Ireland / Dieter Reinisch.
Names: Reinisch, Dieter, author.
Description: Includes bibliographical references and index.
Identifiers: Canadiana (print) 20220223092 | Canadiana (ebook) 20220223254 |
ISBN 9781487545826 (cloth) | ISBN 9781487545833 (EPUB) |
ISBN 9781487545895 (PDF)
Subjects: LCSH: Irish Republican Army – History – 20th century. |
LCSH: Political prisoners – Northern Ireland – History – 20th century. |
LCSH: Northern Ireland – History – 1968–1998.
Classification: LCC HV9649.N67 R45 2022 | DDC 365/.4509416 – dc23

We wish to acknowledge the land on which the University of Toronto Press operates. This land is the traditional territory of the Wendat, the Anishnaabeg, the Haudenosaunee, the Métis, and the Mississaugas of the Credit First Nation.

This book has been published with a financial subsidy from the European University Institute and the National University of Ireland. It is a revised version of a EUI PhD thesis.

University of Toronto Press acknowledges the financial support of the Government of Canada, the Canada Council for the Arts, and the Ontario Arts Council, an agency of the Government of Ontario, for its publishing activities.

To all those imprisoned for crimes they did not commit.

You can chain me,
you can torture me,
you can even destroy this body,
but you will never imprison my mind.

Mahatma Gandhi

By getting that education (on Robben Island), we were actually learning,
ourselves, for the future, not for the present. For the present, it was fight until
the end.

**Sizakele Thomson Gazo, Prison number: 148/64,
a member of the Pan-African Congress of Azania**

Contents

Illustrations

Preface

As I finish the final draft of this manuscript, Ireland remembers the fourteen peaceful civil rights protesters who were shot dead by British army soldiers five decades earlier on Bloody Sunday in Derry. Thousands attended their funerals. One of them was a seventeen-year-old Michael Devine, who remembered: "I will never forget standing in Creggan chapel staring at the brown wooden boxes. We mourned, and Ireland mourned with us. That night more than anything convinced me that there will never be peace in Ireland while Britain remains. When I looked at these coffins, I developed a commitment to the republican cause that I have never lost." Like thousands of his generation, he joined Irish republican guerilla organizations – in his case, the INLA. He was arrested and imprisoned in the H-Blocks of HMP Maze, and on 20 August 1981, he died there on the sixtieth day of his hunger strike. Much has been written about his generation, the internees, and prisoners, and those who died in the prisons. Yet little is known about how they spent their days behind the camp and prison walls – and how they shaped Ireland's future from inside the prisons. This book tells their story.

Acknowledgments

This project started in the hills of Tuscany overlooking the city of Florence in September 2014, after I stumbled over an older article on the Maze prison library in the *Guardian*. Many friends and colleagues offered support and advice that made the journey from idea to book successful. I owe special thanks to my former supervisors, who are not only colleagues but friends: Laura Downs, Alexander Etkind, and Robert W. White. I am especially grateful to my editor at UTP, Stephen Shapiro, who believed in this project since I established the first contact with him and who guided me through the publication process. I also want to thank the three anonymous reviewers and the manuscript review committee at UTP for their valuable comments and suggestions to improve the manuscript. Special thanks also go to Laurence McKeown for permission to reproduce some of the photos he took during a visit to the Long Kesh/Maze site on 8 September 2004.

I am grateful to my friends, colleagues, and everyone who supported me; gave me feedback, advice, and criticism; and made this project a success (in no particular order): Kaan Orhon, Patrick McDonagh, Ciaran Collins, Sean Brady, Nicky Owtram (RIP), Luisa Passerini, Daniel Carey, Anne Kane, Aidan Beatty, Niall O'Dochartaigh, Lorenzo Bosi, Richard English, Carolin Goerzig, Ciaran McDonough, Cristian Cercel, Lucia Martinez, Jim Carroll, Sanjin Ulezic, Sean Moore (RIP), Fergal Moore, Cait Trainor, Kevin Trainor, Georgina Trainor, Carl, Kevin, Patrick Carthy, Philipp Hennig, Fiorenzo Fantaccini, Katharina Meissner-Schoeller, Magnus Schoeller, Felix, Mariusz Kaczka, Dan Hoban (RIP), Helen Aitchison, Liam O'Ruairc, Stefan Berger, Des Long, Annette Long, Matt Conway (RIP), Ruairí Ó Bradaigh (RIP), Manes Weisskircher, Brigid Laffan, Laurence McKeown, Toiréasa Ferris, Anthony McIntyre, Larry, Sean Bresnahan, Seosamh Ó Maoileoin, Maurice Dowling, Josephine Hayden, Róisín Hayden, Lita Campbell, Dermot, Martin McLoone,

Eugene McLoone, Angela Nelson, Geraldine Taylor, Róisín Ni Cha-
thain, Christine Griessler, Ed Moloney, Finbarr McLoughlin, Camilla
Annerfeldt, Victoria Witkowski, Olga Yakushenko, Ekaterina Mity-
urova, Oliver Loksa, Hanita Veljan, Koen Docter, Franco Algieri, Ryan
Crawford, Joern Benzinger, the staff at the National Library of Ireland,
the National Archives of Ireland, the Linen Hall Library, the Special
Collection at NUI Galway, the EUI Library, Nadia Al-Baghdadi and
the whole CEU-IAS team, and Tim Schittekatte and the whole Squadra
Fantastica.

Some of the research for the book was supported by the European
University Institute, Austria's Agency for Education and Internationalization; the Irish Research Council; the National University of Ireland;
and the Institute for Advanced Study, Central European University. In
addition, I had the fortune to write parts of this book as a researcher
and lecturer at the European University Institute, Central European
University, National University of Ireland in Galway, University of St.
Andrews, Ruhr University Bochum, University of Vienna, University of
Salzburg, and Webster Vienna Private University.

Some of the material in the book has appeared in different forms in
a variety of publications over the past years. I am grateful for permission to reproduce material that previously appeared in the *Oral History
Review*, *War & Society*, *Archives: The Journal of the British Records Association*, *Studi Irlandesi: A Journal of Irish Studies*; as chapters in edited
volumes published with Routledge and Springer Nature; and articles
for RTÉ Brainstorm, *Times Higher Education*, *Political Violence at a Glance*,
ORF Science, and The Irish Story. Various sections of this book appeared
in the following journals and edited books:

- "Debating Politics during Confinement: Newly Discovered
  Notebooks of the Sinn Féin Portlaoise Prison Cumann, 1979–1985";
  Archives: The Journal of the British Records Association 56, no. 2 (2021),
  published by Liverpool University Press.
- "Prisoners as Leaders of Political Change: Cage 11 and the Peace
  Process in Northern Ireland"; in Martin Gutmann, ed., *Historians
  on Leadership and Strategy: Case Studies from Antiquity to Modernity*,
  Management for Professionals Series, Basel: Springer Nature, 2020.
- "Political Prisoners and the Irish Language: A North-South
  Comparison"; *Studi irlandesi: A Journal of Irish Studies* 6 (2016),
  published by Florence University Press.
- Dieter Reinisch (2021) "Is Austria a Catholic Country?": Trust
  and Intersubjectivity in Postconflict Northern Ireland, The Oral
  History Review, 48:2, 136–153, DOI: 10.1080/00940798.2021.1941141.

A special thank you to my parents, Wilma and Wolfgang, and my sisters Birgit, Doris, and Elke for believing in me and for all their support throughout the years. Above all, thank you to Melanie, who is always there for me when I need her most.

Galway and Vienna, July 2022

Abbreviations

32CSC / M	32 County Sovereignty Committee / Movement
ANC	African National Congress
BA	British Army
CAIN	Conflict Archive on the Internet
CIRA	Continuity Irish Republican Army
CLMC	Combined Loyalist Military Command
CRA	Civil Rights Association
DUP	Democratic Unionist Party
FARC	Revolutionary Armed Forces of Colombia – People's Army
HMP	Her Majesty's Prison
IICD	Independent International Commission on Decommissioning
INLA	Irish National Liberation Army
IPLO	Irish People's Liberation Army
IRA	Irish Republican Army
IRSM	Irish Republican Socialist Movement
IRSP	Irish Republican Socialist Party
LCR	League of Communist Republicans
LVF	Loyalist Volunteer Force
NICRA	Northern Ireland Civil Rights Association
NIO	Northern Ireland Office
O/C	Officer-in-Command
OIRA	Official Irish Republican Army
ONH / Ó na hÉ	Óglaigh na hÉireann
ORM	Official Republican Movement
OSF	Official Sinn Féin
PIRA	Provisional Irish Republican Army
PLO	Palestine Liberation Organisation

POW	Prisoners of War
PRM	Provisional Republican Movement
PRO	Public Relations Officer
PSF	Provisional Sinn Féin
PSNI	Police Service of Northern Ireland
RIRA	Real Irish Republican Army
RM	Republican Movement
RSF	Republican Sinn Féin
RUC	Royal Ulster Constabulary
SDLP	Social Democratic Labour Party
SF	Sinn Féin
UDA	Ulster Defence Association
UFF	Ulster Freedom Fighters
UUP	Ulster Unionist Party
UVF	Ulster Volunteer Force
WP	Workers' Party of Ireland; also: Sinn Féin – The Workers Party

LEARNING BEHIND BARS

Introduction

In an article for the Belfast-based *Irish News*, Jim Gibney wrote: "I was 17 when I went to my second Easter parade in 1971. My memory of that is a riot, being cautioned by the IRA and wearing a James Connolly badge like it was a fashion accessory to my Wranglers. I later learned about Connolly when I went to prison."[1] Jim Gibney is the former National Organizer of the Irish republican party Sinn Féin. He was first interned in 1971 and later spent six years in prison. He is part of a generation of Irish republican activists and prisoners who were politicized in the early 1970s. In August 1971, the British government launched its internment policy in Ireland.[2] This event marked the beginning of mass incarceration in Northern Ireland. Depending on the sources, at least 20,000 people have been interned or imprisoned for terrorist-related charges or involvement in republican and loyalist organizations on both sides of the Irish border since 1971.[3] Internees were held in large camps without charges or intent to file charges, while prisoners were held in prisons after being charged or on remand awaiting their trial. A large proportion of these young people were imprisoned, and although they demanded to be treated as political prisoners, in fact, they received their political education only once they were in prison.

In this book, I define "political prisoners" as inmates of internment camps and prisons who consider themselves as such. The definition of politically motivated violent prisoners in Ireland has always been contested. Hence, my definition is not a legal definition. However, my definition follows the self-understanding of politically motivated perpetrators and convicts. Since this is a book about Irish republican prisoners, the term "political prisoner" is used for the republican inmates of Irish and British internment camps and prisons evaluated in this study, while I refer to loyalist inmates as "loyalist prisoners." While loyalist prisoners can also be considered political prisoners, I refer to them as loyalist prisoners to avoid conflating their experiences and those of republican prisoners. I, therefore, use "political prisoners" interchangeably with "republican prisoners" and "prisoners of war," which is the term that occurs in Irish republican publications.

I aim to show the relationship between informal political education, including self-organized, informal classes and lectures of Irish republicans, and collective resistance, defending and demanding the Irish political identity in the internment camps and prisons.[4] While the Troubles started in 1968, the mass incarceration of political suspects started only in August 1971. My actors are the individual prisoners belonging to and acting as a collective in these prisons, who made themselves crucial actors in the history of the Northern Ireland conflict. In that sense, I argue that political education was essentially a process of subjectification – the process of becoming a political subject inside and outside the prisons. These Irish republicans were imprisoned with a particular type of subjectivity shaped by their childhood, family, school, and, finally, their political struggle. While they were in prison, their beliefs, feelings, and intentions were reshaped. The self-organized lectures and collective debates formed them politically and strengthened their identity as Irish republican prisoners of war. This understanding enabled them to stage acts of resistance in defence of this developed identity. Self-awareness through self-education empowered young and politically inexperienced individual prisoners to resist as a collective in what US sociologist Erving Goffman calls the total institution that represented the Irish and Northern Irish prison system during the Northern Irish conflict.[5] In essence, this book analyses the significant role in shaping the course of the conflict prisoners played in the internment camps and prisons and examines their contact with the outside movement beyond the high-profile hunger strikes. This story is told by some of these prisoners themselves.

During the 1980s and 1990s, the peace process tried to resolve the conflict in Northern Ireland. Of the many groups supporting this process, one of the most remarkable was the republican prisoners held in internment camps and prisons in Northern Ireland, the Republic of Ireland, and Great Britain. What makes this group remarkable is that they were a collective of political prisoners who were almost entirely politically self-educated. In this book, I focus on the tangible consequence of this self-education: it enabled republican internees and prisoners to influence political developments within their political and military organizations outside the prisons. What is particularly striking is that while Northern Ireland remains "the most heavily researched area on earth,"[6] little is known about life in the internment camps and prisons.

This book, therefore, examines how these republican prisoners lived and became politically aware during internment and imprisonment from 1971 on.

Unlike the republican activists before 1969, those who joined the IRA and Sinn Féin after the outbreak of the conflict in Northern Ireland had looser republican links. Their identity was Catholic and Irish nationalist more than republican.[7] As Jim Gibney recalls, there was no "republican history at all in my family. And probably the way I would define my family would be Catholic."[8] Events on the streets initially politicized activists like Gibney. Still, Gibney only received a systematic grounding in politics and history once he had entered the internment camps and prisons.

In this book, I present the political and informal education of Irish republicans in the internment camps and prisons based on their testimonies. This oral history study is based on thirty-four interviews with Irish republicans who were interned or imprisoned after 1970 in the Republic of Ireland or Northern Ireland. It is the first comparative analysis of Irish republican prisoners on both sides of the Irish border. The majority of my interviewees were members of the Provisional Irish Republican Army (Provisional IRA or PIRA), and a much smaller group of the interviewees were members of other republican groups, like the Official IRA, the Irish National Liberation Army, the Real IRA, and the Continuity IRA.[9]

The informal education and debates within the internment camps and prisons were among the driving forces behind what many scholars have called the politicization/de-radicalization process of the republican movement.[10] As Alex Schmid has shown, the definition of "radicalization" is contested.[11] In the context of the Northern Ireland conflict, the debate mainly emerged around the concept of de-radicalization, in which scholars like Richard English and John F. Morrison see politicization as the driving force behind the de-radicalization of inmates in the internment camps and prisons. Using the writings of the Brazilian philosopher Paulo Freire, Cathal McManus prefers to call this "positive radicalization."[12] Both perspectives share the view that republican prisoners were politicized in the camps and prisons; this politicization led to a shift away from supporting violence. I would argue that both terms are inaccurate. The actions that led the Irish republicans into the camps and prisons – street protests, throwing stones, resisting house raids, building barricades, collecting money for subversive organizations, among others – were political acts already. Hence, the political education the republicans received in the camps and prisons did not lead to politicization, but rather was a process that led them to deepen their political analysis. I, therefore, call this process "political subjectification" rather than politicization.[13] In the case of Northern Ireland, this process led the internees and prisoners to reconsider the tactics and strategies to achieve their ultimate goal: a democratic-socialist, unified Republic of Ireland free from British involvement. While the tactics and strategies undoubtedly changed over the decades, the ultimate goal of replacing the existing states on the island of Ireland with a new form of governance is still a revolutionary act in legal terms. Therefore, the political subjectification of the Irish republicans in the camps and prisons is not a de-radicalization process since their ultimate goal remains radical. However, it did fundamentally impact their perceptions of the conflict. Due to their informal self-education, republican internees and prisoners influenced political developments within their political and military organizations outside the prisons. Hence, the importance of describing how young internees and prisoners developed into political subjects in the internment camps and prisons during the Northern Ireland conflict.[14]

It has often been argued that there is a lack of primary sources used in the study of terrorism and political violence.[15] Andrew Silke commented that "most of what is written about terrorism is written by people who have never met a terrorist and never actually spent time on the ground in the areas most affected by these conflicts."[16] This book is almost entirely based on original interview data that I have collected since 2014. However, the interviews collected in this book will not provide facts, undisputed answers, or even a grand narrative. Instead, I present the evolving identities of political subjects as political prisoners shaped by the developments of their thinking, intellects, and minds during times of incarceration and how they remember these identities and experiences. My book presents a study of memory based on recollections given during personal interviews. Memory is neither right nor wrong – experiences, both individual and collective, shape memory. Furthermore, memory is shaped by environmental, political, economic, and social developments. Finally, memory is shaped by subjectivity and intersubjectivity; it is shaped by the narrator as much as the interviewer. Hence, memory does not narrate facts – it is, moreover, the work of the historian to make sense of memory, namely, creating a new and particular kind of source. Indeed, making sense of memory is what this book aims to do.

I observed seven distinct periods relevant to prisoners' evolution as political subjects in Ireland: three for Portlaoise, the high-security prison in the Republic of Ireland, and four for Long Kesh/HMP Maze in Northern Ireland. Though these were two different prisons run by two different states, the developments were strikingly similar. The first period in Portlaoise was marked by prison protests and hunger strikes between 1973 and 1976/7; the second period after the end of the prison protests was characterized by a liberalization of the prison regime and the development of structured political debate of the Sinn Féin prison Cumann. During these years, the prisoners intensively debated electoralism; the dropping of abstentionism that followed these debates foreshadowed the embracing of the peace process by Provisional republicans in the 1990s. This embrace – in prison characterized by a liberal prison regime that encouraged the prisoners to support the process – is the third phase in Portlaoise.

In Northern Ireland, we witnessed the era of special category status during internment between 1971 and March 1976. Due to short periods of internment, the republicans used their time in the camp to prepare for the continuation of the armed struggle after their release – or escape. This phase ended in 1976 with the introduction of the criminalization policy. From then on, I observed three phases that each shared some similarities with the three phases described in Portlaoise. The first phase of protest between 1976 and 1981 was characterized by a brutal prison regime, isolation, and resistance; the circumstances solely allowed door-to-door lectures. This changed with the reinstatement of de facto special category status in 1982/3. From then on, prisoners had access to reading material and free association. As in Portlaoise, debates arose over the way forward for the republican struggle. These debates were heavily loaded with Marxist rhetoric, which was an essential difference to the situation in Portlaoise. This phase ended abruptly with the fall of the Berlin Wall and the release of Nelson Mandela in 1989/90. From then on, the debates on the peace process evolved within a highly liberal prison regime that encouraged the prisoners to support the process. During these phases, political education was a form of resistance to the criminalization of the prisoners. By politically educating themselves, the republicans found a way of showing the outside population that they were not the same as ordinary criminal prisoners. This understanding of resistance and education let the prisoners use their role in the outside community to become initiators of political change.

The treatment of republican prisoners was arguably the most decisive topic during the conflict in Northern Ireland. Most of these prisoners were still teenagers when they were arrested and charged. The Irish nationalists were not republican fanatics when they resisted British rule in Ireland but young recruits who were radicalized on the streets of Derry and Belfast. One of them was the late Martin McGuinness, who grew up in the Catholic ghetto Bogside before becoming the leader of the Provisional IRA.[17] In an interview before his death, he remembers why he became an Irish republican: "The Duke Street beatings, the attack on Sammy Devenny, and the killing of Cusack and Beattie were the four incidents why I became a republican.... I am a product of British injustice. It was the British and the unionists who made me a republican, not the Christian Brothers."[18] In this comment, McGuinness touches on some aspects discussed in this book. He stresses that his political education did not come from the Congregation of Christian Brothers education – a community that maintained an extensive network of religious schools in Ireland since the early nineteenth century – but from his own experience of British repression on the streets of Northern Ireland after the summer of 1969. This new generation of Provisional Irish republicans was, thus, different from the pre-1969 generations of republicans who were politicized from a young age within their families and by their social background. This post-1969 generation of republicans only received their full political and historical education in the internment camps and prisons, and, as we shall see, the prisoners of this generation made full use of this education. The literature, lectures, and debates established a process that eventually empowered them within – and later also outside – the prison walls. Consequently, many ex-prisoners performed crucial roles in the conflict transformation process in the 1990s and early 2000s.

In the early twentieth century, many Irishmen were radicalized in English internment camps, preparing for revolutionary war in the so-called university of revolution.[19] However, the developments in Ireland since the 1970s demonstrate the opposite.[20] In the Irish arena of the late twentieth century, political prisoners used their time to think, talk, read, and write. While in prison, they prepared for life after their release. The prisoners developed new strategies for a future struggle, but this subsequent struggle would not necessarily be waged utilizing arms. Thus, prisoners organized reading groups, finished Open University degrees, and became community workers after their release.[21] Understanding this process of political subjectification of Irish republican convicts may shed some light on the transformation process of national liberation and non-state wars and insurgencies. To understand this process in Ireland, we need to know what happened in the prisons during these years.

One prisoner held in HMP Maze in the 1980s explains: "Most of the time you'd discuss which kind of Ireland you wanted in jail because when you are out, you have no time.... Mostly in jail, we discussed things."[22] Another prisoner imprisoned in HMP Maze remembered: "We came out of prison very, very politicized about Irish politics, about world politics as well.... I believe because we had the time to do that.

So, people came out of jail very politicized."[23] While the first two prisoners spoke about their experience in the high-security prison HMP Maze during the 1980s, a third prisoner remembered similar experiences from the internment camp in Long Kesh in the 1970s: "I was arrested in 1973 for an armed robbery and jailed in Long Kesh. I was then staying there with a group of people that was heavily politicized. So, I became politically aware very, very quickly.… That politicization process took place only in prison."[24] During imprisonment, former political prisoners had their first contact with political education and literature.

Many of the young activists joined the Provisional republican movement at a young age after the outbreak of the conflict. These activists soon found themselves imprisoned alongside comrades who were demanding to be treated as political prisoners. Under those circumstances, the educational classes organized by the prisoners, the learning of the Irish language, and the organization of a self-acquired prison library was a way to resist the British government's criminalization, which operated in Northern Ireland between 1976 and 1981, by showing the outside communities that, due to their political and historical interest, they were political and not ordinary criminal prisoners.[25]

Becoming political subjects was enabled through debates, readings, and education by the republican prisoners in this restricted space is such a form of resistance. However, the time spent in the internment camps and prisons was not solely a time for political education but often was also a period of rethinking republican principles. Indeed, the time in the internment camps and prisons was particularly crucial for thinking about and formulating what was needed for the next stage of their movement's political and military struggle. This period would see a move away from political violence towards an aspiration to participate in local communities and generate the conditions for conflict transformation, as the following two passages suggest: "During the years in jail, I started to look at politics. In jail, you start to question armed struggle because you have time. You start to look for alternatives. You read about other struggles, Vietnam, Palestine, Cuba.… I don't regret one minute in the armed struggle and in jail."[26] In the second excerpt, a former republican prisoner recalls how he made use of the education he acquired in prison: "When I got released from prison, the last time it was in 1994, I had a different perspective.… From 1994 until these days, I have been involved in political work and agitation, trying to promote the objective of a United Ireland, a political war instead of an armed war. I kept the same objectives and the same determination but a different way to going to win."[27]

A sketch in the booklet "Prison struggle: The story of continuing resistance behind the wire." It shows internment camp activities, such as reading (centre). The original caption reads: "Recreation, constructive pastime or participation in some sort of leisure activity is essential to a POW whether or not he is serving a long or short sentence."
Image courtesy of Dieter Reinisch.

Many prisoners used the knowledge and skills they acquired in prison, either through self-organized lessons, workshops, or formal prison education and the Open University courses, to engage with their communities after their release.[28] Thus, several former prisoners became politicians, social workers, or interface mediators.[29] Without a doubt, the prison libraries compiled by the republicans themselves were a powerful tool in the education process. For instance, the prison library at the high-security prison HMP Maze had some 20,000 books when the prison was finally closed in 2000.[30] Following the closure of HMP Maze, the remaining library was transferred to Belfast and incorporated in the Political Collection of the Linen Hall Library. In an article on collective education in the H-Blocks of HMP Maze, Jacqueline Dana and Seán McMonagle highlight that education represented "crucial steps in gaining freedom."[31] Indeed, the general literature, as well as Dana and McMonagle, paint a picture of "equality," "common society," and "shared development" by organizing "collective educational programmes" based on the writings of Paulo Freire in the internment camps and prisons of Ireland. However, it can be argued that the sole existence of an unelected IRA education officer responsible for the politics, history, and language classes contradicts this notion.

While there is a vast literature on political imprisonment in Northern Ireland, the literature on political imprisonment in the Republic of Ireland mainly focuses on the decades until the 1950s.[32] This is even though, since the outbreak of the Northern Ireland conflict in 1969, a significant number of republican activists have come from the Republic of Ireland, particularly in the decades since the signing of the Good Friday Agreement and the closure of the H-Blocks/HMP Maze in 2000. John Horgan stresses that while dissident paramilitaries confine their armed actions to Northern Ireland, there is a "dominance of the Republic of Ireland in the dissident community."[33] While fewer in number than their Northern Irish compatriots, a significant proportion were Southern republicans during the Northern Ireland conflict.[34] Between 1969 and 1998, over 20 per cent of the Provisional IRA members were convicted in the Republic of Ireland.[35] During the 1970s and 1980s, hundreds of republican prisoners belonging overwhelmingly to the Provisional IRA were imprisoned in the high-security prison Portlaoise. As I suggest elsewhere, these prisoners performed an essential part in the tactics and strategies outside the prisons.[36] Nonetheless, they remain an under-researched subject, with their daily routines largely overlooked apart from former prisoners' studies.[37] Moreover, the daily routine of prisoners has largely been overlooked apart from studies by former prisoners themselves.[38] Mary Rogan reminds us that "there has been no analysis" of political imprisonment in the Republic as compared to Northern Ireland.[39] While historians such as Brian Hanley, Patrick Mulroe, and Gearóid Ó Faoleán have recently published essential contributions to understanding Provisional republicanism in the Republic of Ireland, surprisingly historians have paid relatively little attention to the study of political imprisonment in the Republic during the conflict.[40] The growing literature on imprisonment in the Republic is primarily confined to decades before the outbreak of the Northern Irish conflict.[41]

There is undoubtedly little understanding of political imprisonment in the Republic of Ireland during the Troubles, and our understanding of how internment camps and prisons on both sides of the Irish border operate is guided by official reports, prison authority statements, and governmental documents, as well as memoirs of former inmates and press reports. While the existing literature covers in detail political developments inside and outside the internment camps and prisons, little is known about what internees and prisoners do when locked in their huts and cells. In fact, we know very little of prison life and what happened in prison apart from the period of the prison protests in the H-Blocks of Long Kesh.

The events narrated in this book had a crucial and lasting impact on the transformation of the Provisional republican movement. Political prisoners influenced political developments in two ways: on the one hand, by discussing and developing political positions inside the prison, the prisoners intervened in the political debates of the outside movement. On the other, while prisoners took direct steps of resistance by sparking riots, rejecting cooperation during the blanket and no-wash protests, and embarking on hunger strikes, their influence on outside developments was indirect, for their supporters reacted to the resistance in the prisons. These two forms of agency are shown most vividly in the case of Portlaoise prison. Chapter two discusses the inmates' in-prison subjectivity by telling how collective resistance evolved from the prison protests and how these protests influenced the policy of the republican movement towards their strategies in tackling the criminalization of the prisoners in Northern Ireland. In the years of the prison protest, little focus was given to informal or formal education by the prisoners themselves. In contrast, chapters three and four outline their emerging process of informal education by outlining how the prisoners directly engaged in movement debates outside the prison by organizing themselves in a Sinn Féin Cumann. This structure, the Cumann, oversaw the informal, political education of the prisoners. Republican prisoners started reading, lecturing, discussing, and writing in the internment camps and prisons. Through the collective informal self-education, they empowered themselves.

Subjects are always situated in contested relationships and processes of making.[42] In internment camps and prisons in the late twentieth century, they are formed first by state agencies, in my case the prison authorities, warders, and governors, as well as the British and Irish governments, and, second, by counter-discourses and practices inside and outside prisons, in this case the interaction with comrades in jail, collective actions, and interactions with the political movement outside the prisons. Under those circumstances, the political prisoners influence political debates and decisions inside and outside the prisons. Like Polymeris Voglis and Kieran McEvoy, I argue that the collectivity inside the prisons through the collaborative organization of their everyday life reconstitutes the political prisoners as a subject antagonistic to the prison authorities. Thus, I argue that the transformation of the republican movement in the 1980s and 1990s, supported by the republican prisoners, was the result of an internal debate over how the goals of Irish republicanism could be achieved during the so-called long war.[43] The long war manifested a stalemate, and the prisoners were debating possible exit scenarios while the outside leadership used a section of the prisoners who shared their views to support them publicly on the outside. During this process, the changing politics of the collectivity were interlinked with the remaking of the individual subject.[44] This approach puts me at odds with those who argue that Michel Foucault dismissed the possibility of resistance of the subject.[45] While I use Foucault's theoretical framework to analyse the dialectic of knowledge, education, and resistance in prisons, I go further than Foucault and argue that it is, indeed, possible for the subject, the political prisoners, to resist as a subject if a collective inside the prison supports the subject.[46]

In the book, I use three categories of sources: interviews with former republican prisoners; archival sources from the Linen Hall Library, the National Archives of Ireland, the National Library of Ireland, and private collections; and, finally, the memoirs of former republican prisoners. To collect the data, qualitative expert interviews were conducted with female and male former political prisoners from the following republican factions: the Provisional republican movement (Provisional IRA, Provisional Sinn Féin, Cumann na mBan pre-1986, Na Fianna Éireann pre-1986), the Official republican movement (Official IRA), the republican socialist movement (Irish National Liberation Army, Irish Republican Socialist Party, Republican Youth Movement), and so-called dissident republican organizations (Republican Sinn Féin, Continuity IRA, Cumann na mBan post-1986, Na Fianna Éireann post-1986, Real IRA, 32 County Sovereignty Movement, Republican Network for Unity, Óglaigh na hÉireann). Prisoners belonging to these organizations were held in the following prisons in Ireland: Mountjoy, Dublin City; Portlaoise, Co Laois; Limerick, Limerick City; Castlerea Prison, Co Roscommon (all in the Republic of Ireland); Magilligan, Co Derry; Long Kesh/HMP Maze, Co Antrim; Hydebank, Belfast City; Crumlin Road Prison, Belfast City; HMP Armagh, Armagh City; Maghaberry, Co Antrim; Maidstone (all in Northern Ireland).

Between 2014 and 2018, I conducted thirty-four interviews with former Irish republican inmates of internment camps and prisons in Northern Ireland and the Republic. These interviews are part of my ongoing oral history research on the Northern Ireland Troubles. Since 2010, I have interviewed more than ninety Irish republicans; forty-one of these interview partners are quoted in this book. Some of my narrators were active in various areas or moved between different areas during their activism. Six narrators are West Belfast Provisional IRA members, eight are Provisional IRA members from other areas of Northern Ireland or the Border Counties, and twelve are Provisional IRA members from the Republic of Ireland. Some of these interviewees later left the Provisional IRA and joined dissident republican organizations, whereas three interview partners directly joined dissident organizations. Nine interview partners were members of the IRSP or the INLA, and three women were in Cumann na mBan. Hence, of the forty-one interviews quoted in this book, three were women and thirty-eight were men. Approximately one-third were overwhelmingly active in the Republic of Ireland, while two-thirds were primarily active in Northern Ireland. Of the thirty-eight men, thirty-four are former internees or prisoners. The archival sources include prisoners' writings, such as political documents, communiqué, letters to the editor, or statements. All these writings were produced inside and, overwhelmingly, smuggled out of the camps and prisons as tiny communiqué. Furthermore, many former prisoners – both republican and loyalist – have published memoirs in recent years, and I use this genre as an additional source.

Interestingly, being an outsider to the Irish republican prisoners' community helped me obtain candid interviews despite the subject's sensitive nature.[47] Most of my interview partners gave their first interview to a researcher; thus, building trust was essential to establishing a fruitful conversation that could be audio recorded. I observed two main reasons that established trust in me and my research. First, my go-betweens, or gatekeepers, are well-known and highly respected republicans who served as members of the republican movement for several decades. For example, during the interviews, several interview partners mentioned that they only agreed to meet me because of the person that established the initial contact between me and the narrator. They specifically emphasized that "if he trusts you, I know that I can trust you too."

The second aspect was my appearance and my background. Most of the interview partners had joined the republican movement several decades ago. By contrast, I was still a young PhD researcher at the European University Institute in Florence when developing my first contact with these Irish republicans. Hence, the age difference made it possible that some of these interview partners could have been my grandfathers. This circumstance established a generational hierarchy between the narrators and me during the interviews. In this case, I was perceived, consistent with the typology of Alexander Bogner and

Wolfgang Menz, as "layman."[48] This positioning of the "interviewer as a layman" enabled me, on the one hand, to gain a high level of trust and, on the other hand, experience "*reverse* power relations."[49] In other words, a postgraduate student who could be the son or grandson of most of the interview partners was not perceived as a potential threat to them. However, this age difference can reflect patronizing approaches that would impact the data collection in another research setting. While interviewing Northern Irish politicians, Joanne McEvoy, for example, was approached as "daughter" by some politicians and referred to as "love," "dear," or "lass" by interview partners.[50] My Austrian origin was another feature of my appearance that turned out to play an even more beneficial role in the trust-building process. I will underline this observation with two comments made during both post-interview conversations. The first comment was directed towards the affiliated institution of the initial research. Before pursuing a PhD at the EUI, I had studied history at the University of Vienna. During those years, I conducted my first interviews with Irish republican women. Following a conversation with Eithne,[51] a member of the republican women's wing Cumann na mBan from West Belfast, she offered me another cup of tea and asked:

EITHNE: You said you are studying in Austria?

ME: Yes, at the University of Vienna.

EITHNE: Mhm.… [nodding] You know, that's why I gave you an interview. I speak with you because you are coming from Austria. You are from Europe – you make up your own mind. I am not worried because you are from Europe. I am very worried when students from Britain come and say they want to talk to me, you know. I always wonder why they want to interview me. What do they want to know? Why do they come? What are they doing with the interviews? To whom are they giving the interview recordings? Are they handing it over to someone? You never know! I would never do an interview with any student from Oxford or any of these universities, you know, all the spooks are from Oxford. They are training the spooks there, MI5, intelligence service, they are all there.[52]

Eithne, a republican woman from Belfast who joined the republican movement in the early 1970s and shortly afterwards was interned and, following her release, held various leading ranks within Cumann na mBan, explains that she trusts me more than any other researcher coming from a British institution. Despite lacking any knowledge of my social or family background or my political views on the Northern Ireland conflict, she developed trust in me and assumed impartiality by saying "you are from Europe – you make up your own mind." She further assumes that researchers from British institutions are not only politically biased on the Northern Ireland conflict but also that those from certain institutions are even "spooks" rather than genuine researchers. To be sure, "spook" is a term used in Irish republican circles for British citizens working for British security services such as MI5 or Scotland Yard. In other words, the fact that I was coming from a continental European university convinced Eithne that I am non-partisan and neutral. In contrast, researchers at British universities are, in her opinion, not only biased but, furthermore, possibly MI5 agents rather than researchers.

The second comment reflects on the Christian congregation of the Austrian population. Aoife was a member of Cumann na mBan and its youth wing Cumann na gCailíní during the 1970s in Belfast. She later moved to Dundalk, just south of the border. Following the interview in one of her friends' houses in Beechmount, West Belfast, she told me about her planned summer vacation and skiing trips. She then asked me: "By the way, is Austria, actually, a Catholic country?" Stunned by this question that I had never received from any of my interviewees before, I just stuttered "Yes," which led to her comment "That is good, so you understand what I am talking about."[53] This comment reflects the experience that narrators feel more comfortable during the interview when they feel understood by the interviewer. Yvonne McKenna suggests that the shared background with her narrators allowed them to say things "they would not otherwise have said."[54] In my case, the feeling of security was reinforced since I came from a Catholic country and the interview partner was Catholic. Interestingly, she did not ask me if I am Catholic myself. Instead, she merely assumed that I was practising my Catholic belief. The Northern Ireland conflict is frequently portrayed as a conflict between a pro-British, Protestant majority and a pro-Irish, Catholic minority. Coming from a Catholic country myself was a sufficient reason for my interview partner to suggest that I understand the desires and woes of the Catholic minority, which led to the struggle of the republican movement. The perception that an – imagined – similar background leads to shared world views has been observed by several oral historians, such as Kathleen Blee in her study on women in the Ku Klux Klan. In her introduction, Blee notes: "My own background in Indiana (where I lived from primary school through college) and white skin led informants to assume – lacking spoken evidence to the contrary – that I shared their worldview."[55] Like Blee's background in Indiana and her white skin, my background in a Catholic country led my informants to see me as one of them.

McEvoy made similar experiences, "where the respondent assumes the researcher is on their 'side.'"[56]

Even though asking if Austria is a Catholic country is unusual, it does make sense in the Northern Irish context. In recent years, a contrast between the Western Christian society and the Muslim "other" has dominated public perception. Hence, while people are faced with questions of Christian or Muslim backgrounds, the breakdown into Christian congregations is less familiar, except for the Russian Orthodox church due to its close links with the Putin regime. The importance of the Catholic background becomes even more remarkable, considering the political understanding of the Irish republican movement. While the Northern Ireland conflict is often portrayed as a sectarian conflict between Protestants and Catholics, Irish republicans reject this "Catholic defenders" label. Instead, they argue that they are fighting a national liberation struggle. Consequently, the republican movement rejects the label of a Catholic movement. My interview partner, Aoife, emphasized that she is not practising her religion and that she "would not call [herself] very religious." However, Aoife indeed projected her own religious framework on me, and, although she is not practising her religion herself, this projection shaped her answers during the interview. This phenomenon of people who claim religious affiliation but neither practise nor believe is described by Claire Mitchell as an "ethnic marker" in the Northern Irish context.[57] In other words, despite Irish republican pleas of their religiously non-sectarian ideology, the presence of an interviewer with a non-British, Catholic background gives Irish republican narrators a higher level of security. Consequently, my background in a Catholic country not only built trust between me and the narrator, but it also led her to the conclusion that I, seemingly Catholic, understand the situation and calamities of the Catholic Irish population well, despite the apparent differences in the history and politics of Austria and Ireland.

To sum it up, the interviewer serves as a projection screen for the expectations and fear of the narrator. This projection screen determines, among other factors, the level of trust that is built between the narrator and the interviewer. In my case study, the level of trust is crucial not only to get access to interview partners but also before, during, and after the interview process to get interview material suitable for answering the research question since the organization under study is proscribed as terrorist. Like Ben Crewe, who writes that his "masculine identity and personal circumstances shaped the dynamics" of his own research with imprisoned men, my Austrian background unintentionally shaped my own fieldwork with Irish republicans.[58] The projection of the narrator on the interviewer shaped the whole process of the field research from the first contact with Irish republicans until the conclusion of the last interview. I will not claim that this oral history research would have been made impossible coming from another background, although Paul Arthur notes the success of his interviews with Irish politicians because they trusted him due to his own background.[59] However, considering the comment of "British spooks" trained at the University of Oxford made by interview partner Eithne, I am persuaded that my field research could have seen a significantly different outcome if I was coming from another background.[60] While activists emphasize that their political motivation for republican involvement is not religiously driven, the republicans were raised in a Catholic environment, and thus these subjective experiences shape their answers and attitudes towards the interviewer.

Chapter One

The Irish Prison Arena: Republican Prisoners and the Northern Ireland Conflict

Irish republican prisoners played a decisive role in the history and politics of Ireland throughout the twentieth century. Following the 1916 Easter Rising, thousands of suspected republicans were arrested and shipped from Ireland to the Frongoch internment camp in North Wales. These prisoners used their time in the camp to prepare for the independence struggle following their release, making Frongoch truly a "University of Revolution."[1] Many other prisoners, including Harry Boland, Éamon de Valera, and others, were held in prisons across Britain, such as Dartmoor; also, republican women were held in jails rather than camps. Since then, the political prisoners have determined the course of the Irish conflict on both sides of the border. In the south, the later Republic of Ireland, thousands of republicans were imprisoned during the civil war or interned in the 1930s, 1940s, 1950s, and 1960s by the Irish government.[2] In Northern Ireland, the main prison holding republican prisoners between the establishment of the northern state and the outbreak of the conflict was Crumlin Road Prison in Belfast.[3]

The conflict in Northern Ireland is the longest armed conflict in the Western hemisphere, resulting in more than 3,500 deaths between 1968 and 1998. There were three groups of armed forces involved in this conflict. The first was the British Army; the police force Royal Ulster Constabulary (RUC), later renamed the Police Service of Northern Ireland (PSNI); and the British intelligence services, mainly MI5. The second group were loyalist paramilitary organizations such as the Ulster Defence Association (UDA) and Ulster Volunteer Force (UVF), as well as smaller groups like the Red Hand Commando (RHC) and the Loyalist Volunteer Force (LVF). The political ideology of these groups was unionism. Unionism means the support of the union between Northern Ireland and the rest of the United Kingdom. On the other hand, loyalism is a sociopolitical term that describes working-class unionists willing to take up arms to defend this union. The third group were republican paramilitaries such as the Provisional Irish Republican Army (IRA), the Official IRA, as well as those groups opposed to the current conflict transformation process, like the Irish National Liberation Army (INLA), the Real IRA, the Continuity IRA, and the New IRA. The latter groups are frequently subsumed under the umbrella term "dissident republicans."[4] Irish republicans are Irish nationalists, overwhelmingly Catholic, who support the reunification of Northern Ireland with the Republic. Thus, it is wrong to characterize the conflict in Northern Ireland as religious. As political scientist Joanne McEvoy states, the conflict does not contain a religious element in any real sense, but rather "is about two groups with allegiance to two different national communities. [Hence, it] is about national identity whereby the Nationalist community look to the Republic of Ireland as the 'motherland' whereas the Unionist community looks to Britain as their patron state."[5] Despite recent outbreaks of violence and the obstacles surrounding the recent Brexit negotiations, an attempt to end this conflict with the signing of the Good Friday Agreement in 1998 was largely successful.[6]

The British Army was deployed to the region in the summer of 1969, following violent clashes and pogroms against the Catholic population in the previous weeks and months. Over the following two years, the conflict erupted into open war between Irish republicans, loyalist paramilitaries, and the British Army.[7] This violence brought the local government to a standstill. In an attempt to control the situation, a series of sweeping laws gave the British security forces, the British Army, the RUC, and the Ulster Defence Regiment enormous power to arrest and detain citizens. These new laws permitted the authorities to strike at republican and loyalist activists. The legislation that was to have the most severe impact on the future course of Northern Ireland was the restructuring of the Special Powers Act of 1922 by the local Stormont government in 1971. This restructuring enforced an internment policy allowing the arrest, detention, and imprisonment of activists without trial.[8] On 9 August 1971, the British Army launched Operation Demetrius, interning 342 people in the first 24 hours.[9] In parallel to these developments, English judge Lord Diplock issued the Diplock Report. The findings of this report allowed a single judge to convict any suspected terrorist on the sole basis of his confession procured by any member of the RUC. These legislative changes were followed by abolishing the local parliament and introducing Direct Rule from London in 1972.[10] Furthermore, the Emergency Provisions Act came into being in 1973. This act included that all those detained and convicted to more than nine months' imprisonment were granted special category status,

External cage of compound 19 in the Long Kesh internment camp.
The photo was taken on 8 September 2004. Image courtesy of
Laurence McKeown.

and thereby republican and loyalist prisoners were legally distinct from ordinary prisoners.[11]

This policy change was forced by a hunger strike of the IRA prisoners led by an earlier Belfast republican veteran Billy McKee in Crumlin Road Prison. McKee and his fellow prisoners demanded prisoner of war (PoW) status based on the claim that Irish prisoners arrested after the 1916 Easter Rising had also been granted PoW status by the British government, similar to the imprisoned German soldiers during the First World War. The republican prisoners in Northern Ireland enjoyed a great deal of autonomy due to this special category status. They were, furthermore, exempted from regular prison work; were permitted to wear their own clothes; could receive more visitors, letters, and parcels than ordinary prisoners; and were organized within their own military structures. The internment camp and prison authorities recognized this military structure, and thereby the British government acknowledged the prisoners as different to ordinary criminal prisoners.[12]

In 1975 Lord Gardiner concluded a report that "the introducing of Special Category Status for convicted prisoners was a serious mistake."

The Gardiner Report served as a pretext for the British Labour government to revoke special category status from March 1976 onwards. After that date, prisoners convicted of terrorist acts or membership of republican paramilitaries were treated as ordinary prisoners and held in the newly built H-Blocks. In contrast, those convicted before this date continued to enjoy special category status just yards away in the huts of Long Kesh internment camp. The H-Blocks and the Long Kesh huts formed Northern Ireland's central high-security prison complex HMP Maze, twenty miles west of Belfast.[13] The first prisoner to be convicted after the phasing out of special category status was Kieran Nugent. He entered the H-Blocks on 15 September 1976 and refused to wear a prison uniform. As a consequence, he was thrown into his cell naked. The only piece of fabric he had to cover his body was a blanket. This act of resistance to the new criminalization policy started the blanket protest of the IRA and INLA prisoners demanding to be treated as political prisoners for, as they argued, their struggle was political and not criminal.[14]

The records of how many people experienced time in internment camps and prisons due to the conflict since 1969 are not precise. According to various surveys, the number of political internees and prisoners in Northern Ireland since 1969 ranges from 20,000 to 25,000; some even suggest a number as high as 30,000. However, comprehensive numbers for political imprisonment in the Republic of Ireland since 1970 do not exist.[15] In 2007, Peter Shirlow and Kieran McEvoy published one of the most detailed studies, in which they estimate that 15,000 nationalists/republicans and between 5,000 and 10,000 unionists/loyalists were interned or imprisoned until then.[16] In a later report, the OFMDFM even estimated up to 30,000 former political prisoners in Northern Ireland.[17] However, the OFMDFM report gives neither the data used nor tells the reader how the figure of 30,000 former political prisoners in Northern Ireland was calculated.

Considering its relatively small size of 13,843 square kilometres and population of 1.8 million inhabitants, Northern Ireland has generated a remarkable number of political prisoners from both sides of the divide; to say it in the words of Brendan O'Leary, it shows that an "extraordinary high proportion of Northern Irish working-class Catholic males who matured after 1969 have been through IRA ranks."[18] Ruth Jamieson et al. concluded that former political prisoners make up between 14 per cent and 31 per cent of the male population aged between fifty and fifty-nine, and between 4 per cent and 12 per cent of those between sixty and sixty-four.[19] Still, it must be pointed out that these figures relate only to those who have been sentenced and served time for offences related to the recent conflict.[20] The numbers are much more precise concerning the internment period in the early 1970s: 342 men were interned initially.[21] A total of 1,981 people, among them about 30 women, were interned; 1,875 were nationalists/republicans, and 107 were unionists/loyalists. In sum, it can be suggested that 20,000–25,000 people went through internment camps and prisons for suspected terrorist activities or political involvement of republican or loyalist groups during the Northern Ireland conflict from 1968 to 2000.

The status of republican and loyalist prisoners was a contested area of the Troubles. The question of the perception of the prisoners is crucial to our understanding of the conflict, as Sibylle Scheipers writes: "The question of the applicability of the law became even more important in the war of decolonization in the second half of the twentieth century since … granting POW status to prisoners in those wars was often perceived as acknowledging the political legitimacy of their cause."[22] This question was the cause of most prison protests in both Northern Ireland and the Republic. The men and women arrested for terrorist offences or interned for their political activities in Ireland belonged to various organizations. The members of nationalist paramilitaries of the Provisional IRA, the INLA, and their political organizations claimed a right to special treatment as prisoners of war. On the other hand, the British government rejected the notion that an international war existed in Northern Ireland and, because of that, insisted on treating the prisoners as ordinary criminals under British domestic law.[23] Samantha Caesar argues a strong case for characterizing the Northern Ireland conflict as an international rather than a non-international war under international law. Therefore, she writes that the British government should have continued to grant special category status to the republican prisoners after this policy was phased out in 1975. Accordingly, she concludes that "the revocation of Special Category Status was a mistake."[24]

The republican prisoners are usually referred to as political prisoners by their supporters. Consequently, they were engaged in various prison protests to be recognized as political prisoners and, as such, gain political status within the prison. Over the previous five decades, these protests ranged from blanket protests and no-wash protests for the recognition as political prisoners in British prisons in the late 1970s to solidarity protests in the women's prison HMP Armagh and the Republic's high-security prison Portlaoise to the hunger strikes in 1980/1 and anti–strip search protests in Portlaoise and Armagh to the demand for segregation in Maghaberry Prison in the early 2000s and the recent protests of dissident republican prisoners in Maghaberry Prison.[25] However, while all these different protests are usually summed up as "the struggle for political status," their demands did vary tremendously during those protests. In other words, the claims of the republican prisoners and their supporters have been "neither consistent nor unambiguous."[26]

The category of Prisoner of War is based on the 1949 Geneva Convention on the humanitarian laws of war and its amendments of 1977, known as Protocols I and II. These Geneva Conventions and their additional protocols form the core of the international humanitarian law, which regulates the conduct of armed conflict and seeks to limit its effects. The 1949 Convention could not apply to republican prisoners, as they were not engaged in conventional warfare; however, its 1977 Protocol II dealt with rebellions and guerrilla warfare. Nonetheless, there is no political status in domestic or international courts, and even taking legal precedents into account, republican prisoners never had Prisoner of War or Political Prisoner status, Liam O'Ruairc argues.[27] So, when republicans refer to their official recognition as political prisoners in Northern Ireland during 1972 and 1976, they mean essentially special category status.[28] The granting of this special category status was de facto recognition of the British government that the prisoners were engaged in politically motivated acts and thus distinguished from "ordinary decent criminals."

The situation in the Republic is similar to the one in Northern Ireland. In the Republic, IRA prisoners have been held in the high-security prison Portlaoise. The Irish government also de facto recognizes the validity of the cases of the republican prisoners.[29] Hence, for lengthy periods during the past four decades, both the British government and the Irish government have acknowledged the political motivation of unlawful acts by republican prisoners as opposed to "ordinary criminal" prisoners. Consequently, Clive Walker has argued along those lines, writing that "The disparate claims to some form of special treatment for convicted republican prisoners can be rejected with confidence as almost totally without foundation in domestic or international law. However, this formalistic legal conclusion in no way pre-empts the answer which might be given on the basis of moral or political considerations. As the history of Ireland has repeatedly shown, law and justice are by no means inseparable companions."[30] Contrary to Walker, Samantha Anne Caesar argues that "Under international law, as it exists and applies to Britain today, the IRA prisoners of the 1970s and 1980s would be entitled POW status. Even if the conflict was classified as non-international, the IRA prisoners still should have been afforded some distinguished sort of status, because the British government derogated from Common article 3 when it instated internment and Diplock prosecutions. For that reason, the British government should have retained special category status for the IRA under international law as it did, in fact, apply at the height of the Troubles."[31] Andrew Silke explains: "Even using the term 'political prisoner' is shunned [by governments]. Terrorist prisoners rarely describe themselves as 'terrorists'. Instead, they portray themselves as soldiers, freedom fighters, volunteers, partisans, the resistance (at least in their own minds if nowhere else). Normally they bitterly contest any effort to describe them as criminals. Many, though, will refer to themselves as 'political prisoners'."[32]

What Silke describes is also the case in the Irish context since republican activists and their supporters usually refer to all republican prisoners as political prisoners. Going one step further, Silke analyses the UN framework and concludes that under this framework, most terrorist prisoners can be "reasonably referred to as political prisoners, though, not surprisingly, most governments prefer to avoid this term out of fear that it might transfer some apparent legitimacy to the terrorists and their cause."[33] Contrary to Silke's observation, Peter Shirlow et al. use "paramilitary prisoners" and "politically motivated prisoners" for both loyalist and republican prisoners.[34] Similarly, Tracey Irwin distinguishes between "political prisoners" and "ordinary prisoners." According to her, political prisoners justify their behaviour on political grounds, whereas ordinary prisoners are unable to do so.[35] Nonetheless, following Silke's argumentation, I will use the term "political prisoners."

The main factors distinguishing recruits of contemporary extremist organizations are ideology and education in general and higher education in particular. Diego Gambetta and Steffen Hertog show that engineers are overrepresented in Islamist terrorist organizations and frequently among right-wing extremist movements in the developed world. Furthermore, graduates in the humanities and the social sciences will disproportionately join left-wing extremist groups.[36] Conversely, I argue that recruits of national liberation movements in Europe are educationally disadvantaged. Thus, activists of national liberation movements develop their interest in political education in prison. Their developing interest in political and historical debate leads them to higher education by enrolling in university degrees, such as Open University. To illustrate my argument, I am using the Irish republican movement during the first decade of the Northern Irish conflict as an example. In particular, I look into the knowledge production of Irish history and the Irish nationalism of activists. Thereby, I aim to understand what knowledge of Irish history and nationalism they had when joining republican and nationalist organizations and what knowledge they obtained while active within these organizations.

Former republican prisoners tell their story more successfully in public than other groups involved in the conflict. There are three reasons for that. First, republicans are portrayed as being more interested in politics than loyalists. Second, prisoners put much effort into informal (self) education and, later, formal education; this provides the prisoners with the necessary skills to publicly tell their stories. Third, specific local communities in Northern Ireland consider political prisoners as their heroes and martyrs.[37] Morrison writes that "historically, the prisoners have been among the most trusted and revered actors with the Irish republican movement."[38] While I will discuss the third point later, I will first examine the political and historical education of former republican prisoners before their first arrest.

Analysing the internees and political prisoners offers valuable insights into this group's social structure and educational background. Thus, several studies show that most political prisoners were young men when first sentenced;[39] precisely, two-thirds were twenty-one years of age or younger when first imprisoned, and 72 per cent spent five or more years in prison.[40] For example, a study of forty republican ex-prisoners in North Belfast shows that 50 per cent had no qualifications, 27.5 per cent held a GCSE or equivalent, 2.5 per cent had A-levels or equivalent, and 20 per cent had a degree.[41] Indeed, while 50 per cent of these prisoners had no qualifications when imprisoned, another study conducted with sixty-four republican ex-prisoners shows that 53 per cent gained academic qualifications during imprisonment.[42] Furthermore, Michael Ritchie's study of 640 republican ex-prisoners from West Belfast shows that nearly two-thirds were unemployed before being interned or arrested.[43] As Laurence McKeown recounts, it was not "a hotbed of revolutionaries" during the early days of the Long Kesh internment camp. Contrary to the idea of a revolutionary place, he writes that most of the internees had not arrived at prison educated in Irish republican history and ideology. Instead, the internees "largely responded to the situation on the ground, in their streets and community. Most of them were in their late teens or early 20s and more interested in lectures and discussion about guns and explosives than politics." Consequently, Long Kesh was "not really a highly politicized environment" at that time.[44] In essence, the majority of the republican ex-prisoners were very young men when first interned or imprisoned (under twenty-one), they served a long time in the internment camps and prisons (more than five years), and most of them had no secondary education at all.

Considering these characteristics and previous research, the republican internees and prisoners can be classified into two categories following the different paths of their involvement. The first category is republican activists who were active in republican organizations before the outbreak of the Troubles in 1968/9. These activists were attracted to republicanism by political ideology and biographical continuity. Most came from republican backgrounds and gained political and historical education from their parents and friends. The second category is those republican activists recruited after the outbreak of the conflict. Although, contrary to the pre-1969 recruits, these activists were driven by a feeling of "defending the nationalist/Catholic people," they furthermore had very little or no political education and knowledge of Irish history and republican ideology.

The republican movement in the 1970s did not provide structured educational classes for their young recruits. While young recruits joined the youth organizations Na Fianna Éireann for boys and Cumann na gCailíní for girls, they received training in transporting, parading, drilling, and the use of weapons. Individual local recruitment officers or comrades occasionally provided boys and girls with books of a historical and nationalist nature, but there was no political educational program for recruits. For example, Anthony McIntyre joined Official Fianna Éireann in 1974, when he was sixteen. In that year, he was arrested for the first time and brought to the Long Kesh internment camp. Asked how he would describe his political education when joining the republican movement, he said:

> Very little, you know, everyone had some political knowledge, but I wasn't politicised....
>
> DR: *When did you leave school?*
> I finished school at fifteen. I think it was three days after my fifteenth birthday that I left school and i started working. I had a very poor education, not that I wasn't offered any good education, but I was intellectually lazy. I was interested in other things. I didn't have a great concentration span for things that didn't attract my attention. I could become bored easily. But I read, and I was articulate enough for my age....
>
> DR: *Did the republican movement offer education classes when you joined?*
> No, they offered me a rifle, experience of the street, their experience, their advice. They didn't train me properly. I don't blame them because I was eager for – they didn't offer me any education, no. When I went to prison, they were talking about *Éire Nua*, and I remember my friend Davy Clinton sitting down and reading *Éire Nua*.... So, there was no educational programme, no attempt to cultivate intellectual debate, in my view. There were Irish classes, but there were no political education classes, and political education was not encouraged in jail at that time.[45]

McIntyre's account shows that the republican movement was either unable or unwilling to provide political education to its recruits in the early 1970s. The year 1974 was a bloody one, and the republican movement was in ceasefire talks with the British government. In that period, the Provisional republican movement was more concerned with winning recruits to carry on their war against the British Army and the RUC than politically and historically educating their new members. McIntyre had received a conservative education at school and had been introduced to events like the 1916 Easter Rising and the War of Independence. However, as he mentions, he was only politicized due to his experience with the war when growing up in Belfast. This "experience of the street" that interview partners such as McIntyre refer to was one of the reasons for the developing political awareness of teenagers and young adults in Northern Ireland during the 1970s. McIntyre only started reading and developing an interest in politics when interned. There, as he mentioned, he read his first political book – an autobiography of Angela Davis. He got that book from a fellow inmate. McIntyre immediately established a keen interest in politics and history and became educational officer of the IRA in the H-Blocks in the 1980s. He also started Open University courses in prison and defended a PhD at Queen's University Belfast after his release. McIntyre became a republican because he had experienced repression on the streets. Yet his systematic political education came only later when comrades sparked his interest in reading and discussing in jail. He subsequently embarked on a journey that led him from teenage street rioter to a PhD student at Belfast's Queen's University. McIntyre is only one of many Irish republican activists who made this journey.

For the most part, the narrators from Northern Ireland tell that the political and historical education during the 1970s was rudimentary. Due to the sectarian policy of the local government since partition and the segregated school system, children received no historical or political education in school. The Christian Brothers schools were an exception. However, the conservative and Catholic character sparked Irish nationalist identity among the pupils rather than the quality of the teaching. Therefore, children's historical and political understanding before their first imprisonment remained superficial even after joining political organizations. Indeed, the "experience of the street" sparked historical and political interest and knowledge among them. I identified two areas where nationalist children developed their political and historical knowledge. The first area, as mentioned, is a conservative and Catholic education in Christian Brothers schools. The second area is family and friends.

Northern Ireland's capital is Belfast, historically a nationalist rather than a republican city. The republican movement in Belfast was weak before the outbreak of the conflict in 1968. The republican movement circled around a few families with strong republican traditions. Hence, many of the new, young recruits after 1969 had no republican background whatsoever. Therefore, these young people had not received a historical or political education from their families. Since most of them left school as early as possible, they also did not receive higher education. Notably, uninterested in reading in general, and politics and history in particular, they only became politicized by experiencing the conflict. Gerard Hodgins grew up in the nationalist Andersonstown neighbourhood of West Belfast and joined the republican movement in 1971. He outlines his historical, political, and nationalist education at that time:

> First of all, I had no education whatsoever in regards to Irish republicanism. I couldn't have told you about the 1916 Rising or any of these events because in my school, what we learned were the Kings and Queens of England, you know. Irish history wasn't taught, although it was a Catholic school, but that was the deal. The Catholic Church stuck with the Unionist government in Stormont…. So I learned my Republicanism through the events that were happening around about me in the early 1970s and also through the books I was reading, you know, I read all these classics, Dan Breen's *Fight for Irish Freedom*, [Tom] Barry's *Guerrilla Days* in Ireland and stuff like that.[46]

Hodgins's comments are typical for the interview partners who joined the republican movement in the early 1970s. Like most interviewees who grew up in the nationalist ghettos, they stress that they had little knowledge of politics or republicanism when they became involved in the movement. Hodgins joined the youth movement Provisional Na Fianna Éireann. He tells me that he got some reading material from Fianna after joining but received no systematic political education from them:

> When I first joined, it was the junior IRA called Na Fianna Éireann, and one of the first things was that they gave me two books. The first one was called *Down Dublin Street*s, it's an old wee book about the Rising, and another wee book called *Tragedies of Kerry* by Dorothy McArdle. *Tragedies of Kerry* I remember reading it, and it had a massive impact on me; I had no idea of the savagery of the Civil War. I had no idea about the Civil War, I never really [knew], I never grew up in a republican tradition; a lot of it was new to me.[47]

Hodgins became radicalized because of his experience with the conflict. Like many later republican prisoners, such as Jim Gibney or Danny Morrison, he attended political rallies, civil rights marches, and anti-internment protests; he witnessed arrests, curfews, and house raids but had received no structured political or historical education. However, despite stressing that he had "no education whatsoever in regards to Irish republicanism," the experience of riots and repression on the streets was the first political education that he received – not through books and classes but action and experience. This "experience of the street" radicalized him, and as a result, he joined the republican movement. As a new member, he occasionally got Irish nationalist and historical books. Nonetheless, through books about Irish nationalist history, such as the 1916 Easter Rising, the War of Independence, and the civil war in 1922/3, he developed an understanding of his own political struggle in the 1970s. Politics is a way of understanding the world. For these young men, history was another way of making sense of what was happening on the streets of Northern Ireland. Thus, street politics was the first way of understanding the conflict. It was a way of understanding that school was unable to give them.

Since the partition of Ireland, the school system has been a hotbed of segregation. As Kevin Rooney notes, "the vast majority of Protestants attended Protestant only (also known as 'controlled') schools; likewise, most Catholics attended Catholic only (or 'maintained') schools."[48] A significant number of my interview partners attended Christian Brothers schools. These schools are institutions run by the Congregation of Christian Brothers, the Irish Christian Brothers, the Institute of the Brothers of the Christian Schools, or the Lasallian Christian Brothers. In the 1970s, there were nine Christian Brothers schools, half of them in Belfast. Gerard Murray grew up in the Markets area of South Belfast. He went to one of these Christian Brothers schools and joined the movement in the 1970s. He is an activist of the Irish Republican Socialist Party (IRSP). He remembers:

> First of all, the area I lived in, the area I grew up in, was obviously turbulent, and in 1969 I was just turning into my teens and becoming aware of what was happening. I didn't understand the full scenario of what was about to unfold, but being taught a lot of Irish history and a lot of Irish language in school by the Christian Brothers sort of aroused some sort of interest and understanding, albeit on a small scale because of, I was only after turning a teen when 1969 came. But romanticism was, I suppose, part of it. You know, when you listen to the history of the Irish, 1916 and different things like that. So, it seemed that it was only partly for the cause that

I went down this road.... I saw this all unfold, the raids, the teargas, the peace lines going up. So I was in an area where I got easily influenced, but I do believe that the teaching from Christian Brothers gave me some sort of awareness, some sort of romanticism, some sort of understanding that it was only a matter of time that I was going to do going down that road. But there were others in my school who go the same teaching but lived in different parts of Belfast and didn't actually come into contact with what was happening.[49]

Like other interview partners, Murray explains his understanding of the events and his knowledge of Irish nationalism and history, what he calls "romanticism," with his education in a Christian Brothers school. The Irish nationalist education Murray and others received in the Christian Brothers schools is underlined by the fact that they learned the Irish language in school. However, the Christian Brothers school education did not spark children's interest in the republican movement, but it helped them interpret events from an Irish nationalist point of view. This interpretation paved the way towards their recruitment into republican organizations.

The primary source for the nationalist education of children from a republican background were their families. Children from republican families grew up with Irish nationalist culture. While their preferred political and historical knowledge sources were their parents, their social environments also formed their nationalist views. In other words, these children lived their social lives among other republican families. They joined republican youth organizations at a very early age and learned marching, drilling, and parading and participated in functions and other social events. However, as they were marching and drilling with their republican youth organizations on the one hand and spending their time with friends at republican social events, their nationalist education came from their parents and not the republican organizations. For example, Peig King was a teenager in the 1960s and joined the republican girls' organization Cumann na gCailíní. King came from a republican family and remembered: "On the weekends, there was a small hall on Parnell Square, not where you had number 44 later, it was on the other side, so when you go straight up from O'Connell Street, you pass by the monument there and on the other side there used to be an office of Sinn Féin. There were two empty rooms, and one was for meetings, and the other one was for social nights, and we always went there dancing, you know, céile dancing, the traditional Irish dance. And so, it happened that I went on to do other things."[50]

While King joined the republican youth organizations when she was still under the age of ten and spent her weekends with friends dancing to Irish music at a Sinn Féin office, it was her family and friends and not the movement, as she noted in her interview. The movement gave the young recruits practical lessons in transporting and parading and provided them with social contacts, but they did not offer systematic Irish history and politics classes.

The Irish Republican Socialist Movement (IRSM) split from the Official republican movement in 1974/5. The IRSM considered itself a Marxist-Leninist organization from the 1980s on but initially, at least, disavowed some aspects of Marxist politics. Contrary to the Provisional republican movement, the IRSM's political wing IRSP and its youth wing, the Irish Republican Socialist Youth Movement, organized mandatory and regular education classes for all members in the late 1970s. Fra Halligan joined the IRSP when he was fifteen years old in the early 1980s. Halligan grew up in West Belfast opposite the then newly opened office of the organization, the James Connolly House. When he contacted the organization, the first thing he remembers was that members gave him pamphlets to read. Asked about educational classes, he says:

> It was totally different to the sort of nationalist type republicanism that was on the go, you know, that was very much Catholic church-based and very much near, sort of almost moving towards a right-wing sort of stance. There was never any talk of the working class, there was never any talk of Connolly, there was never any talk of certainly anything outside Ireland, like Frank Ryan and the Spanish civil war or Cuba or anything like that. It was all about removing the British occupation from Ireland....
>
> *Can you remember how these political lectures and courses were organized?*
>
> Well, they took place every Monday night from seven o'clock until nine, and as a member, you were sort of expected there, always to be there. Each Monday night was a different topic, mainly around Seamus Costello, the founder of the party, and certainly James Connolly, Fintan Lalor, Peadar O'Donnell, and Frank Ryan and people like that. There was an examination of the major events in Irish history, from Cromwellian times to the 1934 Republican Congress and so on.... You know, the whole Irish Church's role, Irish nationalism, Joe Devlin, the AOH, the GAA, so there was a multitude of things covered. But, also, theory from Marx and Engels and Lenin and as the party had declared itself at an Ard-Fheis[51] as being a Marxist-Leninist organization. There were a lot of young people, including myself, who didn't really understand what Marxist-Leninist meant, and some older people just said it's all right, just follow the tradition of

Connolly. So, within the IRSP, there was a great melting pot that accepted as well that it was okay to be slightly outside of the party line by being committed to Connolly and not as much so to Marx and Lenin.... So it was very interesting, you know, some became very boring, but it depended really on who was giving it and that changed over time, and it was more an informal discussion and conversation that was allowed to happen, and that seemed to educate and help people to understand a lot better. Certainly, all aspects of republicanism and socialism were covered.... They were encouraging people, and we were reading different books and different pamphlets and so on. There were people who were obviously writing their own stuff, you had Jim Lane in Cork and Professor Jim Daly and people like that, and they were coming into the room, and you met them, and we were listening to their experience going back to the 60s. It was education but also very informative and interesting.[52]

Halligan speaks enthusiastically about the classes and lectures of the IRSP. He outlines the differences between his own organization and its socialist views on the one hand and what he considers as the "right-wing stance" of the Provisional republican movement on the other hand. Nonetheless, while he criticizes other organizations for the nationalism and ignorance regarding international events, the historical topics covered by the IRSP were also all of Irish nationalist nature, albeit Irish socialist or Irish socialists active in other countries, such as Frank Ryan in Spain. Still, Halligan is right that other republican organizations did not put a similar emphasis on the structured education of their membership. The reason for this can be found in the self-characterization of the IRSM as a Marxist-Leninist organization. These smaller organizations put greater emphasis on political and theoretical debate than broader national liberation movements.

Many prisoners received their first systematic political education following their imprisonment. One republican prisoner says that "you would read stuff and you would get knowledge that you would never have got otherwise in that respect."[53] The prisoners themselves organized these classes. For example, Tommy McNulty, originally from Dungannon in County Tyrone, served time in Belfast Prison, Mountjoy, Curragh, and Portlaoise. He talks about the situation in Portlaoise Prison: "You had the like of Daithí Ó Connell and Ruairí Ó Brádaigh. You had some very intelligent, well-read, old Southern republicans. And I went to many lectures and many political discussions. I learned a lot from them."[54] The initial classes organized by the prisoners were Irish language classes, discussions on political documents of the republican movements, such as *Éire Nua*,[55] and lectures. The lectures were mainly historical, dealing with Irish history and the history of the republican movement since the 1790s. Furthermore, internees and prisoners read political books from the prison libraries. These books were shared among the inmates.

The young prisoners received their first political education in prison from other inmates by organizing debates and lectures and reading political literature. The prisoners used this newly acquired knowledge by participating in political and cultural debates outside the prison walls. The prisoners had three ways to spread their views among their supporters. First, prisoners wrote letters to national and political newspapers and magazines. Second, the prisoners issued statements through their PRO. The prisoners wrote these letters and statements on cigarette paper; these tiny communiqués were then smuggled out of prison during visits. Third, during the peace process in the 1990s, the prisoners' representatives could meet with representatives of the republican movement; furthermore, prisoners supportive of the peace process from the Republic's Portlaoise Prison attended Sinn Féin AGM. Between the 1970s and 1990s, the prisoners ignited political change within the republican movement. New political directions started following the ceasefire in 1975.[56] Support for these new developments arose from internees in the Long Kesh internment camp.[57] The educational classes, organized by the internees and prisoners themselves, were central for discussing and developing new strategies. The Brownie letters, widely attributed to Gerry Adams, are the first prisoners' publications mirroring these debates in Long Kesh.[58] Notably, the debates within the prisons have played a "significant role in shaping the strategies and tactics of the Movement."[59]

In Northern Ireland, young recruits of republican organizations in the 1970s had no higher education but a developed political consciousness. There is too little data available for the situation in the Republic to make similar conclusions. Due to their experience of the conflict, young Irish republican recruits had a developed political consciousness. Through self-education and informal classes in prison, these young activists made use of this political consciousness. This process of becoming a subject during their imprisonment empowered them to shape political debates outside the prison walls to become leading activists in their community. These activists radicalized in particular circumstances because of the internment of their parents, civil rights protests, street closures, curfews, or constant house raids. These events were their political education, and the national narratives they heard from family, friends, or Catholic schools channelled this radicalization towards their involvement in the republican movement.

From the 1980s on, prisoners organized their own classes and sub-scribed to Open University courses. Thus, many prisoners obtained higher education and academic degrees while imprisoned. Addition-ally, a disproportionate number of former prisoners became involved in community activism, were elected politicians, and promoted cultural initiatives, such as the Irish language. Even the OFMDFM acknowledge their role, saying that "many ex-prisoners, since release, have played active and positive roles in conflict transformation processes within republicanism and loyalism."[60] Donnacha Ó Beachain calls the phenom-enon of former Irish republicans turned moderate community workers holding elected offices "politicians by accident."[61] However, rather than being an accidental development, the self-education during imprison-ment and the use of this newly acquired education to influence political events was a conscious attempt by actors of the conflict.

Former republican prisoners hold an outstanding role within public life. Being a former IRA prisoner gives kudos within nationalist com-munities. This view of prisoners as heroes within their communities who gave their lives for the struggle to defend their communities is comparable to the image of martyrs. In fact, former prisoners, particu-larly former Blanketmen, are seen as living martyrs. They are hailed as heroes within their communities because they spent time behind bars "for their community."[62] This image of "heroes" develops against the background that most prisoners face considerable psychological and social difficulties following their release.[63] Previous research by Adrian Grounds and Ruth Jamieson,[64] Kieran McEvoy et al.,[65] and Peter Shirlow[66] has examined the impact of imprisonment on republican ex-prisoners. All studies show that ex-prisoners suffer from mental prob-lems and post-traumatic stress disorder.

Local communities in Northern Ireland consider political prisoners as their heroes and martyrs. Morrison writes that "historically, the pris-oners have been among the most trusted and revered actors with the Irish republican movement."[67] Another example that underlines the community's support for the political prisoners is that the prisoners' "definition of themselves as volunteer soldiers was largely shared by their communities."[68] To be sure, republican prisoners and loyalist pris-oners do not belong to a marginalized and socially excluded group. In fact, they are seen as heroes in their local community. David McKittrick writes for the *Independent* about youth in Belfast in the year 2009: "But kids still see paramilitary veterans strutting about their districts, notic-ing their status and their sometimes expensive lifestyles. Many loyalist figures were not just killers but also gangsters, ostentatiously sporting chunky jewellery, revving around in 4x4s, holidaying in Dubai. Sadly but inevitably, some kids adopt them as role models, admiring them as men of power and stature. One small boy asked what he wanted to be when he grew up, replied: 'An ex-prisoner.'"[69]

Given that, Maurice Goldring stresses the critical role of the political prisoners in their community's struggle. According to Goldring, one of the main aspects of the struggle is to make martyrs, the two groups who are turned into martyrs of their community are, on the one hand, the dead activists of the movement, and on the other hand the political prisoners; he explains:

> In the newsletters produced by *Coiste*, the ex-prisoners republican organi-sation, you find the slogan "Fifteen thousand prisoners, one hundred thousand years in jail" repeated constantly. From a strictly military point of view, this slogan is an aberration: it is an admission of defeat and of the opponent's victory. Normally in a war, the propaganda puts emphasis on the number of enemy prisoners and enemy victims rather than those of one's own side. However, neither the IRA nor ETA publishes literature where it is written: "1500 enemies killed, 15,000 wounded and £2 billion in material damage"; or "three journalists killed, five local councillors exe-cuted." The purpose of armed struggle is not an impossible military vic-tory, but foremost the creation of martyrs. The celebration of martyrdom revolves around two main areas: the graveyard and the jails.[70]

While these remarks are characteristic of the republican prisoners in Northern Ireland, the situation in the Republic of Ireland remains starkly different. The position of the former political prisoners in their community differs between the two Irish states. The former prisoners have a stronger position and adopt leading roles within their commu-nity in Northern Ireland, whereas they were less able to perform simi-lar roles in the Republic. Furthermore, the republican prisoners in the Republic were considered less relevant for the movement's strategy by the republican leadership itself than the prisoners in Northern Ireland. Matt Treacy was imprisoned in Portlaoise Prison during the late 1980s and early 1990s. He worked for Sinn Féin in the 2000s; however, he fell out with his former comrades over political issues and has since become a fierce opponent who regularly gives his opinion in online blogs. I interviewed Treacy when he was still a paid employer of Sinn Féin. He interprets the role of the Southern prisoners in the following way:

> No one took us seriously at that time. We were not important for the move-ment. We were not the prisoners in the North, in Long Kesh or so, we were in the South, in Portlaoise, and no one in the movement cared what we

were saying. But they gave us the feeling that we were important and sent people to jail, and they made us feel important, and we sent statements out, and there were delegates to the Ard-Fheis, and we thought we had an input, but in fact, they were just using us for their own gains. I think that was very dishonest.[71]

In other words, it is unsurprising that the republican prisoners had a less-powerful stance within their own communities in the Republic compared to their fellow ex-prisoners in Northern Ireland if one considers that the republican movement itself gave the Southern prisoners the feeling that they were less important for the struggle than the Northern prisoners.

Chapter Two

"Portlaoise Is an Example for This": Portlaoise Prison Protests, 1973–1977

The 1981 hunger strikes of Provisional IRA and Irish National Liberation Army prisoners are a defining moment in Irish history that brought the Troubles to a broader international audience.[1] Moreover, they set Sinn Féin on track to become a mass movement that eventually embraced the conflict transformation process over the following decades.[2] The circumstances which led to the hunger strikes in Northern Ireland started with the move of the republican prisoners from Mountjoy Prison in Dublin to Portlaoise Prison, Co Laois, in autumn 1973. To examine the two hunger strikes in 1980 and 1981, we need to understand Irish republican imprisonment throughout the Northern Irish conflict on both sides of the Irish border.

During the fours years from 1973 to 1977, political prisoners aligned to the Provisional republican movement carried out a series of protests, including hunger strikes, in the high-security Portlaoise Prison. Provisional IRA prisoners were separated from other prisoners in Portlaoise. While there was at times contact with other, more minor republican factions, such as Saor Éire and the INLA, prisoners belonging to the Official IRA did not participate in these protests. In the 1970s, several prison unions emerged that demanded a prison system reform.[3] The socialist-leaning organizations Saor Éire, INLA, and the Official IRA cooperated with these groups to improve the conditions for all prisoners; moreover, groups like the Official IRA considered all prisoners as victims of the capitalist system. On the contrary, the Provisional IRA made a clear distinction between them and other prisoners not motivated by political actions. When the Irish government considered housing members of the prison unions together with socialist-leaning republican prisoners of Saor Éire, these and similar approaches were rejected by the Provisional prisoners.[4]

The prison protests in the Mountjoy and Portlaoise prisons coincided with the coalition government of Fine Gael and Labour under *Taoiseach*

(Prime Minister) Liam Cosgrave. Until 1973, the government was led by Fianna Fáil. This party was founded in 1926 by former members of the IRA who fought in the 1916 Easter Rising, the War of Independence, and the civil war. It considered itself the "republican party," and several of its cabinet members showed sympathy for the struggle of the Catholic minority in Northern Ireland. In 1970, Minister of Justice Mícheál Ó Móráin resigned amid an alleged plot to supply Northern republicans with arms. His successor, Desmond O'Malley, served in office from April 1970 until the new government's inauguration in 1973.[5] In 1977, the Fine Gael/Labour coalition was, again, replaced by a Fianna Fáil executive.

The early 1970s was a time of expansion of the prison system in the Republic of Ireland.[6] Whereas the prison population had declined from about 25 average daily prisoners per 100,000 of the general population in the early 1940s, reaching its lowest point of 10 average daily prisoners in 1958, the renewed outbreak of the conflict in Northern Ireland in the late 1960s also had repercussions for the penal system in the Republic.[7] In 1972, the average daily prison population reached 35 per 100,000, increasing to 53 in 1985.[8] New prisons for adult males were opened, and plans were to build a new women's prison.[9] In the words of Mike Tomlinson, these were "very troubled years in the South's prisons, with escape attempts and the build-up of a well-organized group of political prisoners."[10] The outbreak of the Troubles brought further challenges to the prison system through an influx of republican prisoners.

Since the independence of the twenty-six counties, which became the Republic of Ireland, and the Irish Civil War in 1922/3, the Dublin government had criminalized republican activists who continued their fight for a unified Irish Republic. These republicans were initially known as "anti-Treaty republicans" because they rejected the Anglo-Irish Treaty that gave the twenty-six counties independence and divided Ireland. The repression of republicans remained severe until the 1970s and after. As Mark Findlay argues, a section of prisoners with radical politics and direct association with revolutionary organizations on the outside was "a constant threat to the Irish state." The state's awareness of this threat urged the Irish government to criminalize republican prisoners.[11] After the independence of the twenty-six counties in 1921, these republicans were held mainly in Kilmainham Gaol in Dublin (1920s), Portlaoise Prison (until the late 1940s), and the Curragh Military Camp in Co Kildare (1940–60). Portlaoise Prison did not house republican prisoners again until the early 1970s. When the Troubles erupted in 1968, Mountjoy Prison was the main prison holding republicans in the Republic.[12]

In the 1970s, the Irish state introduced a new strategy; this was "criminalization." In 1972, the second Prison Act was introduced. While the first one in 1970 focused on the modernization of the prison system to rehabilitate, the later one reflected "a general hardening of attitude towards republican activity."[13] Findlay argues that the government of the Republic "used the army systematically to screen certain sections of the population and arrest and intern certain 'suspects' for varying periods without trial."[14] Examples of this criminalization policy were the introduction of Section 31 of the Broadcasting Authority Act (1960), which banned the voice of members of Sinn Féin and the Provisional IRA from the national broadcaster RTÉ; the reactivation of the Special Criminal Courts in 1972, the equivalent of the Diplock courts in Northern Ireland; benches with three judges; non-jury courts; the less rigid rule of evidence; and the reversal of the onus of proof in certain circumstances.[15] In 1974, the Prison Act of 1972 was extended for another three years under the new Fine Gael/Labour coalition and was extended again in 1977.[16] In essence, the developments in the Republic's prisons echoed those in Northern Irish prisons; the systematic protest by prisoners against this criminalization foreshadowed the later H-Blocks struggle. Under these circumstances, prison protests unfolded in Mountjoy and, later, Portlaoise Prison.

In the autumn of 1969, the republican movement had split into an Official and a Provisional wing; a significant fraction of the Mountjoy prisoners belonged to the armed wing of the Provisionals, the Provisional IRA. The Officials were socialist orientated, whereas the Provisionals followed a nationalist ideology. By 1973, 130 people had been arrested and convicted for republican activities. Most of them were detained in Mountjoy Prison and the Curragh Military Centre, while Portlaoise had also been reopened to house some political prisoners. These prisoners brought the Northern Irish conflict into the Republic's prisons by demanding the right to be treated as prisoners of war (PoWs).

Historically, republicans rejected the label of "criminals," and by doing so, they underlined that they were political activists and not terrorists. Following the 1916 Easter Rising, the British government had granted Irish prisoners held in Britain the same PoW status as German First World War prisoners. However, this situation changed with the outbreak of the Troubles. Thus, the newly arrived prisoners in Mountjoy also demanded PoW status from the government. In July 1972, William Whitelaw, who had become the first secretary of state for Northern Ireland in March, introduced special category status for both republican and loyalist prisoners following the hunger strike of senior Belfast Provisional Billy McKee. The Republic of Ireland government followed one year later. In the summer of 1973, following a hunger strike that lasted twenty-two days, privileges that amounted to special category status were granted to the republican prisoners in Mountjoy.[17] John Lonergan, the former governor of Mountjoy and Portlaoise, acknowledges this situation in his memoir: "In the decades before the outbreak of conflict in the late 1960s, IRA prisoners had automatically been granted political status."[18] This status changed again with the transfer of the prisoners from Mountjoy to Portlaoise in 1973. Thus, both in the Republic and Northern Ireland, the status and treatment of republican prisoners remained contested throughout the conflict. On the particular situation in Portlaoise, Findlay wrote that "the press argued that through the wide use of solitary confinement and the strict regime effected in Portlaoise when compared with other prisons, the government was de facto according to these inmates' special political status and, as a result, should treat them as being a special category."[19] As in Northern Ireland after the 1981 hunger strikes, the Irish government recognized de facto political status despite not officially referring to the prisoners with this term.[20]

The years 1972 and 1973 were a period of high tensions characterized by small and short protests by republicans in Mountjoy, the Curragh, and Portlaoise.[21] That year also witnessed several escape attempts from the various prisons, some of which proved successful. The most significant of these happened in October 1973, when three leading Provisional IRA members escaped by helicopter.[22] This escape caused much embarrassment to the government, both on a national and an international level, and, as a result of the protests and escape attempts, all the republican prisoners were moved to Portlaoise within days. The Irish government considered Portlaoise a higher-security prison more suitable for housing subversive prisoners. Thus, after more than two decades, Portlaoise once again became the main prison housing political convicts in the Republic.

The transfer of the prisoners from Mountjoy to Portlaoise happened soon after the escape and was ill prepared. The prisoners were not informed about their transfer beforehand, and upon their arrival in Portlaoise, they reported that some of the cells were still under construction. Nevertheless, a total of 130 prisoners were transferred to Portlaoise. The two main reasons for this transfer following the helicopter escape in the autumn of 1973 were that, first, Portlaoise had soldiers stationed on its roofs and outside its walls, making escape more difficult; second, Portlaoise had mesh covering the yard, making the landing of a helicopter impossible, unlike the utterly open yard of Mountjoy.

In the 1970s, riots and hunger strikes were the two preferred forms of prison protest used by republicans before the start of the blanket

protests in September 1976. The republican use of hunger strikes originated from the British suffragette movement in the early twentieth century.[23] The first republican to die during his hunger strike was Thomas
Ashe in 1917. Altogether, until 1946 a further seven republicans died on
hunger strike. Around the time the republican prisoners were moved
from Mountjoy to Portlaoise, in England, the republican prisoners Mar-
ian and Dolours Price embarked on their hunger strikes.[24] Their aim
was to be transferred back to Ireland. Both women were subsequently
force fed.[25] However, since Thomas Ashe's hunger strike, Irish authorities had not used force feeding.[26] Thus, while republican hunger strikes
originated from the same political tradition, the hunger strikes in England and Ireland took different paths.

The most common use of hunger strikes by republicans was to protest their classification as criminals. For example, when authorities
refused political prisoner status to the suffragettes in the 1910s, they
went on hunger strike. Republicans took similar action to demand their
treatment as political prisoners of war from the 1910s until today.[27] The
republican newspaper *An Phoblacht/Republican News* explained the tactic of a hunger strike by republicans as follows: "Hunger-strike is the
last resort for prisoners. It is a supreme test of will-power, a decision
that calls for the ultimate self-sacrifice. It is the final means of protest
against an unbearable, intransigent regime when all other means of
protest have gone unheeded."[28] Accordingly, this action was also taken
to protest conditions and their classification as criminals during the
Portlaoise protests.

Portlaoise Prison is today the only high-security prison holding
republican prisoners in the Republic. It is situated in the County Laois
town of Portlaoise and was opened in 1830, making it Ireland's oldest
prison still run by the Irish Prison Service. Its experience with republican prisoners dates to the period following the Easter Rising in 1916.
During this time, Portlaoise housed several people convicted of republican activities. Following the end of the War of Independence, the
newly formed government of the Irish Free State took over the prison
from the British authorities. Until 1948, when it was closed due to its
deteriorating conditions following a study by the Labour Party, Portlaoise Prison regularly held political prisoners.[29] It was reopened for
republicans after the start of the Troubles, and the conditions inside the
prison remained a constant cause for tensions. There were two waves
of protest against the conditions during the 1970s and 1980s. Hunger
strikes characterized the first wave; this phase started in 1974 and
lasted until March 1977. The second wave was characterized by protests
against strip searches of prisoners and visitors; it started following the

conclusion of the hunger strikes in the H-Blocks when the republican movement again moved their attention from the Northern Irish prisons to the prisons in the Republic of Ireland and lasted throughout the 1980s. In this chapter, I address the first wave of protests.

On 15 March 1972, eleven political prisoners were housed in a separate wing. These prisoners belonged to three different groups. They were Saor Éire prisoners Patrick Dillon, Joseph Dillon, Martin Casey, Brendan Walsh, Seán Morrissey, and Finbarr Walsh; Provisional IRA prisoners James Hazlett, Michael Walls, and Liam Fagan; and Official IRA prisoners James McCabe and Roland Giles.[30] One year later, seventy-one prisoners were affiliated with the Provisional IRA in Portlaoise.[31]

The staff at Portlaoise Prison had no experience in dealing with these prisoners, and tensions arose immediately, especially when the prison authorities refused to grant special status that had been won by the prisoners in Mountjoy that summer. Seosamh Ó Maileoin was one of the prisoners transferred from Mountjoy to Portlaoise. He remembers: "Portlaoise was a much tougher place than Mountjoy. We were just moved, very quickly.… I think they were completely unprepared; they didn't know what to do with us in Portlaoise.… The warders were very aggressive, and we had fewer rights there. In the beginning, they couldn't cope with the situation. It was not like Mountjoy, [it was] tougher."[32]

However, the Department of Justice (henceforth DoJ) document states that "all PIRA/OIRA inmates of Mountjoy and Curragh were transferred to Portlaoise under a very liberal regime."[33] In fact, the prisoners had lost the privileges they had previously won by embarking on various prison protests in Mountjoy in 1972/3; however, following days of intense negotiations between management and prisoners, special category status and all other concessions previously granted in the Curragh camp and Mountjoy were also introduced in Portlaoise. According to the DoJ, the situation in Portlaoise after the granting of rights was as follows: The prisoners had free association all day; had access to each other's cells; were locked up at 10 p.m.; were granted unlimited visits, cigarettes, letters, newspapers, parcels, and unlimited quantities of craft materials; and musical instruments and craftworks were allowed in the cells.[34] Contrary to this, Behan writes, "as the 1970s began, conditions in Irish prisons were grim. Most prisoners had no in-cell sanitation and had to 'slop out.' Prisoners spent over fifteen hours in their cells, and there were limited productive out-of-cell activities."[35]

The relatively peaceful atmosphere that followed a compromise between prisoners and authorities was short lived. Following the transfer of "subversive prisoners" to Portlaoise, the tensions and regular clashes between prison staff and republicans led to the reinforcement of the physical security of the prison in four ways. First, armed guards patrolled the perimeter walls day and night; second, barbed wire had been mounted extensively around the prison; third, perimeter security was further ensured by a military presence of both soldiers and equipment; and, fourth, on each segregated landing with the prison, officers of the Garda Síochána, the Irish police, complemented prison personnel. Prison officers in the Republic were unarmed; therefore, members of the police and the army assisted in guarding Portlaoise. Consequently, the prisoners pressed for reforms. They particularly objected to five issues: deprivation of free association and access to other prisoner's cells,[36] requirements to wear prison clothing, lack of suitable visiting facilities, absence of proper toilets, and lack of sufficient exercise facilities. While some of these issues could be solved, others continued to be disputed throughout the 1980s, such as closed visits; furthermore, issues like the requirement to wear prison clothing reflected, together with the prisoners' protest tactics, the developments in the H-Blocks.[37] It was under those circumstances that the prison protests in Portlaoise unfolded.

The prisoners embarked on the first protest in Portlaoise, a solidarity action for republicans held in England in March 1974.[38] Although this protest was not directed against the prison administration in Portlaoise, it highlighted the internal discipline of the Provisional IRA prisoners, who were described as a "close-knit, highly organized group" by the authorities.[39] In August 1974, the Provisional IRA organized a mass escape. Nineteen prisoners escaped from Portlaoise.[40] Consequently, a large amount of money was spent on improving security in and around the prison. Furthermore, there was a gradual erosion of the rights gained the year before, which "led to further trouble."[41] That meant that searches of the cells increased, letters and books were restricted, and food parcels and the right to craft materials were withdrawn.[42] The removal of these rights resulted in heightened tensions within the prison. On St. Patrick's Day 1975, the PIRA prisoners organized an escape attempt in which prisoner Tom Smith was shot dead by snipers guarding the prison.[43] George McDermott, imprisoned in Portlaoise from 1974 until 1990, remembers: "The atmosphere soon changed after that. The regime came down very hard after that. There were lockups for months. Shortly after that, in the North, they brought in criminalization."[44]

The simmering tensions in Portlaoise exploded in riots in the days after Christmas 1974, followed by a hunger strike in the following month.[45] During this riot, the prisoners took several hostages. Dan Hoban took part in this riot and recalls:

> When the riot took place …, they haven't given us our conditions, and it was boiling up and boiling up, and the next thing was that there was a riot in the jail and there were prison officers taken as hostages.… Leo Martin from Belfast was the O/C in prison, and I was the adjutant, and I was selected to go out by all the prisoners to negotiate with the governor.… I went through a line of screws with batons and everything, and I went in to negotiate with him, and I had the only certain option to negotiate with him, so the talks broke down between us.… Then they came with the power hoses, and they broke down the barriers at the bottom of the prison, and they battered us back with the high-power hoses.… We had the cell doors sprung so they couldn't take us individually and beat us; I say what they would have done if they got us locked up in the cell.[46]

As adjutant general, Dan Hoban was the second in command of the Provisional IRA prisoners. He had already been interned in the Curragh Camp in the 1950s and imprisoned in Mountjoy in the early 1970s. Hoban was elected to represent the prisoners on various occasions, including the hunger strike that followed these events.

During the protests in December 1974, 27 prison guards were held hostage for 6 hours by around 140 prisoners. The prisoners used doors, mattresses, and furniture to barricade themselves inside a cellblock of the E-wing that housed republicans. The prison authorities summoned six hundred police officers and army soldiers to surround the building. During the negotiations, the prisoners issued a list of demands. Additionally, they hung a large white sheet from a window with "Fight repression" written on it but gave up without a fight when riot troops moved into the prison. Following the conclusion of this riot, prisoners complained about the brutality of the prison officers during the riot.[47] Nonetheless, they lost further rights: the lock-up time was changed from 10 p.m. to 8 p.m., and only one book was allowed in the cells at a time.[48] In response to the riot, a permanent Gardaí presence was maintained in prison, and a new governor, William Reilly, was appointed. Over the following weeks, conditions further deteriorated. Hanley quotes a Gardaí source, writing that "while the prisoners' complaints were dismissed as propaganda, a Garda later admitted that 'things went on we'll say in searches … that shouldn't have gone on … there were episodes that were fairly severe, that shouldn't have happened.'"[49] As a direct consequence of this situation, eight prisoners embarked on a hunger strike on 3 January 1975. The numbers on hunger strike doubled within a fortnight.[50] In a press release, Sinn Féin explained:

> Six republican prisoners have been on hunger strike since 12.00 noon on January 3 last. That means that at 12.00 noon today, they have completed 40 days on a diet of water and salt and entered on the 41st day. Eight other prisoners have been on hunger strike since January 13, which means that they have now completed 30 days' fast....
>
> Mr William Whitelaw conceded special category status to both republican and loyalist prisoners in the North in June 1972.... The Coalition government in Dublin refuses to grant republican prisoners what the British have conceded in the Six Counties.[51]

The strike lasted for forty-four days and only ended after Pat Ward was admitted to the hospital in critical condition.[52] Dan Hoban remembers: "Many men went on that hunger strike, including Pat Ward; that was his third hunger strike. The hunger strike really had its toll on him when it finished, and he was on the brink of death like when the hunger strike was over."[53]

On the thirtieth day of the hunger strike, the prisoners were moved to the Curragh Military Hospital, and on the forty-second day, the conditions of two hunger strikers, Pat Ward and Colm Daltún, deteriorated seriously, with doctors believing them to be within hours of death. However, following public pressure, government officials entered into negotiations with the prisoners, and, on the forty-fourth day, the government agreed to restore some form of special category status. Hoban was Ward's negotiator during this hunger strike, and he recalls a conversation that he had with Ward's brother, who tried to convince him to take Pat off the hunger strike:

> That was a very silent time in jail, in prison because you were called to go out to negotiate, and they might get you out of the cell at 12 o'clock at night when they think that you'd be at your weakest and they try to break you down to agree to something.
>
> Even during all that period, they sent in Pat Ward's brother, and I got out of my cell. It was half eleven at night, and I had to go out into the visiting boxes to meet Pat Ward's brother. I sat here at the table, and you're sitting there, and I moved in, and this is Pat Ward's brother, and I shook hands with him, and he said to me: "Are you going to let my brother die?" You know, straight across the table, like he wasn't a republican, but the authorities were using him. So, I say: "I feel, I can understand how you feel.... Your brother is a personal friend of mine. We were in the battle

for Irish independence together, and your brother has entrusted me as his negotiator during his hunger strike. And what you are asking me to do, if I do what you are asking me to do, I would no longer be a friend of your brother. I appreciate your brother's friendship very much. Sorry, I cannot ease your request. There is no point sitting across the table crying to me. I appreciate your brother's friendship to me is very important. We are in this battle together, and I cannot do it for him."

And he went away, and Pat Ward was getting very weak then. Then the hunger strike was called off, they got certain demands they were looking for, and Pat Ward was shifted to hospital. He was very weak. You had all sorts of stuff like that.[54]

The prisoners announced: "Following discussions on a confidential basis between the prisoner's representatives and the prison authorities, a satisfactory settlement has been reached in the dispute which led to the hunger strike, and we are happy to announce that the hunger strike has now ended."[55] The twenty-nine-year-old hunger striker Ward is quoted as saying "another victory [for the republican prisoners]."[56] However, the interpretations of this "settlement" starkly differed. While Joe Cahill said that "the IRA men had won political status," a government spokesperson denied this claim, and a subsequent statement read that: "Certain matters which were not matters of principle as far as the government was concerned were resolved satisfactorily. The Minister for Justice is pleased with the outcome," whereas the IRA statement read: "Following the discussion on a confidential basis between prisoners' representatives in Portlaoise and the prison authorities a satisfactory settlement has been reached in the dispute which leads to the hunger strike, and we are happy to announce the hunger strike has ended."[57] A report of the DoJ from 1981 claims that the hunger strike "ended after 38 days following concessions of a well-stocked tuck shop, two late nights per week to 10.30 p.m., etc."[58] In essence, the republicans argued that the concession of these demands de facto meant "political status," while the government argued that these were merely well-defined concessions, and thus the government did not back down to the republican demand of "political status." Nevertheless, both sides were right and could claim a propaganda victory for themselves.

During an escape attempt in March 1975, prisoner Tom Smith was shot dead. Following this incident and the discovery of explosives in the prison, the authorities immediately suspended all visits for prisoners and, when visiting rights were eventually restored, they replaced the old open-visit system with a new closed version. For the next decade, visits were to take place in a box resembling a cage. A table separated the prisoners from the visitors, and from that table, two wire grilles, two feet apart, ran to the ceiling. On the inside of both grilles were sheets of Perspex. A prison officer sat in a cage at the end of the table to monitor all the conversations and take notes.[59] In 1976, two extra officers were placed on visits, one directly behind the prisoner and one behind the visitor. Any mention whatsoever of the conditions with the prison resulted in a warning that the visit would be terminated. The closed visits continued after the end of the protests in 1976. It was only in 1984/5 and 1987 with the regime change that closed visits, strip searches, and night searches were finally phased out.

As a result of strip searching, another hunger strike began in October 1975. Pat Ward and Colm Daltún again undertook this hunger strike; however, it ended after only a few days. It had begun to protest the beating of a young prisoner, Martin Ferris, from County Kerry. Ferris was beaten by military police when he resisted the strip searching before medical treatment in the Curragh Military Hospital. During the autumn months, the situation for the prisoners had worsened. In a press release dated 14 December 1975, the PIRA-linked Irish Republican Information Service (IRIS) complained about the "inhuman conditions" in Portlaoise, referring to a statement smuggled out of prison. In this report, written by then Provisional IRA O/C in Portlaoise, Dáithí O'Conaill, the prisoners informed about a confrontation with prison officers on 25 November:

> Within an hour, the following punishment was inflicted on all political prisoners: a) Removal of all furniture and beds from cells; b) Deprivation of exercise, ablutions, laundry, recreational, craft, library and TV facilities; c) Banning of all visits, mail and newspapers; d) Withdrawal of shop facilities; e) Harassment of prisoners by frequent searches and threats to strip men naked; f) Denial of access to Chaplains and legal advisers; g) Collective fining of all political prisoners of £3.50 each without their consent....
>
> The governor ... instructed his warders to carry out an orgy of destruction, removing beds from the cells and smashing hundreds of tables and lockers. The punishment resulted in prisoners eating and sleeping on the floors.[60]

O'Conaill was one of the leaders of the Provisional IRA in the 1970s. He had joined the IRA at the age of seventeen, and over more than twenty years, he was repeatedly imprisoned – he escaped from the Curragh internment camp in 1958 – or was driven into hiding. He joined a delegation that met with the British secretary of state for Northern Ireland in 1972 and played a leading part in the negotiated ceasefire of

1974/5, but after it failed, he was discredited and was gradually supplanted by Provisionals from Northern Ireland. During his imprisonment in Portlaoise, he was the Provisional IRA O/C in prison. He and his adjutant Liam Kelly issued three demands to the governor on 2 December 1975.[61] In particular, they demanded a "public sworn inquiry into the management of Portlaoise Jail."[62] This one and other demands were not met and, as a result, prisoners rioted after Christmas 1975. In January 1976, prisoners held a solidarity hunger strike with a republican, Frank Stagg, in England. Concerning the conditions in Portlaoise, they issued several demands; a statement by the Government Information Service read: "A group of prisoners in Portlaoise Prison have indicated that they propose to refuse meals in furtherance of certain demands … : removal of the metal grille in the visiting room; provision of facilities for education; increased parole facilities; permission to engage in craftwork in cells; in return of chairs to cells (removed at the end of November because chairs had been used to make weapons in riot situations)."[63] On 2 January, the IRIS reacted to this statement and informed that "Tension is still running high in Portlaoise since November 26th, when prisoners were deprived of all furniture, visits, mail and reading. The situation has been aggravated by the refusal of compassionate parole to two prisoners.… All Provisional prisoners will take part in the hunger strike. Recent press reports of a split in the jail are complete without foundation. The prisoners were never more united under their own elected leadership."[64]

Although this was only a temporary hunger strike, the prisoners were stretching their muscles in opposition to what prisoners Dáithí O'Conaill and Liam Sean O'Ceallaigh called "the Pinochet-style regime in Portlaoise."[65] Later in 1976, a similar comparison with Chile was also made in the *Sunday World*.[66] Then, in February 1976, IRIS again informed the public about the "brutal treatment of prisoners" and "state 'violence' in Portlaoise Prison." The statement claimed that the prisoners had nothing but a mattress in their cells and had been "eating their food off the floor since Friday, 20 February 1976."[67] In the summer of 1976, the situation further deteriorated when three prisoners escaped during a court hearing. The prisoners had used explosives smuggled into the prison to blow a hole in the courthouse wall. This incident led to intensified strip searches and a reduction of visits. In protest, the prisoners attempted to burn the prison on 21 July. As a result, the two late nights and the free access to the landing and other cells were withdrawn. Although it was forbidden to speak about the conditions in prison during visits, the stories of released men have led Fr. Denis Faul of Dungannon, Co Tyrone, "to say that men coming out of Portlaoise

are more socially disorientated than ex-prisoners from any jail in the
North or in Britain."[68] Hanley writes that, in another article, the *Sunday World* claimed that the inmates were treated "worse than in any
other regular prison ... in the EEC [the forerunner of today's EU]."[69] In
1976, Garda believed to have prevented a bomb attack on the governor
of Portlaoise. However, in October, a suspicious object was reported,
and when the Gardaí investigated it, a booby trap bomb exploded,
killing Garda Michael Clerkin. While the PIRA denied involvement,
it heightened the tensions.[70] Republicans killed around forty people
in the Republic during the 1970s, including Fine Gael Senator Billy
Fox, the first member of the Irish Senate killed by the IRA since 1927,
British Ambassador Christopher Ewart-Biggs, and five Gardaí. On the
other hand, loyalists killed fifty people in the Republic during the same
period.[71]

The situation in Portlaoise eventually exploded in a hunger strike
in 1977. Prisoner Patrick Casey from Dundalk, Co Louth, outlines the
situation that led to the hunger strikes in a prison statement to Fr. Piaras
O Duill:

> I was imprisoned in Port Laoise prison from the 13th January 1975 to
> April 23, 1977.... In July 1976, when the escape took place from Green
> Street Courthouse, the craft shop was closed, and an attempt was made to
> introduce strip-searches, but the prisoners resisted these.... All personal
> possessions of prisoners were taken from the cells, watches, photos, personal letters, clothes.... Men were beaten about their cells, and many were
> injured. I could hear the cries of the men as they were being beaten up. I
> was stripped forcibly every night and every morning during that week.
> I was allowed no letters in or out and no visits. My wife or relatives did
> not know what was happening....
>
> As a means of alerting our relatives and the public, we staged a protest
> in prison by burning the mattresses in the cells.... The only food we got for
> the two days in the cells was a cup of tea and dry bread on one occasion.
> There were no toilet facilities....
>
> Each prisoner was sentenced to one month (31 days) solitary confinement ... , loss of 14 days remission, loss of all privileges and each fined £41....
> Because of these conditions and in order to draw public attention to them,
> twenty of my comrades began a hunger strike on March 7.[72]

This statement and other republican accounts are propaganda statements aimed at the republican support base and must be read in this
regard. However, on 20 March, the *Sunday World* also reported "random
strip-searches, beatings, harassment and solitary confinement."[73]

On 7 March, twenty Provisional IRA prisoners went on the fast, which lasted forty-seven days. The *Irish Press* reported at that time that there were, in total, 134 republican prisoners; they included 82 Provisional IRA, 12 "dissident" Provisionals, 7 Official IRA, 18 Socialist Republican Alliance Group A, 11 Socialist Republican Alliance Group B prisoners, and 4 dissidents from the Socialist Republican Alliance.[74] The prisoners on hunger strike were Kevin Mallon, Tyrone; Seamus Swan, Wexford; Joe Ennis, Cavan; Mick Brody, Clare; Liam O'Mahony, Laois; Jim Nolan, Tipperary; John Carrol, Offaly; Martin Ferris, Danny O'Sullivan, and Brendan O'Doherty, all Kerry; Phil O'Donnell and Jim Ferry, both Derry; Tom Bannon and Sean McGettigan, both Monaghan; Kevin Walsh and Bobby McNamara, both Limerick; Daithi Ó Conaill and Jerry Quinn, both Dublin; and the two remand prisoners Tom Keenan and Fintan Hearty, both South Armagh.[75]

The initial demand for the hunger strike was for a public inquiry, but several other demands were soon put forward.[76] On 18 March, the prisoners issued eight demands: 1. the right to free association, 2. an end to degrading and humiliating strip searches, 3. an end to solitary confinement, 4. open and respectable visits, 5. the right to engage in craftwork, 6. the right to educational facilities, 7. adequate recreational and exercise facilities, and 8. the right to communicate with the legal advisor of choice.[77] While twenty prisoners started the hunger strike, fewer than a dozen stayed on until the end. Kevin Walsh remembers that

> Every memory is to do with food. I remembered stuff I had forgotten about. Beautiful dinners my mother made me, beautiful cakes she made.… There was a fella next to me, and he'd have nightmares every night – dreaming that you were after breaking your fast. It happened to me too. I remember one fella, he was only seventeen. He was actually eating the toothpaste in his sleep. He was eating the blankets in his sleep, and he thought he was after breaking it. We were all eating the blankets because we were dreaming, we were eating, and you'd fall asleep, and you'd be chewing away at the blankets.[78]

The then president of Sinn Féin, Ruairí Ó Brádaigh, who had himself embarked on a hunger strike in Mountjoy Prison in June 1972, said "that men were being turned into vegetables and broken mentally in Portlaoise. They had been sentenced by the special non-jury court to imprisonment for alleged crimes: 'No one is entitled to punish or torment them further, yet that is what happening.'" Ó Brádaigh also addressed whether the outside movement directed the hunger strikes: "It has long been recognised in the republican movement down through history that no one has the moral right to order another on hunger-strike."[79] In this short statement, Ó Brádaigh raises several relevant points. First, he stresses that the hunger strikes were not directed outside. Instead, the decisions were made from within the prisons. This claim is strengthened by former prisoner Vivion Hayden from Dublin. Hayden was imprisoned in Portlaoise during the hunger strikes and emphasized that the prisoners themselves decided to start, and later end, the protests. The decision to join the hunger strike was voluntary: "They passed a list around, and everyone who wanted to join could join. It was usually the younger ones who had no family or children outside."[80] By saying that the prisoners were not ordered from the outside movement to go on hunger strike, Ó Brádaigh was reacting to claims made by the government. The days before the hunger strike had started, a document had been found ordering prisoners to go on hunger strike. Yet, the fact that the prisoners themselves drew up this document did not emerge.[81] A press statement from the DoJ read: "A document found in the course of a routine search of Portlaoise Prison yesterday indicates that some of the main group of prisoners there are likely to be instructed by their leaders to stage a hunger strike early next month."[82] Republicans continuously denied this claim. The front page of *An Phoblacht* read: "It was the prisoners who decided to make the protest against the jail conditions. It was they who decided to end it."[83]

Second, Ó Brádaigh underlines both violent and passive resistance periods forerunning the hunger strikes. Third, he mentions "extensive publicity outside." However, public support for the hunger strikers was limited, and Ó Brádaigh's claim of "extensive publicity" was exaggerated, and the actions inside Portlaoise "had only a limited impact on the unfolding prison struggle north of the border."[84] Bernadette O'Hagan, the wife of J.B. O'Hagan, who was on hunger strike in 1971, remembers being "annoyed to learn that nothing had been organized in support of the men to highlight their grievances, as it was thought it was too early. But I thought otherwise."[85] O'Hagan says that when she went to the Sinn Féin Office in Dublin, only to be informed that there were no preparations for a public campaign, seven prisoners were already nineteen days into their hunger strike.

On 22 April, the hunger strike ended after forty-seven days without concessions, following a visit to the prison by Bishop James Kavanagh. However, he promised improvements in the future.[86] An editorial on the front page of *An Phoblacht* said: "Through the intervention of Senator Michael Mullen, Bishop James Kavanagh, Auxiliary Bishop of Dublin, visited the republican prisoners on hunger-strike in the Curragh Camp today, 22 April, at the request of the aforementioned, the prisoners agreed to call off the hunger-strike at 8 p.m. this evening."[87] Kevin Walsh remembers:

> I remember the evening Daithi O'Connell and Kevin Mallon came around to say it was ended they had to wake me up. I'd say I'd have just fallen asleep and died. It ended with negotiations. Now, Kevin Mallon could answer that better, but it ended, in a sense that the Government didn't admit they gave anything but within six weeks, we had the whole lot back. Well, we never got the proper visiting conditions but the clothes. They were trying to make us wear the uniform. We had a more or less free association, and we had the right to wear our own clothes and stuff like that.[88]

Throughout the year, the Fianna Fáil government improved conditions in the prisons.[89] Yet, these new developments were not enough for the republican prisoners who started to refuse all privileges except visits in September. The prisoners demanded free association and an end to strip searching. In an internal report, the authorities noted a danger of a riot in prison. Therefore, to ease the tensions, the prison authorities ended the strip searches, lock ups were agreed for 8:30 p.m., the prisoners were granted one late night every five to six weeks, tapes and records for language studies were allowed in the cells, and the tuck shop was improved. The concessions convinced the prisoners to end their protest.[90] As a result, commentators have interpreted the Portlaoise hunger strikes as a failure. For example, Darrach McDonald wrote in *Hibernia* shortly after the end of the fast: "The effects of the Portlaoise hunger strike will be felt for some time by the Provisionals. For those who took part, the physical effects will also be quite severe – Portlaoise was the first hunger strike by republicans when twenty men lasted over forty days. Kevin Mallon has, in the past four years, spent over 120 days without food, and the possible effect of the latest experience both on him and Dáithí O Conaill will affect the leadership inside and outside Portlaoise."[91]

While the prisoners did not attain their ultimate aim of political status, they had secured de facto special category status, and the conditions unquestionably improved over the four years of protest. Following the end of the protests, prisoners could wear their own clothes, and they could associate at breakfast. However, they were not allowed to receive any parcels, and no teaching staff were allowed in the jail – although self-study was permitted, and prisoners could also organize their own seminars and lectures.[92] Considering this, the prison protests were successful insofar as the prisoners achieved most of their demands. In

Northern Ireland, the blanket protests had started in the H-Blocks, and republicans were shifting their attention from the Republic's prisons.

In 1978, the prisoners again made a series of demands that were all rejected. Whereas the conditions improved throughout 1977/8, the prison authorities retained five security measures: periodical searches of the prison, strip searches, wire mesh barriers in the visiting room, access to craftwork only permitted if prisoners would agree to be strip searched, and free association only during periods of recreation. Furthermore, Patrick Cooney, the Minister of Justice, noted presumably in the spring or summer of 1977 that "allegations of brutality or inhuman treatment are totally false and without any foundation whatever." He claimed that: "Prisoners have outdoor recreation with facilities to play football, volleyball and handball. At indoor recreation, they can play cards, chess, draughts, table tennis, watch television and have four pool tables. Prisoners are well bedded, well-fed and warmly clothed."[93] The Minister of Justice's outline shows an improvement of the conditions. The document of the DoJ noted that "it is clear that the regime is a benign one and markedly different from that enjoyed by ordinary criminals."[94] Therefore, the government observed that "since the phasing-out of Special Category status [in Northern Ireland] there has been a marked decrease of tensions in Portlaoise. This may reflect the fact that conditions there are now appreciably better than in the Maze."[95] Different treatment from the ordinary criminal convicts was the primary demand for republicans. As soon as they had achieved it, the focus shifted towards self-organization in prison; among these steps were the setting up of a Cumann, that is, a local branch of the political party Sinn Féin, and the Irish-language wing.

The Portlaoise protests and the recognition as de facto political prisoners in the Republic had an often-overlooked impact on the prison protests in the Northern Irish prisons between 1976 and 1981. The first aspect is the role the prison struggle performed in the politics of the Provisionals during the Northern Ireland conflict. Although the protests did not ignite a broad popular campaign, they were nevertheless successful insofar as, ultimately, the demands had been met. The Northern Irish prisoners were also granted de facto political status following a short hunger strike of forty prisoners in 1972. However, this political status was removed in 1976, sparking the blanket and, later, the no-wash protests and eventually the 1980/1 hunger strikes.

The campaigns for political status and better conditions in the prisons of the Republic and Northern Ireland were similar. In both cases, protests lasted for nearly four years, which attracted relatively little attention from the public and were on the brink of failure. Ruairí Ó Brádaigh confirmed this in an interview on the results of the hunger strike in 1980: "The campaign was going nowhere. We knew that a new factor had to be introduced."[96] This new factor was the hunger strikes. This tactic had already been used to successfully conclude the long-lasting protests in Portlaoise for the Provisionals, as most of their demands were granted.

The second aspect, often overlooked, concerns the place Portlaoise occupied in the governmental and public debates surrounding the Long Kesh/Maze dispute. For example, in 1978, merely one year after the conclusion of the Portlaoise protests, Fr. Alec Reid of Clonard Monastery in Belfast addressed the Minister of State at the NIO, Don Concannon. Reid pointed to the government of the Republic as an example of how to deal with republican prisoners in Northern Ireland: "As you know, they do not, in principle, recognize political status for prisoners, or give any special status to any prisoner, but they so manage the affairs of their prisoners that they are able to avoid the kind of confrontation we are experiencing here. Portlaoise Prison is an example for this. The approach of the authorities in the Republic and the way they have managed to handle their prison protest are worthy, I believe, of serious and detailed examination because they may give helpful guidelines."[97]

Archival papers demonstrate that the British government studied the previous prison protests in Portlaoise, mainly how the Irish government solved the issues with the prisoners and how the situation within the prison developed after the end of the protests. An internal document of the British government compared the conditions of the prisoners in the Northern prisons and camps, such as H-Blocks/HMP Maze, Magilligan, Hydebank, and Armagh, with the conditions of republican prisoners in Portlaoise. Another British document compared the Northern prisons with Portlaoise and the conditions in other European countries. The information on Portlaoise included in these documents was obtained directly from the Irish government in intergovernmental briefings.[98] As the rumours of a hunger strike in the H-Blocks and the Armagh Women's Gaol intensified, "a British official visited the Department of Justice in Dublin on 6 and 7 October to investigate how the Irish authorities dealt with their paramilitary prisoners in Portlaoise Prison."[99] Sir Leonard Figg compiled another report on the effect of the hunger strikes in the Republic of Ireland.[100] The comparison between the protests in Portlaoise and the H-Blocks was also picked up by public commentators, such as the editor of the *Irish Press*, Tim Pat Coogan. In a letter to the *Guardian* on 31 October 1980, Coogan argues that the H-Blocks/Maze crisis could be solved by granting the prisoners the same rights as the Irish government had granted the Portlaoise prisoners:

In fact, of course, the substance of the five demands of the protesting republican prisoners in Long Kesh has been conceded in the Republic's Portlaoise gaol since 1977.... [The p]rison conditions in Portlaoise where protests, fasts, explosions, and a general state of near-riot over the issue of how IRA prisoners should be treated had created a situation which in some ways resembled the tensions generated by the H blocks.

One of the general considerations motivating the incoming Fianna Fail administration was the fact that a sizeable section of the population in the Republic perceived that the motivation of the prisoners, while it led them to commit criminal acts, was not that of ordinary criminals, and had to be judged against the backdrop of the physical-force tradition in Ireland and specifically the conditions in Northern Ireland which had involved these young men in violence in the first place.

Since that accommodation was reached, Portlaoise has faded out of the Irish consciousness in a way which the H blocks could also do if a similar solution were pursued.[101]

In this letter, Coogan stresses that demands of the H-Block prisoners were already conceded to the Portlaoise prisoners in 1977 when the prisoners were appeased, and the three and a half years of violent protests and hunger strikes had ended. This conclusion resulted from direct negotiations between the prisoners and the authorities of the Irish government, who recognized the need to solve the tensions in the prisons. By emphasizing the Irish government's insights in this regard, Coogan implicitly refers to the British government, which publicly stressed that no negotiating with republican prisoners would take place. Coogan concluded that the situation could be smoothed by negotiating and granting concessions, and the prison struggle thus "faded out" of public consciousness, if the British government would follow this example. In an editorial piece, the *Guardian* responded to Coogan: "Mr Tim Pat Coogan's letter today points to the solution at Portlaoise as a model for the Maze. His newspaper has urged the British Government to look again at the Younger Committee's proposals for improving the prison regime as a whole. At this crucial stage, every idea should be explored. But it is our understanding that the Portlaoise prisoners were not given what the Maze prisoners are demanding – concessions which would distinguish them from 'non-political' prisoners."[102]

Though the impact of the Portlaoise protests in resolving the H-Blocks hunger strikes remains unclear, the protests in the Republic undoubtedly informed the politics of the British government and the Provisionals alike. After the 1977 hunger strikes, the authorities informally recognized the paramilitary chain of command, which internally structured each of the segregated groups in Portlaoise and evolved a dispute-resolution process.[103] Following negotiations between the republican prisoners and the British government, de facto political status was also recognized in Northern Ireland. However, a similar dispute-resolution process developed only after ten prisoners had died on the hunger strike. While their demands were not formally granted, republican prisoners had gained special status on both sides of the Irish border from 1983.

The Portlaoise protests largely coincided with the period of special category status for the prisoners in Northern Ireland and ended with the phasing out of this special category status. The Portlaoise protests and the situation in Northern prisons were interlinked for five main reasons. First, the Portlaoise protests started because of the refusal of political status won in Northern Ireland. Second, prison protests in Portlaoise were successful insofar as they improved the conditions of the prisoners in the long run. When special category status was phased out, this showed the prisoners in Northern Ireland that their demands would only be met by embarking on protests. Third, the hunger strikes in Belfast in 1972 and Portlaoise in the following years resulted in the de facto recognition of political status for the prisoners. This recognition was the prisoners' primary demand when they started their hunger strikes in the H-Blocks in 1980 and 1981. Fourth, in the run-up to the 1980/1 hunger strikes, the Provisionals organized a broad-front support campaign, including independent activists and members of other republican groups to rally popular support.[104] This contrasted with the Portlaoise protests that were uncoordinated and unprepared, thus remaining marginal.[105] Fifth, the British and Irish governments regularly shared information on the conditions in the prisons during the protests in Portlaoise and the H-Blocks.[106] Under those conditions, it is fair to say that the Provisionals learned from the Portlaoise protests and used this experience during the years of the H-Block protest.[107]

The recognition of the paramilitary structure of the prisoners was an additional aspect that eased tensions in the debate. It was not until after the 1977 hunger strikes that the conflict could be solved, which enabled a smooth running of the prison. After these hunger strikes, the authorities informally recognized the paramilitary chain of command that internally structured each segregated group.[108] The governor of Portlaoise said: "We meet their O/Cs every so often. Each group elect an O/C every three months, and they come in here. We discuss grievances and problems. It generally works pretty well."[109] Former Portlaoise governor John Lonergan remembers the same situation in his memoirs: "The Provisional IRA prisoners had an OC (*oifigeach ceannais*) or commanding officer and a deputy OC who acted as spokesmen for their members.... The spokesmen came to see me on a regular basis, at least once or twice a month."[110] This situation is similar to recognizing de facto political status in the internment camps before phasing out the special category status in March 1976 and post-1983 in the H-Blocks.

Chapter Three

"No Prisoner Has the Right to Advance the Education of Another": Education in Portlaoise Prison

From the beginning of the conflict in Northern Ireland, educational facilities were demanded by republican prisoners held in Portlaoise Prison. This demand was expressed by the small number of republican prisoners held in Portlaoise before the arrival of the bulk of the prisoners from Mountjoy and Curragh. To make their voices heard, this small group of prisoners formed a Political Prisoners Committee and elected an adjutant to represent them. This elected adjutant was Seán Morrissey from Saor Éire, the most significant faction inside Portlaoise. In the prisoners' name, he formulated eighteen demands and issued them to the governor on 12 February 1972. Their primary demand was to have their own landing and that "we be given cells adjoining each other." In other words, the republican prisoners demanded segregation from ordinary prisoners as well as their own, separate space within the prison. Demand 17 was related to prison work and recreation; it said that "instead of doing the conventional work we be allowed to do leatherwork, match work, craft, Irish classes and study."[1] A "Note for the Minister's Information" from the same month describes the situation as follows:

> 4. [They] have all privileges of untried prisoners. They wear their own clothes, do not work, may have a daily 15-minute visit from not more than 3 relatives or friends, have unlimited correspondence, books, newspapers and can augment the prison diet from outside.
>
> 5. In addition, although they do not work they are allowed to associate and recreate from about 10.00 a.m. to 12.00 noon and from shortly after 2.00 p.m. to after 4.00 p.m. They have a room with a radio and a television which they can use during these periods as well as during the regular recreation period from 5.30 p.m. to 7.30 p.m. In the mornings, they also use a small exercise yard where they can play basketball, and the handball

alley is made available to them as well. In the afternoon, they have the use of the corrective training unit exercise yard where they can play football or handball.

6. They have asked for full "political treatment", recognition of their "political status", association in the evening up to 9.30 p.m. or 10.00 p.m. (for Irish classes?), an official issue of radio sets in their cells, rashers and eggs three times a week and "Crumlin Road [the prison in north Belfast holding loyalist and republican prisoners] standards" generally.…

8. Staff could not cope with late evening association. They can have their Irish classes morning or afternoon in their association room. One of them is competent to teach Irish. Only convicted prisoners serving twelve months or over are allowed the privilege of radios in their cells and then it must be a small transistor of their own. If they wish to get in additional food – rashers and eggs included – they will be facilitated about cooking it. An electric kettle is being supplied to the association room.…

11. They are troublesome since then and they march military fashion about the place. At the moment, 2 refuse to wear prison clothes and these 2 with 2 others refuse to work. There have been demands for "political" recognition, exemption from prison clothing and work, accommodation in adjoining cells, cell doors to be open during the day, freedom of association in each other's cells, private craft work in their cells, unlimited letters (this is accorded in practice to all prisoners in respect of incoming mail), food parcels, and "Crumlin Road conditions".[2]

This document shows that the small group of republican prisoners in Portlaoise Prison enjoyed wide privileges during the early 1970s. They could wear their own clothes, have daily visits, and were exempted from prison work. Furthermore, they could associate with comrades, hold meetings, and organize Irish classes. This treatment shows that the prisoners enjoyed de facto political status. The importance of learning Irish and the influence of older prisoners in running the republican landing were obvious.

Developments in the Northern Irish camps and prisons strongly impacted the prisoners in Portlaoise. When the prisoners were granted political status in Northern Ireland, the Portlaoise prisoners also demanded "Crumlin Road standards" for themselves. This acknowledgment would not have meant a significant improvement of the already very liberal conditions but recognition of their outside struggle. In the years after the transfer of the political prisoners from Mountjoy and Curragh, access to education was a frequent cause of tension. Cutting access to the library, books, and learning materials was often the first punishment for prisoners who protested degrading conditions in prison. In a press statement published by the Irish Republican Information Service at the height of the tensions between prisoners and warders on 14 December 1975, the republican movement informed the media about such restrictions by using its nom-de-guerre "P. O'Murchu, Runaí." Since the IRA was an illegal organization in both Irish states and Great Britain, the republican movement used pen names to secure their PRO (Public Relations Officer) Department members from prosecution. The most widely used pen name was "P. O'Neil"; *Runaí* is the Irish word for "secretary." The communiqué read: "The following week the Governor ruled that all educational facilities, lectures and debates were banned, together with correspondence courses and Dept. of Education examinations. The Dept. of Justice ruled that no prisoner had the right to advance the education of another."[3] These rulings meant heavy restrictions on the formal and informal education of the prisoners and restrictions on free association and political debates. Such limitations of debates during periods of protest aimed at hampering the decision-making process of the prisoners and was, probably, aimed at disuniting the prisoners and their strategies during the protests. An undated, handwritten letter by the imprisoned vice president of Sinn Féin, Dáithí O'Conaill, who was promoting education among prisoners, complains: "I have learned on Friday that the Dept. of Justice has ruled that no further lectures, debates and discussions will be tolerated here. The ruling is that 'no prisoner has the right to advance the education of another'. This is a severe blow to the programme of teaching the Sinn Féin political, social, regional and cultural policies and a setback to Des Ferguson also, who was about to start a course in woodwork. As you know, Sinn Féin literature is banned because it is considered 'subversive'."[4]

Following this handwritten letter, O'Conaill, the then OC of the PIRA prisoners, and his adjutant Liam Seán Kelly issued a statement entitled "Lectures banned in Portlaoise Jail." The statement read:

Three months ago, the Governor told Mr. O'Conaill that he would not allow Sinn Féin literature because in his (Mr O'Reilly's) view the material was "subversive" when it was pointed out to him, the Governor, that he had neither the right nor the competence to adjudicate in such matters, and that Sinn Féin literature was openly on sale to the public, Mr O'Reilly under-took to get an Official from the Department of Justice to discuss the matter.

No Official came to the Jail, and following a query on Dec 5th the Governor informed the Prisoners O/C and Adjutant that the Dept. of Justice had ruled that no prisoner had a right to advance the education of another and no lectures etc. would be tolerated. Already correspondence courses

are banned and requests to sit Dept. of Education exams in the prison have
been contemptuously dismissed.

The Governor's decision has been greeted with rage by the Political
Prisoners, it is seen as a further attempt to degrade republicans and treat
them as less than human.... A series of eight lectures on [republicanism]
was concluded a month ago and a keen interest was taken in them by both
Warders and Police....

The republican prisoners are treating with utter contempt the ruling of
the Dept. of Justice. An ambitious programme of winter debates has been
drawn up and will begin next week with "Freedom of Speech" an analysis
of Mr Cosgrave's address to the RTÉ authorities.[5]

As this statement informs, republican prisoners had organized a
systematic lecture program. These lectures were a step forward in sys-
tematizing the informal prison education, which consisted of individual lectures during the first years after the transfer of prisoners from
Mountjoy in 1973. Instrumental in the attempt to set up a lecture series
was imprisoned Sinn Féin Vice President Dáithí O'Conaill. However,
a notable difference between this lecture series and the later lectures
organized by the Sinn Féin Cumann was that these lectures were under
the guidance of the IRA and not the Cumann, as we shall see.

Following years of protests, the heightened tension within Portlaoise Prison slowly reached public attention. On Monday, 25 April 1977,
the *Irish Times* published "A day in the life of a prison Provisional,"
bringing the situation within Portlaoise Prison to a broader audience
than the republican movement could reach. The article mentions education, informing the reader that "attempts at organizing classes and
debates have failed because of the overcrowding and noise in the room....
Unless everybody was involved, they [do] not work and inevitably
not everybody was involved, and so they failed."[6] While the reporters
wrote that "attempts at organizing classes and debates have failed,"
no mention was made of any restrictions on organizing classes by the
prison authorities. Later, *Irish Press* journalist Pat Holmes wrote the
article "Inside Portlaoise," informing that "facilities for work and education, other than craftwork, do not exist at the prison." He continued:
"The cells we saw contained many books. The books are ordered from
the County Library for the prison, and the governor also orders a wide
range of educational books as requested by the prisoners. Visitors are
not allowed to bring books to prisoners. Such books could possibly contain codes and must be prohibited for security reasons, we were told."[7]

Around the end of the protest, "friends and relatives of the political
prisoners in Portlaoise Jail" published an appeal outlining the prisoners'

demands. The demands embraced four areas: spiritual welfare, educational facilities, recreational facilities, and general demands. Regarding "educational facilities," it read:

> Various attempts to run educational classes in the jail have been prevented by the governor. He has refused to allow correspondence courses, educational tapes and records, drawing equipment and textbooks, a room for study, lectures and debates, etc. and permission for examinations to be held in the prison. An educational body has been set up with facilities in Mountjoy and other prisons however such facilities do not obtain in Portlaoise. Offers by outside teachers, both clerical and lay, to give lectures in the prison have been turned down by the governor. Since most of the 90 prisoners are between the ages of 18 and 30 the suppression of educational facilities is a great hardship which will have a lasting effect on them. The policy of the authorities is one of forcing the prisoners to vegetate.[8]

The accounts of the journalist and the prisoners' relatives slightly differ. However, all accounts stress that classes and lectures could not be held, whereas different accounts give different reasons for this. The second media report from November shows a relaxation of the prison regime. While still unable to hold classes, many prisoners had a considerable number of books in their own cells that had been ordered through the prison library. This ordering of books through the library became the primary source for preparing lectures and classes following the formation of the Sinn Féin Cumann in the following year.

Since the free association was restricted and classes, lectures, and other educational facilities were subject to the restriction as punishment during the height of the protests, education was among the main demands of the prisoners during this time. Father Piaras Ó Dúill from Dublin was a human rights activist during all periods of prison protests in the 1970s and 1980s. Following the end of the Portlaoise hunger strikes, he wrote an analysis on these hunger strikes entitled "Portlaoise Prison – Why there was a hunger strike." In this document, he identifies three main areas that lead to the outbreak of the protests. These were strip searching, visiting conditions, and education. Regarding educational facilities, he wrote:

> No education allowed:
>   Educational facilities are forbidden in the prison, not indeed by the prison rules but by the prison authorities.… Lectures, whether by outside lecturers or by chosen prisoners are forbidden. The prison Governor's reply to this request was: [unbelievably] "No prisoner is entitled to further

the education of another." Educational books are also forbidden as are all classes, debates, correspondence, basic teaching aids such as drawing equipment, textbooks, cassettes and records....

When addressing a clerical ecumenical conference in March last, Fr. Faul said that the ex-prisoners he had met from Portlaoise Prison were more socially disorientated than ex-prisoners from either Six County or British jails. It is my own opinion that the worst prison in these islands is that of Portlaoise.[9]

Ó Dúill sums up that the lack of educational facilities combined with the frequent use of solitary confinement harmed the psychological well-being of released prisoners. A later document by Ó Dúill again stresses the demand for educational facilities. In this paper entitled "Denial of Educational Facilities in Portlaoise Prison," he informs that the re-introduction of educational facilities was included in the agreement that had ended the February 1977 hunger strikes. However, it had still not been implemented in the autumn of the same year. He writes that "to date, the following requests of the prisoners have been met by blunt refusals and total indifference" before listing five points:

1. A request to have a room available for classes, lectures, debates etc. has been refused outright by the prison governor. He also refused to re-open the Recreation room closed since last March.
2. The authorities will not allow correspondence courses to prisoners wishing to do Leaving Certificate and G.C.E. examinations....
3. Basic teaching aids such as drawing equipment, textbooks, cassettes and records are banned completely. Many prisoners who are individually studying languages are working under great hardship because of the refusal of the authorities to permit courses on tapes. Educational books seized last December by the authorities have not been returned to the prisoners.
4. Offers by outside teachers to give lectures in the prison have been turned down by the prison governor. Lecturers have been given access to Long Kesh for the last couple of years while this facility is being denied strenuously by the Portlaoise authorities.
5. An offer by Anco[10] to conduct courses in the prison has also been rejected. Many of the prisoners are young apprentices who could be greatly assisted by Anco. In Mountjoy prison, Anco courses are being conducted for non-political prisoners. This is progress. But there seems to be a determination on behalf of the authorities in Portlaoise prison to create conditions where prisoners are forced to revolt. It is such use of institutional privilege that forces more

and more people to identify themselves with those who have been pushed to violence.[11]

In this document, Ó Dúill develops a relationship between the denial of educational facilities for the prisoners and their resistance against the prison authorities, which ultimately led to three hunger strikes in the previous years. It is also noteworthy to draw attention to his comparison of the situation between Portlaoise and Long Kesh, north of the border. In subsequent years, this comparison was used regularly by media and internal Irish and British government correspondence but not by the republican movement itself. Instead, Irish republicans and their supporters shifted their full attention from Portlaoise to the protests in the H-Blocks following the settlement in 1977 in the Republic and the start of the blanket protest in 1976 in Northern Ireland.

Following the end of the prison protests, the regime was significantly relaxed, and educational facilities such as the library, private books, course material, and free association to hold meetings and lectures, were made available for the prisoners. The prisoners were woken up around eight o'clock in the morning. They were then brought to the bathrooms, given breakfast, and led to the yard. Following the morning sports, those prisoners who did craftwork could use the remaining time until lunch for meetings, discussions, learning, and reading. Similarly, there was time to hold meetings, lectures, and work in the prison library in the evening. The nights were used for reading until the warders switched off the lights.[12] Matt Leen from Tralee, Co. Kerry, was imprisoned in Portlaoise Prison from 1979 to 1983 and described a day in the prison:

Your cell door was opened at 8 a.m., you had breakfast then, and you'd wash and wash the cell and few things like that. The only work we did was to clean our own landings; we didn't work for the screws.[13] At 10 a.m., we went out to the yard. Every fellow had his own agenda; I could play handball, walk around the yard. There were workshops there, leather workshops and timber workshops and you could go there. There were plenty of things to do; if the day was wet, you could watch a film. Dinner was at 12:30 p.m.; you would be locked up until 2 p.m. On every landing, there was a hot press where the dinners were brought up prepared; you collected your dinner and brought it back to your cell. You had about ten minutes before the lockup, so a lot of fellows ate their dinner with the fella from the next cell and things like that. At the weekend, you could buy food, like steak, the prison would cook that for you. In the afternoon, you could go back to the yard. On a fine day, you would have lads sunning themselves; there would also be football matches and handball. It all got us through. You would go back in at 4 p.m., and you would be locked up for an hour. You would be out again from 5 until 8 p.m. You could then go up to the workshops, particularly in the winter when it was dark early. There was lovely stuff turned out there like wallets and belts, tables, mirrors and that type of thing. You could lace wallets in your cell, but the rest of the work was done in the workshops.[14]

While the description of a day in the prison is similar to the descriptions of other prisoners in Portlaoise Prison between the end of the prison protests in the 1970s and the late 1980s, Matt Leen does not mention any education facilities or reading time during his interview. Instead, he devotes a fair amount of time to sports and yard activities. Indeed, other prisoners mentioned that Matt Leen was a devoted GAA player and was an outstanding goalkeeper in the Gaelic football tournaments organized in prison. However, when asked if prisoners organized education classes, he said:

Yes, they did, there were Irish classes, Jim Monaghan organized a class one day, it was actually an explosives class, one fellow went to the class thinking it was about construction as it was advertised as an "Engineering class", when he came out he said: "It was blowing things up not building they were teaching ye in there". There were very good lectures. Whenever Gearoid MacCarthaigh gave a lecture, there was a full house because Gearoid lived through all of this. Gearoid was locked up in the 1940s, '50s, '60s, '70s and '80s. His lectures were unreal. Gearoid was giving a lecture one night on the 1940s, there was this infamous Special Branch man Dinny O'Brien, he was notorious for chasing down republicans, he and his brother Paddy had fought in 1916, and in the Four Courts[15] in 1922, Gearoid said that on the day O'Brien was shot by the IRA he was wearing a bulletproof vest, but he didn't have a bulletproof hat. Liam McElhinney from Co Tyrone also gave very good lectures. Liam was also the OC, and I count him as a most honourable man. He knew his history about every part of Ireland. There was another fellow. I gave him a copy of the book *Tragedies of Kerry*, and I said read this tonight. So, he came out in the morning out of the cell and said: "Who dreamt this up? This never happened". – "Well", I said, "if you don't know your history, this is what happened in Kerry, Kerry is in Ireland too."

But what I found with some of the Northern people is they knew some of the histories of their own areas, but they weren't too well up on the history of the rest of the country. It's important to have a full knowledge of Irish history. If you're in jail, first of all, you have to believe in what you're there for, and your time won't be half as hard. If you don't believe in what you're there for, you will suffer. There were a lot of them in there, and they didn't know what it was all about.[16]

Leen remembers individual lectures that prisoners gave. However, he shows no awareness of systematic classes organized by the prisoners, nor does he say anything about who organized these lectures. Another sign that education was not systematically organized is the mention of the book *Tragedies of Kerry*, a book about the Irish Civil War in 1922/3. Leen is himself from Kerry, suggesting that he may have read this book before his sentence. In other words, Leen may have been reluctant to show enthusiasm for the classes offered in prison, but his main criticism is that prisoners from Northern Ireland had little knowledge of Irish history because, what was almost shocking for a Kerry man, they had no knowledge of the Civil War in County Kerry, as described in the book by McArdle.

Dan Hoban was a republican prisoner during all three decades between the 1950s and 1970s. He served as a second in command in Portlaoise Prison and was a negotiator during various prison protests. Thus, due to Hoban's experience as a prisoner and his leading role within the republican movement, his views can be interpreted as representative of a faction within the republican movement of that time, namely, traditional Southern republicans. During the interview, Hoban explained his understanding of what was expected from republican prisoners during their sentence, he said: "What I always considered as the prison was that you got over your prison sentence in the best way you could, and at the end of your term, if you could come out of prison the same man as you went in, you had achieved something. Because when you were a prisoner, any rank you held outside vanished. You know, you were no longer making a contribution to the struggle for freedom. You just did your time as best as you could. That was my reading of it."[17]

Hoban's understanding is that the focus of the prisoners was to finish their sentence and come out the same republicans as they went in. He argues this because prisoners lost their ranks in the IRA when imprisoned and thus made no further contribution to the struggle from within the prison. This argument springs from a military viewpoint and neglects the political work done by prisoners in later years. Furthermore, although losing their ranks within the outside movement, prisoners held their own ranks and maintained their own structure within the prison; as mentioned above, Hoban was general adjutant of the Portlaoise prisoners himself.

Hoban gives the impression that the political prisoners were not interested in education, although he mentions that "some prisoners liked reading." Indeed, books and additional educational material were regularly part of the negotiations between prisoners and authorities. For example, in 1974, prison authorities reduced the number of books prisoners could receive and keep in their cells after the escape of nineteen prisoners. However, in September 1977, tapes and records for language study were allowed in the cells.[18] Around that time, prisoners joined the landing with high skills in Irish, and these prisoners promoted the language among their comrades, which resulted in the setting up of a separate Irish language area on the top of the landing.[19] Hoban was released from Portlaoise Prison in the mid-1970s. A report issued by the Department of Justice from the late 1970s explains the regime in Portlaoise; under the headline "Remission," it reads: "One-quarter remission of sentence may be earned for 'industry and good conduct'. The industry includes education. Teachers are not provided at Portlaoise, but books are upon request. Prisoners may study in their cells, but the movement of books is carefully monitored. The formal position is that prisoners are not allowed to educate each other, i.e., they can study individually in one of the study rooms, which allow for 4 students each or in their cells. However, when prisoners come together as for example, in recreation, they would clearly be in a position to converse."[20]

The rules and regulations state that prisoners were not allowed to "educate each other." However, as the same documents suggest, that rule was merely a "formal position," and since the free association was possible during certain times, prisoners were indeed able to educate each other, give lectures, and hold discussions.

In 1981, the prison protests in Northern Ireland reached new heights. While prisoners had been on blanket and no-wash protest in Long Kesh since the phasing out of special category status in 1976, in later years the women in HMP Armagh joined the protests. In the autumn of 1980, the first hunger strike failed to solve the situation, and thus Bobby Sands led a second hunger strike in 1981, which resulted in the death of ten Irish republican prisoners until it was eventually called off in October 1981. In the same year, a document compiled for the Northern Ireland Secretary of State compared the prison regime in HMP Maze and Portlaoise Prison. It showed a significant improvement of the Portlaoise prisoners' situation compared to the situation described by Father Ó Dúill and the prisoners' relatives in 1977. The relevant parts dealing with educational facilities and the access to classes say that:

Work

Private study an alternative to work. Can study individually in the study room (Max 30). No formal lectures – book, tapes and video available. No teachers.

Association

Prisoners locked up at dinner and tea time and from 8.30 pm to morning. 1 late night up to 10.30 pm every six weeks. Breakfast, work and recreation times, limited no. of prisoners may come together, e.g. 65 PIRA take outdoor recreation, 30 may study together. During breakfast cell doors are open, and prisoners in any landing (about 50 cells) may congregate in each other's cell for the period – normally 3–4 in any one cell. Prisoners are not allowed free movement in the prison.[21]

The document concludes that the department approved these conditions of justice on 3 September 1981. According to this document, the prisoners could associate freely, organize lecture debates, and hold classes on an informal basis. However, formal education by external teachers was not allowed. Nonetheless, the new regime permitted prisoners to organize their own political education and debates. This change was a significant step that furthered the work of the Sinn Féin Cumann and the establishment of the Gaeltacht landing, as we shall see later.

In the biography of former Portlaoise prisoner Martin Ferris, who became Sinn Féin TD for Kerry after his release, the author J.J. Barrett writes that in the early period during the protests in the 1970s, the prisoners only had access to the books available through the prison library. However, Ferris remembers that access to books made life in the prison much more accessible, although one had no choice over the reading material. Nonetheless, the prisoners sometimes had access to political literature and history. In total, they could borrow three library books per week. Ferris explains that after the last hunger strike that had ended on 26 and 27 April 1977, the "conditions did improve, albeit slowly." He remembers two significant improvements among other, more minor, changes. These were, first, the recognition of the IRA structure in prison and, second, the abolition of body searches of the prisoners. Strip searches continued, however, causing further tensions in the early 1980s. He continues to write that the conditions in Portlaoise remained the same between the end of the hunger strikes and 1982. Although there were minor improvements, the strip searching, closed visits, and beatings continued. Prisoners resisting these strip searches were subject to solitary confinement. However, the phasing out of night searches significantly improved the prisoners. Prisoners strongly objected to the practice of strip searching, and the republican movement regularly reported on this inhumane practice in their periodicals. However, the prisoners did not seek direct confrontation with the prison authorities on this matter, nor did the outside movement prepare a campaign to protest the strip searches until the end of the hunger strikes in the H-Blocks in the autumn of 1981. As outlined in the previous chapter, the focus was on supporting the Blanketmen and the hunger strikers in Northern Ireland between 1976 and 1981.[22]

The relatively quiet period from the end of the wave of protests in 1977 ended abruptly with violent clashes during a general search of the prison on Sunday, 30 October 1983. This search made headlines in the news at that time. The Department of Justice reported six injured prison officers and two injured prisoners, while Sinn Féin reported eighty injured prisoners. In his biography of Martin Ferris, who was not imprisoned in Portlaoise at that time, Barrett writes about the clashes on that night:

> The initial incident began after the prisoners had been locked up at din-nertime, 12:45 pm. Officers were ordered to search two cells and strip-search the occupants. Searches during the lock-up or at night were totally unacceptable to the prisoners, and up until then, it was a practice long discontinued by the officers. In addition, this search came on a Sunday, and this meant breaking a previous agreement that no cell searches were to be carried out on Sundays. It was the only day of the week the prisoners could get some respite from these searches and relax. There was a stand-ing policy to resist any such searches as a unit, as well as resistance by the individuals subjected to the searches.[23]

Strip searches and cell searches were common during these years. The prison administration broke a previous agreement by conducting the searches on a Sunday. It was, nonetheless, a break in the prison authorities' policy to keep the tensions low in the prison. Thus, the col-lective resistance to these searches might have been an indication that the republican movement was once again turning its attention south of the borders following the end of the prison protests in Northern Ireland. After the violent clashes, Governor O'Reilly met with the OC, Francis Lucas Quigley, and the IRA adjutant, Paul "Dingus" Magee. During these talks, O'Reilly informed the prisoners' leader that all the cells would be stripped of their contents as a punishment for banging on doors. The republican movement blamed then governor O'Reilly for the conditions and compared the prison with Nazi concentration camps – a ridiculous claim despite the hardship in prison – and one of the prison officers, Larry O'Neill, vice-chairperson of the Portlaoise branch of the Prisoners' Officers' Association, is reported as saying, "if Hitler wanted generals today he would find plenty of them in Portlaoise." However, the reign of Governor O'Reilly soon came to an end and thus so did these violent clashes. The clashes on 30 October 1983 were the last physical confrontations between prisoners and warders of this scale in Portlaoise, and conditions improved dramatically in the mid-1980s.[24]

The Irish government introduced a prison reform in Portlaoise called the "humane containment policy." While economic considerations were given as the official reason for this move, the policy changes came parallel with similar improvements in Northern Ireland from 1983 onwards; introducing these changes foreshadowed the beginning of the conflict transformation process. Moreover, since the Irish and British governments were in direct contact discussing the prisoners' situation in Northern Ireland and Portlaoise throughout the conflict, the reform of the prison regime in Portlaoise and the H-Blocks likely represented an agreed move by both governments to hasten the transformation of the republican movement.[25]

Throughout the 1980s, conditions improved, strip searches and closed visits ended, and educational facilities were made available to the prisoners to hold debates, lectures, and formal education. In Portlaoise Prison, the "humane containment policy" included an educational program and "negotiation, and a good working relationship would replace the baton and the boot.... The strip-searching was phased out.... This still left the issue of inhumane closed visits. They too disappeared from the system shortly afterwards."[26] Originally from Dungannon in County Tyrone, Tommy McNulty served time in Belfast Prison, Mountjoy, Curragh, and Portlaoise. On the situation in Portlaoise Prison, he explains: "You had the like of Dáithí Ó Conaill and Ruairí Ó Brádaigh. You had some very intelligent, well-read, old Southern republicans. And I went to many lectures and many political discussions. I learned a lot from them."[27] As these accounts by various prisoners, such as Ferris, Hoban, Leen, and McNulty, show, the lectures and discussions were not systematic or compulsory, and they mainly focused on historical topics.

While lectures and debates in the 1970s were unsystematic, the introduction of regular and more formal classes and lectures only started with the formation of the Sinn Féin Cumann in 1978/9 after the prison protests.[28] This Cumann formation coincided with the relaxation of the prison regime, and the rules and regulations for education in 1980 were as follows: "Prisoners in Portlaoise Prison do not have the teaching service which in the case of other prisons is provided by the local Vocational Education Committee. They may, however, study privately."[29] The passage that prisoners were not permitted to "educate each other" included in the earlier document had been removed in the later rules and regulations. Indeed, the prisoners made full use of these new privileges through the Cumann.

In later years, the prison governor allowed university lecturers and teachers into the prisons. Brendan McCaffrey was born in Roslea, Co Fermanagh. He spent time in Crumlin Road Prison, Long Kesh, and Portlaoise. He remembers lectures from UCD and other institutes teaching in prison: "They used to send lecturers in from UCD. Finish up, Brian Maguire and another fella used to come in. They were painters. They were lecturers in NCAD. So, they used to come in every so often, like, try and teach you. But I think they learnt more off us than we learnt off them because Maguire used to copy some of my stuff."[30]

McCaffrey is one of the few Portlaoise inmates who mentions external lecturers. His comment that these lecturers "learnt more off us than we learnt off them" suggests that the prisoners showed little enthusiasm for the formal education offered by the prison service; moreover, the prisoners were more articulate than the teachers and as advanced. Pat Treanor from County Monaghan spent time in Mountjoy and Portlaoise Prison in the late 1970s and 1980s. He was one of those conducting Open University degrees: "You could do Open University courses, and the library would facilitate in getting the necessary books, the reading list in for you. I did psychology and sociology at A-Level standard. There were others that had an interest and liking for languages. Seán McGettigan learned five or six languages."[31] Treanor only discusses his own degrees and does not mention other prisoners who did Open University courses.[32] Instead, when mentioning the education of other prisoners, he gives their interest in learning Irish as an example. This comment and the one from McCaffrey above indicate that only individual prisoners used the formal education courses in Portlaoise. While informal debates and lectures organized by the prisoners themselves were not restricted during the 1980s, the prison authorities placed obstacles in the way of prisoners who wanted to receive a formal education. These obstacles could be one of the reasons why only a small number of prisoners decided to finish formal degrees in Portlaoise Prison compared to the internment camps and prisons in Northern Ireland. In an interview with the republican newspaper *An Phoblacht/Republican News* published on 22 November 1984, Seán Mulligan, who served eight years in Portlaoise, explains:

> Educational facilities are also bad, though recently a few teachers have been allowed in, all the petty restrictions that are enforced before a prisoner is allowed to go to a class makes it virtually useless. A lot of the men study on their own and have passed exams by correspondence when it is allowed.

Some of them have been waiting for more than two years for an answer to requests to do courses. It is a way of pulling prisoners off doing anything worthwhile. The prison authorities hope you will just give up.[33]

In another interview from that time, prisoner John Carroll recounts similar experiences regarding the educational facilities available in prison: "There have been a lot of improvements in this area, but there is still much to be desired. The only exams the man can take are Inter and Leaving cert and 'O' and 'A' Levels. No correspondence courses are permitted for higher courses, and no lecturers are allowed in. The reason given is 'security', but it's really because they couldn't be bothered censoring all the stuff."[34]

The fact that only individual prisoners used the formal education courses and conducted Open University degrees is in stark contrast to the prisoners north of the border. In Northern Ireland, many prisoners undertook Open University degrees during the 1980s and 1990s. The contradiction between the acceptance of formal education in the Northern and Southern prisons will be discussed later in this book. In Portlaoise, education was unsystematic and not compulsory for the prisoners in the 1970s. The focus of the republican movement was that prisoners remain solid republicans during their sentence – there was no attempt to use the prisoners for political advantage or to include them in internal debates within the outside movement. However, individual prisoners organized lectures and discussions; this situation changed with the introduction of formal Irish languages classes and the formation of the Sinn Féin Cumann in prison.

Chapter Four

The Harvey/McCaughey/Smith Cumann: Sinn Féin in Portlaoise Prison, 1978–1986

In August 1973, Sinn Féin established its first Cumann in Mountjoy Prison, Dublin. In an attempt to politicize the IRA prisoners, this Cumann was later reorganized at a meeting of republicans in Portlaoise Prison in 1978. The Sinn Féin Cumann in Portlaoise held a central position in the political and social life of the republican prisoners during the 1980s. Before the establishment of the Cumann, the focus of the republican movement was on keeping the prisoners "solid republicans," as former prisoner Dan Hoban describes it. This interpretation means that no effort was made to use the prisoners for political advantage or to include them in internal debates within the outside movement during their sentence. This situation ultimately changed from the mid-1970s onwards, both in Portlaoise and Long Kesh.

In 1986, the majority of the Sinn Féin Ard-Fheis voted in favour of dropping the policy of "abstentionism" from the constitution of Sinn Féin.[1] Abstentionism meant that elected candidates of Sinn Féin would not take their seats in any of the parliaments in Dublin, Belfast, or London and instead would represent their constituency as delegates of the Second All-Ireland Dáil established in 1921.[2] Traditional Southern republicans formed the leadership of the republican movement from the split between the Officials and the Provisionals in 1969/70 and the takeover of a new Northern-based leadership in 1983; three years later, they split the movement and formed their own organization.[3] The Portlaoise Cumann ceased to exist around the 1986 split of the republican movement. The reasons for the decline and the abandoning of the Cumann remain unclear.

While the republican prisoners always maintained the military structure in the internment camps and prisons, in the late 1970s, the Provisional republican movement decided to organize the prisoners as Cumainn (local branches) of its political wing, Sinn Féin. The formation of this Cumann was an integral part of the political self-awareness process of the Provisionals. However, while a Cumann had existed in Mountjoy Prison, it ceased to exist with the transfer to Portlaoise; it was only after the conclusion of the prison protests in 1977 and the granting of most of their demands to the prisoners that the situation improved to a stage in which the Cumann as a functional body could be reorganized.

A Cumann is the smallest entity of Sinn Féin. It works on a local level and can be formed by at least five full members of the organization. The constitution of Sinn Féin explains the work of the Cumann as: "Through local Sinn Féin members establishing themselves in their local community on local issues, thereby gaining the confidence of those involved in local affairs." Membership of Sinn Féin can only be obtained through membership of a Cumann. Thus, in the case of Portlaoise Prison, all prisoners who were members of Sinn Féin had to be members of the Cumann; in other words, there were no Sinn Féin members outside the Cumann. The Cumann sends two delegates to the annual Ard-Fheis (AGM) of Sinn Féin – however, impossible for members of a prison Cumann. Nonetheless, the Portlaoise Prison Cumann members received and debated all motions put forward at the Ard-Fheis; they could also comment on these motions. Furthermore, every Cumann of Sinn Féin elected an officer board. This officer board consisted of a Cathaoirleach (chairperson), a Leas-Cathaoirleach (vice-chairperson), a Rúnaí (secretary), beirt Cisteorí (two treasurers), and a public relations officer (PRO). This officer board was elected annually at a special meeting held on written notice within fourteen days after the termination of the Ard-Fheis.[4]

The first Sinn Féin prison Cumann was formed in the D-Wing of Mountjoy Prison in August 1973. The organizer of this Cumann was the republican prisoner Donal McCarthy from Cork. Apart from him, seven other prisoners are named as initial members of this Cumann. However, the exact number is unclear because no written accounts from this Cumann in Mountjoy Prison remain. A republican prisoner wrote a brief history of the Mountjoy Cumann; he explains that Donal McCarthy had the idea to form a Cumann in Mountjoy in honour of Séamus Harvey. Harvey was an IRA member from West Tyrone who had been arrested near the border in June 1973 and was on remand in the D-Wing of Mountjoy Prison. In July, Harvey got bail, and upon his release, he reported back to the local temporary commander of the IRA since the local O/C had recently been arrested. Harvey was appointed O/C himself, and a fortnight after his release, he transported a bomb towards Castlederg in County Tyrone. The bomb went off prematurely, and both men died on 10 August 1973.[5] The report of the prisoner says:

> Anyway, it wasn't very long after that when Donal McCarthy approached some men in the "Joy" (Mountjoy) with the idea that a Cumann should be formed to honour the memory of Seamus Harvey, as he was a popular comrade in the Unit (he had a great interest in football & played often in the jail) I must say, Donal went about the inmates in a very bad way, he talked it over with this one and that but still kept it all very "hush, hush"....
> The meeting was held in the Rec. on "D.I" & the Cumann was founded – Donald McCarthy was Secretary & Donal DeBarra, Chairman – I remember Joe Laughlin was also a member – the main work of the Cumann was education groups + meetings on the "Éire Nua" booklet + the idea of Co-Ops etc. [It was named the Seamus Harvey Cumann.] When we came here in Nov. '73 – I recall the Cumann meeting a few times & also a few debates etc.[6]

As this report suggests, this Cumann was not a properly functioning entity, for it met irregularly and performed no visible role within the prison population. However, it held some meetings and started a political discussion on essential republican documents, such as the *Éire Nua* policy. *Éire Nua* was a policy document adopted by Sinn Féin in the early 1970s. It called for a united and federal democratic Ireland with Athlone as its capital and remained the main Sinn Féin document outlining a solution for the conflict until it dropped at the Ard-Fheis in 1983.[7] Nonetheless, the transfer from Mountjoy to Portlaoise further affected the work of the Cumann. The stricter prison regime and the ongoing protests of the prisoners made it impossible to continue the previous work of the Cumann, and it went into decline over the following months. The report says: "Due to the later state of affairs here, the Cumann went into decline – it would have been impossible to keep it going between Hunger Strikes, protests, lock-ups etc."[8]

The reorganization started in 1978. The inaugural meeting of the Cumann was held in January 1978, and according to the prisoners' report, it was "well attended."[9] According to the minute books, there were fifteen prisoners in attendance, approximately 10 per cent of the prison population held in Portlaoise at that time.[10] The Mountjoy Cumann was initially named the Seámus Harvey Cumann; yet when the Cumann was reorganized in Portlaoise, the names of Seán McCaughey and Tom Smith were added.[11] Seán McCaughey was an IRA member who died on hunger strike in Portlaoise Prison on 11 May 1946; Tom Smith died during an escape attempt from Portlaoise Prison on St. Patrick's Day 1975.[12] Since then, the name of the Cumann had been "The Seámus

Harvey/Seán McCaughey/Tom Smith Cumann Sinn Féin Portlaoise Prison." The Irish name of the Cumann was "to be used in all official letters etc."[13] Pat Treanor from Monaghan was arrested in Co Galway in 1975 and, after a short spell in Mountjoy, transferred to Portlaoise, where he was involved in reorganizing the Cumann:

> We started off the process of setting up a Cumann and doing education on Sinn Féin structures and policies. I think I might have been chair or secretary of it for a while. Out of that, there were more detailed debates around aspects of policy, economic policy, the whole issue of equality and feminism. Some people would have gone off and done research on other struggles – Algeria, Vietnam and places like that. And then they would have done a talk to the rest of the prisoners. Geróid McCarthy from Cork agreed to do a lecture on the IRA from the Thirties on. It was a great education for us all because you would never have heard it first-hand.[14]

As Treanor recalls, they focused on organizing lectures and debates for all prisoners on the republican wing. As in the earlier years, the talks were unsystematic, and many imprisoned republican veterans, like Geróid McCarthy or Dáithí O'Conaill, held lectures about previous periods of the republican struggle. In addition to the regular lectures, the Cumann organized commemorations, particularly Easter Commemorations to commemorate the 1916 Easter Rising, and debated on Sinn Fein business, such as the motions of the annual Sinn Féin Ard-Fheisenna (AGMs). For instance, in the spring of 1979, the Cumann organized a function to honour the one hundredth birthday of Irish republican icon Patrick Pearse. In the same year, the Cumann also organized annual Easter Commemorations.[15] The constitution of Sinn Féin demands that Cumainn hold an AGM following every Ard-Fheis to elect a new officer board, consisting of a chairperson, vice-chairperson, PRO, secretary, and treasurer. The Sinn Féin members also held this AGM in Portlaoise.

It was usually those who were already members of Sinn Féin before being arrested who joined the Cumann in prison. Seosamh Ó Maileoin from County Westmeath was imprisoned twice, first in Mountjoy during the helicopter escape, which resulted in his transfer, together with all other republican prisoners held in Mountjoy and Curragh to Portlaoise; he was released shortly afterwards. His second spell in Portlaoise was longer and lasted from 1980 to March 1986. During this time, he was an active member of the Cumann. He remembers: "I was always a very political person, so it was no question for me to join the Cumann when I arrived in Portlaoise…. For me, I always considered the political part as very important. I was always politically interested, I read a lot, in the cell I read and collected newspaper cuttings, but, you know, also before, local history, and so."[16] He continues explaining the work and the running of the Cumann:

> I got involved with the Sinn Féin Cumann inside. We were a small group.… Out of the one hundred or so prisoners, we would have a dozen people or so directly involved in the running of the Sinn Féin Cumann. Cyril MacCurtain was one of them from Limerick, Liam McElhinney, and so. There were people who wanted to take seats (in Leinster House), and I got a shock. There were two people I couldn't depend on among the people I thought I could depend on. Jim Monaghan, no, Jim never hid the fact that seats should be contested. Now, I kind of admired him for it in one way because he was open about it. Joe Reilly would have been another who was lukewarm.… But we held our meetings, and we held lectures, and Jim used to give lectures on everything and anything, Socialism, Communism, every "ism" going, Jim was brilliant in giving lectures. We gave lectures; then, on 1798, we had one on 1916. I remember myself writing a pageant for 1916. I based it on Michael O'Hanrahan and called it the "The Swords Man in the Brigade." The lectures would be held every month. We wouldn't have a huge crowd. Some of the people that weren't directly involved in the Cumann wouldn't come to the lectures.… Jim Monaghan gave a number of lectures, so did Cyril MacCurtain, who naturally would have given some of the lectures, and also Liam McElhinney used to be brilliant. Liam was from Donegal, and Cyril was from Limerick. But there were two people who were very "anti" any moves towards accepting seats. There were two in particular, well, there were others too, but they were particular. Every time in Portlaoise, I was a member of the Staff. I was the Quartermaster, which meant I was looking after the cigarettes.… That was the main thing of the Quartermaster at that time, cigarettes. Clothing, if it came in it, could come to my cell as well. I did all of that stuff. On another occasion, I was the Finance Officer; I was the Landing Officer.[17]

Ó Maileoin was not only member of the IRA staff in prison, but throughout the years, he was also involved in the running of the Cumann in various positions. Pat Treanor explains that the focus of the Cumann was the organization of lectures and debates. As Jim Kavanagh remembers, these lectures were held by a small group of volunteers. Kavanagh was originally from Wexford but was an active Provisional IRA member in Belfast. He first spent time in the internment camp Long Kesh and afterwards from 1975 to the autumn of 1982 in Portlaoise Prison: "I am sure people would volunteer that they would give a talk on this and that and a Q&A afterwards. It was more that kind of thing that people volunteered; it was not really formal. I think people enjoyed them.… In retrospective, it seems more important than we thought it was at that time."[18] These lectures could be attended by all prisoners, not only members of the Cumann: "For the number of people that were in it, it was certainly not enough in the Cumann. I am not really sure because you didn't hold meetings like an ordinary Cumann on the outside. As you were not planning activities or anything, you know. It was more or less only organizing debates and things like that. You would get support for these debates, to be honest. Now there was always a fairly good turnout."[19]

Prisoners who volunteered to give these lectures were either republican veterans who spoke about their previous struggle in the republican movement or younger prisoners interested in historical and political topics. If any prisoner wanted to prepare a lecture on a specific topic, the prison library was the main focal point for gathering material, as Seosamh Ó Maileoin tells: "There was a library there. The librarian there at that time was a warden. He was good. If you got a book in from outside with a hardcover, if you wanted to get this book, the hardcover was to be removed. Your letters were stamped, you had to leave your letters open before going out, and they were stamped coming in. But any book you wanted on any subject they got you through the library. I ordered any book I wanted through the public library."[20]

While censorship was still apparent in the 1980s, the prison regime had significantly relaxed following the prison protests in the late 1970s.[21] As prisoners remember, there was hardly any censorship of books, only hardcovers were removed, and pornographic material was forbidden. All other books and magazines could be purchased through the prison library.

Matt Leen, who had worked as a post office clerk, was sentenced to seven years, of which he served four years and three months between 1979 and 1984 in Portlaoise for his part in the robbery of Tralee Post Office in 1978. In his interview, he also informed that he was a member of the Sinn Féin Cumann in Tralee, Co. Kerry, before being sentenced. He immediately joined the Cumann in prison: "Well, you know, I was a member of Sinn Féin before, I was in my Cumann here and, you know, it was like, I continued what I did, but, you know, now just inside the prison. I was Sinn Féin, and there was the Cumann, so I joined them."[22]

Interestingly, although I met and interviewed more than one dozen former Portlaoise prisoners, there was not one single prisoner whom

the Cumann recruited within the prison. Indeed, as far as my interview partners and contacts are concerned, only those who had experience with Sinn Féin activity outside the prison joined this Cumann. Jim
Kavanagh explains why he joined:

> You were looking for things to do, and this was something that was stimu-
> lating.… You had conversations and all right that, but for the most part,
> you stayed within your own groups. You were walking along with the
> same five or six fellas that were in with that. For me, politics were always
> the thing. The military side was always there to achieve a political aim.
> That wasn't an end in the mean; it was a tactic. That is all it was.… You
> were left with no option, but if it was something that you could achieve
> in any other way, that was great like, but it wasn't at that time, certainly
> wasn't. There was no other option.[23]

Kavanagh considers himself a political person and prioritizes the
political struggle over the military – the latter being purely a tactical
means to further political goals. Seosamh Ó Maileoin considered joining the Cumann inside Portlaoise as an obvious step. Asked why he had
joined the Cumann, he said:

> I don't know. I might have been in Sinn Féin outside. I just did it, and it
> was very interesting and very well run all these lectures and talks. We
> would have our ordinary meetings that would be boring enough, but the
> talks and the lectures were very interesting, depending on the subject and
> who held it. We couldn't at that time send motions, but I am not sure.
> Yeah, we couldn't; that was it. We were a Cumann inside, but we were
> totally isolated inside. But we got papers in each week and correspond-
> ence.… The Cumann was, I would not say, disregarded. It was function-
> ing for years and years. I don't know before I came in. It could have been
> very different in Mountjoy in the earlier years.… I thought it did good
> work.… I probably heard that there was a Cumann, and so I got involved.
> But for a long time, when I moved to Portlaoise, it was very disorganized.
> It took a bit of time until we got furniture and all the things set up, the
> craftwork and all this.[24]

He remembers the work of the Cumann as follows:

> Mostly it was just organizing debates and lectures and stuff like that.
> That was mainly it and passing on books and pamphlets, and all that was
> coming in. You know, we had our own paper we used to produce once a

month. It was some sort of a political magazine with political articles in it, and it would have things that were going on in the jail and a bit of craic[25] in it as well....

Do you remember the size of Cumann or the number of people involved?

I am not really sure.... [We had debates on] things like the influence of the church during Irish history and things like that and people's reaction to that. It was forty years ago, so it is hard to take out individual debates that happened, you know. It was always very interesting because you had a very diverse group of people in there. You wouldn't know what people were turning up. I managed to offend everyone by condemning God and James Connolly in the same sentence. [laughing][26]

A central part of the work of the Cumann was the teaching and promoting of the Irish language. One prisoner remembers that prisoners gave Irish classes immediately after the transfer from Mountjoy to Portlaoise.[27] The frequency of these early classes is vague; another inmate, however, reports that the situation improved following the hunger strikes in 1977 and the prisoners were from then on allowed to organize their classes and lectures.[28] Nonetheless, while inmates taught each other Irish in the early days, it was only in 1979 that a more serious attempt was made to promote the Irish language among the prisoners. This new development was primarily initiated by a new prisoner, Cyril McCurtain, from Limerick.[29] McCurtain was a fluent Irish speaker and a Sinn Féin member who immediately joined the Cumann in Portlaoise. In this position, he was elected to the officer board of the Cumann and initiated the formation of a Gaeltacht.[30] In 1982, prisoner John Carroll told the republican newspaper *An Phoblacht* about the Gaeltacht landing:

> We recently set up a Gaeltacht wing in prison, which meant a complete change-over of cells. Irish has made great progress in the jail over the last few years, and between fifty and sixty are now attending classes.
>
> On the Gaeltacht landing, which contains twenty men, only Irish is spoken. In association, any language may be spoken. No pressure is applied to anyone, and this is probably one of the reasons why it has made such great headway. When I went in, I hadn't a word of Irish, and now I speak it fairly fluently.[31]

This Gaeltacht area was situated on the top floor of the landing, and everyone there was encouraged to use as much Irish as he could. Prisoners who spoke Irish or wanted to learn Irish could ask the prison authorities to be transferred to one of these cells.[32] While it is known that this Gaeltacht was set up in 1979 or early 1980 and performed a vital role in the political and social life of the prison in the first half of the 1980s, it is unclear when it ceased to exist. Matt Treacy, who was imprisoned in Portlaoise from May 1990, said that the Gaeltacht landing had already ceased to exist by the time he arrived in the prison.[33] Pat Treanor was imprisoned in Portlaoise while the Gaeltacht landing existed. He gives an account of the role of the Irish language and the Gaeltacht area during these years:

> The language was important. I would have had a bit of Irish before that, although I would never have been confident enough to speak it. As part of working in the Civil Service, I would have done night classes and went to the Gaeltacht for a period of time. But there were people there who were very, very enthusiastic about the language, like Coireall MacCurtáin,[34] Joe Ennis, Johnny Johnson (who was from Dublin but had worked in Belfast for a period), and many others including Jim Lynagh,[35] [his brother] Colm Lynagh then when he arrived in. The best way to make sure that we could advance our Irish or improve on our Irish was to set up a Gaeltacht. So, there was a Gaeltacht set up on the top landing, on the fourth landing in the jail. The first day we moved to it, there were nineteen people who either had Irish or had thought they had enough to speak Irish all the time. And to help others then, there were Irish classes. There had been Irish classes run before that, where, if you were any good at all at the Irish, you were given the green book. Progress in Irish, I think it was called. You were asked to take five or six others and teach them. You know, have your class for an hour every morning, four mornings a week or three mornings a week, or something like that. So, those classes were ongoing, and when the Gaeltacht was set up, that's where people were progressing to. As soon as they felt good enough to start using it, they moved to the Gaeltacht, and you could only speak Irish there.[36]

Treanor's account underlines the importance of the Irish language in the daily routine of the prisoners by holding regular Irish-language classes and setting up the Gaeltacht landing. The number of prisoners willing to join this Gaeltacht landing was nineteen, thus higher than the roughly one dozen prisoners organized in the Sinn Féin Cumann. These numbers can be interpreted as revealing a greater interest in maintaining Irish culture than advancing the political understanding of the conflict in prison. Furthermore, the possibility of setting up a Gaeltacht landing and the liberal movement between the landings show a significant relaxation of the prison regime during the 1980s compared to the 1970s.

The prisoners in this Gaeltacht area on the top landing organized a wide range of cultural activities. Among those were Irish-language classes, the publication of the Irish-language prison newspaper *Macalla* (Echo), and the organization of Irish nights.[37] These Irish nights were introduced in 1984 and were held twice a year. During these nights, lectures were given in Irish, sometimes prisoners performed plays in Irish, and Irish songs were sung.[38] They were organized by the Gaeltacht Committee, which consisted of three prisoners and was elected by all prisoners on the Gaeltacht landing. This structure is one of the differences between the Gaeltacht areas in HMP Maze and Portlaoise. While an elected committee ran the Gaeltacht in Portlaoise, the Gaeltacht areas in HMP Maze were run by the educational officer of the IRA, whom the IRA O/C of the prison appointed. Another difference between HMP Maze and Portlaoise was the selection of the prisoners for the Gaeltacht areas. For example, in Long Kesh, the prisoners themselves selected members for the two Gaeltacht huts, whereas the prisoners who wanted to join the Gaeltacht landing in Portlaoise had to ask the prison authorities to be transferred there.[39] Thus, while the prisoners on the Gaeltacht landing could voice their objection or approval of any prisoner asking for transfer through their O/C, the prison staff made the final decision.

Although the Gaeltacht area ceased to exist during the 1980s, the prisoners continued with the Irish classes following its closure. For example, when John Crawley arrived at Portlaoise in 1984, the Gaeltacht landing still existed. Crawley was originally from the United States and had no Irish before imprisonment; nonetheless, he thinks he learned Irish "very well in prison." During our interview, Crawley stressed the importance of the Gaeltacht landing in Portlaoise as a "national thing" because the Irish language is – in his view – "a republican and nationalist element." He furthermore remembers that he did most of the reading and studying after lock up during the night.[40] Matt Treacy says that the prisoners were unlocked at 8:30 in the morning and could decide whether to go to the gym, the yard, or do classes such as Irish or learning for Open University degrees. He stressed that all prisoners did a lot of reading and writing. This education was possible because every prisoner could order two or three books through the prison library per week.[41] There were no restrictions regarding reading material, "any book on any subject" could be ordered, except hardbacks, for security reasons.[42] Seán Óg Ó Mórdha remembers that classes were held twice a week for one hour each during the mid-1990s.[43] So although there was a great emphasis on promoting the Irish language, former prisoner turned academic and political advisor Treacy does not think the Irish classes in Portlaoise had the same "meaning" as those in Long Kesh/HMP Maze, for in the "North [they were] more identifying."[44]

Following the prison protests and the hunger strikes in Portlaoise, the Irish classes became a central feature of the daily life of the prisoners, which originated in the founding of the Gaeltacht landing in 1979/80. For some years, this Gaeltacht landing was, along with the Sinn Féin Cumann, the prison's cultural and educational pivotal point. However, following the split in the republican movement in 1986, the Gaeltacht landing also ceased to exist. The reasons for its cessation are, however, unknown. Nonetheless, the prisoners continued with the individual learning of the Irish language, self-organization, and official Irish-language classes throughout the 1990s. Consequently, many republican prisoners gained fluent Irish-language skills while imprisoned.

The learning and speaking of the Irish language by the republican prisoners were forms of strategic resistance both within and outside the prison walls. While imprisoned, the republican convicts had three ways to promote the Irish language. First, they pushed the Irish language through publications. Among these publications were republican magazines and newspapers published outside the prisons, such as *An Phoblacht* or *Saoirse*, and magazines they published themselves. These magazines were, for example, *Scairt Amach* (Shout Out), published from 1989 onwards; *Irish Bheag* (Little Magazine), published from 1987 onwards; and *An Glór Gafa* (The Captive Voice), published from 1988 onwards.[45] Second, through visits, newspaper reports, and their own publications, republican prisoners made their supporters aware of the importance of the Irish language for their struggle. Third, they generated an Irish language–friendly environment as a result of this.

Following their release, they continued promoting the Irish language, once again on three new fronts. First, ex-prisoners became active in grass-roots initiatives. Second, they started teaching Irish-language classes, partly motivated by idealism and the need to earn an income. Third, ex-prisoners supporting Sinn Féin could lobby for the language through republican politicians supporting the peace process and, thus, generated additional funding for the Irish language in Northern Ireland. Although this may be true, the revival of the Irish language in Northern Ireland is less linked to the financial funding of the language as agreed in the Good Friday Agreement of 1998 than to the release of the Irish-speaking prisoners and their activism in grass-roots cultural campaigns. Likewise, I am afraid I have to disagree with MacGiollaChríost, who writes that "Irish, as the peculiar language of Irish republican (ex-)prisoners, enters the public domain via murals."[46] In fact, the Irish language entered the public domain, not via republican murals but cultural, community-orientated activism by former republican prisoners.

While there are few substantial differences in the development of Irish in Long Kesh/HMP Maze and Portlaoise, the situation of the ex-prisoners in the revival of Irish in Northern Ireland and the Republic of Ireland stands in stark contrast to each other for four reasons. First, the position of the former political prisoners in their community differs between Northern Ireland and the Republic. Due to the colonial context, the former prisoners have a stronger position and perform leading roles within their community. In contrast, the post-colonial situation in the Republic of Ireland does not allow them to perform similar functions. Second, fewer grass-roots initiatives promote the Irish language in the Republic of Ireland than in Northern Ireland. Accordingly, former prisoners have fewer opportunities to become active in these initiatives. Third, the Irish language is an official language in the Republic of Ireland. In contrast, in Northern Ireland, Sinn Féin lobbies for language support. It sells any Irish language and culture funding as a "victory" against the Unionist community.[47] Fourth, the republican prisoners in the Republic were considered of lesser relevance for the strategy of the republican movement by the republican leadership itself than the prisoners in Northern Ireland. Hence, while the Southern republican prisoners could debate and express their opinion in public, Matt Treacy interprets the role of these Southern prisoners in the following way:

> No one took us seriously at that time. We were not important for the [republican] movement. We were not the prisoners in the North, in Long Kesh or so, we were in the South, in Portlaoise, and no one in the movement cared what we were saying. But they gave us the feeling that we were important and sent people into jail and they made us feel important, and we sent statements out, and there were delegates to the Ard-Fheis, and we thought we have input, but, in fact, they were just using us for their own gains, you know. I think that was very dishonest.[48]

In other words, it is unsurprising that the ex-prisoners had a less dominant position within their communities in the Republic compared to their fellow ex-prisoners in Northern Ireland if one considers that the republican movement itself gave the Southern prisoners the feeling that they were of lesser importance for the struggle.[49]

In the early 1980s, the Cumann remained active as an entity of ten to twenty republican prisoners. This situation changed dramatically in the run-up to the republican split in 1986. Due to this decision to drop abstentionism, the republican movement split, and a minority formed the political organization Republican Sinn Féin (RSF) and the military organization Continuity IRA. Several prisoners also left the republican movement but did not align themselves with RSF or the Continuity IRA but instead formed the League of Communist Republicans. In the run-up to the split, the outside IRA leadership started influencing the Cumann and ordered an extraordinary Ard-Fheis to be held in the name of the Cumann, although all Provisional IRA members had to be in attendance and discuss the dropping of abstentionism. Vivion Hayden remembers: "We had this meeting, and most of us were there. I think there were about 90 or maybe 100 prisoners there. And we discussed abstentionism, well, I was not prepared, I mean, I supported the dropping, but I didn't take part in these debates, you know, all the guys were discussing these things weeks before and afterwards and so on but my focus was on other things. But, yeah, I was at that meeting and, yeah, we discussed it, you know. That was a meeting of all republican prisoners, and the leadership wanted it."[50]

Conversely, Seosamh Ó Maileoin explains that this was not an IRA meeting but an extraordinary AGM of the Portlaoise Cumann, a claim supported by the notes in the Sinn Féin Cumann minute books.[51] Ó Maileoin was a Cumann member in the years leading to the split in 1986:

> I was finance officer at the time the O/C of the prison decided to meet the Sinn Féin Cumann. Now, I was the secretary of the Cumann – No, I could be wrong, I may not have been the secretary, but if I was not the chair, I was the secretary. I had to be the secretary or hold some position within Sinn Féin at that time, and he wanted to meet three [of us]. So, whatever I was, I was one of the three. And we went to a cell, and the O/C was there, and the adjutant and the quartermaster and he said: "Sorry, we have a meeting there" and I said, "I am here" and he said: "What are you doing here?" So, I said that I am involved in Sinn Féin, and he was the O/C of the prison, and he did not know. So, that is the interesting thing that I wanted to get across to you. We would have been functioning for a very long time, and he was not even aware of who was what. They had got instructions from outside to meet with us and decided to call an extraordinary Ard-Fheis, and everyone was to attend.[52]

In this passage, Ó Maileoin raises three essential points. First, he strengthens the claim made by other prisoners that many IRA members were unaware of the members of the Cumann. Second, he underlines the superiority of the IRA over Sinn Féin in prison by mentioning that the IRA staff called a meeting with Sinn Féin representatives, and the former told the Cumann members to hold a Sinn Féin Ard-Fheis. Third, the outside IRA instructed the prisoners to conduct an Ard-Fheis. Similarly, many of the PIRA members in prison did not even know of the existence of the Cumann. Vivion Hayden, for example, remembers the activities of the Cumann, but he did not realize that a Sinn Féin Cumann organized them: "Yes, there were these lectures and all these things going on. I attended it, you know, not in 1985 because I had other things to do, you know, but, before and I enjoyed it, history, and this and that. Many people attended these lectures and meetings. I think there was a special committee for it, but I don't know who organized it. I suppose O/C or the [IRA] staff, but I don't know."[53] Asked if he remembers the work of the Cumann in prison, he replied:

> A Cumann? No, there were committees for this and that, as far as I know. But I don't know, maybe, you know, people organized this and that, and there was a group of people very active, and they were very into politics and so but, a Cumann, no, well [pause] I don't know. Maybe, you know, as I said, I was busy with other things in 1985 and maybe, I mean, if it was formed around that time, it's possible that there was a Cumann and I didn't know it because at that time I was busy with other things, you know.[54]

This answer is similar to the one given by other IRA members in Portlaoise. While they attended Cumann activities, such as lectures, commemorations, or Irish nights, they thought these activities had been organized by committees set up by the IRA officer board on the landing and not the Cumann. Although some were members of Sinn Féin, the prisoners were organized in a military structure inside the prison. Jim Kavanagh sees this relationship between the IRA structure and the Cumann work as the reason for the subordinate role of Sinn Féin:

> It didn't have a big role apart from that because, at the end of the day, you were in an army structure, and the army was the big thing in the prison, and it had to be because you had to maintain discipline. You know Jim Monaghan; he was one of the "Colombia 3" and Jim Monaghan was O/C at one stage. There was a certain course of action planned, and Jim and his staff just went to each man and group and told them what was happening. Somebody said to him: "That is not very democratic. We haven't discussed this." And Jim said: "Of course, it's not democratic, I am the O/C and we are the staff, and this is what we decided, and that's it." Jim was a funny fella, I must say. He was one I ever heard in favour of taking seats [in the Irish Parliament in Dublin, Leinster House]. That was what he

always favoured like.… It wasn't behind people's back that was the way forward he saw, especially after the hunger strikes [in Northern Ireland in 1981]. I had a lot of time for him. He was a very genuine fella. He wasn't like [Gerry] Adams, sneaking around behind people's back.[55]

Like Kavanagh, prisoner Ó Maileoin mentions the debates on abstentionism in the run-up to the split:

People that never bothered with Sinn Féin [were there at the meetings]. As I said, we were a small, little group. We were so small; I don't want to say we were insignificant because, you see, when Jim Monaghan gave a lecture, he could have had thirty or forty people, but other times you wouldn't have the numbers, and the O/C of the prison didn't know that I had a joint membership. So, I was going as a Sinn Féin member, but I was also a member of the staff, but I wasn't part of the staff to meet the Sinn Féin crowd at the time.… So this meeting was called, and it was an instruction from outside, and we were to discuss abstentionism. Now, we would have been very pro-abstentionist, and this is where Cyril MacCurtain and Liam McElhinney and these and they were very, very – and it was just to be discussed. Now, if there would have been one hundred people at it, there might have been ninety-five in favour of abstentionism. You know, at that time, that was it.[56]

Ó Maileoin thinks that most prisoners favoured continuing abstentionism at that time. However, individual prisoners, like the influential Cumann member Jim Monaghan, who was years later arrested in Colombia and convicted for providing military training to the FARC, were against it. Therefore, the outside opponents of abstentionism were trying to influence the prisoners, for the support of the prisoners would guarantee that a majority of the Cumainn delegates at the 1986 Ard-Fheis of Sinn Féin would follow the proposal to end abstentionism. In fact, no political and strategical changes of the republican movement could be imposed without the support of the prisoners, who enjoyed a prominent position of authority within the movement and their communities. Ó Maileoin continues to tell how, in his opinion, the outside IRA manipulated the Sinn Féin Ard-Fheis inside Portlaoise:

But coming back to the Sinn Féin meeting, the staff was not aware of who was who. They knew that there was a Sinn Féin Cumann but not who was involved. It was an instruction from the outside, and that was the start of the rift.… The extraordinary Ard-Fheis was held to discuss abstentionism.… Everybody was instructed to go there.

But it was a Sinn Féin Ard-Fheis, and the Cumann only had …

Everybody was at it, everybody. They approached the Cumann to call it, and the instruction was to attend. They were probably going to get a feeling at that time. I don't know. There would definitely have to be a number of non-Sinn Féin members there. Now, a number of people were in both. You could have been in Sinn Féin and not in the IRA and vice versa but in most cases, most people were in both at the time. There was another thing at that time. We used to hold weekly meetings, that was not Sinn Féin that was ordinary [IRA] staff, ordinary landing meetings.

We all meet once a week just to discuss things and give us a general talk.… Things were discussed, general talking, maybe work for [the prisoners' support organization] Cabhair, whatever had to be done.… Then, an instruction, the O/C called a meeting one time. This was going for a number of years, and out of a sudden, out of the blue, any prisoner that had broken during interrogation and talked, and bear in mind, they were accepted inside, they were to be ostracized, they were not to be part of this meeting. So, they could be five of the thirty here or seven there, and that was the instruction and the order. I didn't like it. The fact is that from the day one they came in, they were to be debriefed, and they had been accepted up to this. We were all one; we were all prisoners. We were all equal.… But for whatever reason they talked, maybe they were not strong enough, or they were young and hadn't gone through any anti-interrogation training or that. From this day on, they were to be blacklisted, and I didn't like it at all.… I came in, and it was put to us, and there was no conversation on it.

Things were not running too well, too smooth at that time; there was a little bit of unease about it. There was an election due for the O/C. "Dingus" Magee was O/C at that time, and he pushed forward this extraordinary Ard-Fheis. And there was an election due, and he was naturally running again, and he was taking orders from the outside naturally. The outside, in general, never interfered, an O/C was elected, and the outside ratified it, you know. They left the appointment of the O/C to the staff. I was in the cell one morning, early, and this man knocked on the door, Jim Monaghan. And they were attempting to go against the sitting O/C, and Jim came up with a paper in his hand. He said: "I am running for O/C. Will you sign this?" And I was on the staff at that time, and I said: "Oh well, you want to get rid of the regime." And I signed the paper, and Jim went away, and he went across to the O/C who was direct across my cell and gave it to him. I walked out ten minutes after, and Jim was bitter. So, what happened was that the outside imposed an O/C on us, Gerry Rooney, and there was no voting on it! Gerry was a good fella, a nice fella, a Belfast man. He would have been accepted by all, but there was a lot of bitterness, and Jim probably would have gotten it. I said to you before, Jim never made any secrets about abstentionism and where he stood on it. I would not agree with him, and I would be very against him on that, but I was prepared to sign that thing for him on that day, and I did it.... Gerry Rooney became O/C, and that was it. The outside had made this decision, but I am sorry that I can't give you the exact dates.[57]

In this lengthy excerpt, Ó Maileoin describes how the outside republican leadership influenced the prisoners inside. First, they instructed that all republican prisoners, no matter if they were in Sinn Féin or not, should use a Sinn Féin Ard-Fheis for a cover to discuss abstentionism. Then he explains that the outside IRA faction imposed an O/C on the Portlaoise prisoners. This O/C was from Belfast, and the IRA faction that was the driving force behind political and military changes outside had its support base around Gerry Adams in Belfast. In other words, this faction used their power to impose on the prisoners in Portlaoise an O/C loyal to them; their opponents who later formed RSF and the Continuity IRA were the older Southern-based leadership of Sinn Féin. Ó Maileoin concludes:

Gerry Rooney became very prominent afterwards with Gerry Adams' group in the Midlands; he contested elections.... Everything happened so quickly, the election was called, and when Jim threw his name in the hat, I think the outside became alarmed, and they went back to where it was and appointed Gerry Rooney. And the interesting thing was that I was appointed back to the staff, I think Gerry appointed me as finance officer, and I thought that was strange. I was the only one who came back as an existing member of the staff to come back under the new regime of Gerry Rooney. I don't know if this is of any use to you.[58]

Jim Kavanagh was already released when the split happened, but he experienced the preparations for it and shared Ó Maileoin's views:

We had our own Sinn Féin Cumann, and we would organize lectures and debates and that, every week there would be something. And strangely enough, the people that would never turn up at a debate or a lecture are the same fuckers who now sit at Leinster House, the likes of Martin Ferris and all those. They went on and on that "I am an [Irish republican] Army man. I don't want nothing to do with Sinn Féin or politics." And now they are sitting in Leinster House. That's not an accident that they weren't interested in that side of things. The military side was just a tactic to achieve things. To them, the [Irish republican] Army was enough of its own like. They didn't go beyond that, and that's why they were so easy to persuade by Adams and them because they had no political base for what they were doing.[59]

Kavanagh and Ó Maileoin joined RSF after the split in the movement in 1986, while Ferris became a Sinn Féin TD. Martin Ferris, whom Kavanagh mentions, gives a contrasting view of the split in the republican movement. At the time of the division, Ferris was serving the second year of his second sentence in Portlaoise. His biographer J.J. Barrett writes: "Ferris and the other Kerry political prisoners in Portlaoise were made aware of the forthcoming meeting of the breakaway Sinn Féin wing. There was a great concern that Sinn Féin in Kerry was about to split irretrievably once more, as some very well-known and respected republicans seemed intent on following the alternative Republican Sinn Féin course."[60]

RSF had support in Kerry, a county known for its traditional republican support base, and the Kerry prisoners attempted to use their authority as prisoners to weaken the RSF position in their area. When the Kerry branch of RSF held a meeting of all county members in the Ballygerry House Hotel in Tralee, Ferris's hometown, on Sunday, 23 November 1986, over fifty people attended. They represented eleven Cumainn and elected a Kerry Comhairle Ceanntair, a ruling body for the whole county. Eleven Cumainn, represented by fifty people, indicates significant support for the RSF position in the area. Among the designated RSF members of this body was also former Portlaoise prisoner Matt Leen. In attendance were prominent republicans, including the former president of Sinn Féin, Ruairí Ó Brádaigh. Barrett writes that "Martin Ferris was about to nail his colours to the mast with a decisive intervention. A statement signed by Ferris and the other seven Kerry prisoners was read to the meeting."[61] The statement read:

> We wish to clarify any ambiguity that may exist among Kerry republicans and republican supporters as to the position of IRA prisoners (Portlaoise Prison) with regard to the recent decision by Sinn Féin to end its policy of abstentionism in future Dáil Elections. As Óglaigh na hÉireann personnel, we accept the decision taken by the General Convention of the Irish Republican Army (October 1986) as being absolute. Equally, we fully support the democratic decision of Sinn Féin taken at the Ard-Fheis (2 November 1986). We pledge our complete loyalty to the aims and objectives of the republican movement. We wish also, to make known our position regarding the post-Ard-Fheis walk-out by a small number of republicans, and the subsequent formation of a group calling itself "Republican Sinn

Féin". This breakaway group has no sanction whatsoever to speak or act on behalf, nor have they any authority to run functions or take up Christmas collections or any other collection, in the name of prisoners, or Prisoners' Dependants. We view their activities, sincere though they may be, as harmful to our just cause. It is our earnest wish that those who joined this breakaway group would reunite with our comrades, strengthening all our resolves and determination in securing the unity of our Country and freedom for our people. Our commitment to a 32 County Socialist Republic is total.

Signed: Martin Ferris (Ardfert), Paddy Boyle (Tralee), Billy Kelly (Tralee), John O'Sullivan (Listowel), Peter Sugrue (Listowel), Michael Browne (Fenit), Paul Magee (Tralee), Angelo Fusco (Tralee).[62]

The statement was previously published in the local newspaper *Kerry's Eye* on 20 November 1986. It reaffirmed the commitment of the prisoners to establish the United Socialist Republic. While the statement also stresses that the new breakaway group RSF had no legitimacy for most of the IRA and Sinn Féin had supported the dropping of abstentionism, the most substantial claim is that the new group had no authority to work on behalf of the prisoners. This claim was an attempt to damage the new group seriously. As I mentioned before, republican prisoners hold a prominent position among their supporters. The Kerry prisoners were aware of their position and used it to strengthen the majority faction outside the prison. Ferris was the initiator of this statement; therefore, his name appears as the first signatory. This intervention was his first prominent public display of political allegiance with the leadership of the republican movement around Gerry Adams and Martin McGuinness. Barrett concludes: "His activity and input from behind the high limestone walls of Portlaoise Prison would mark him out as a crucial cog in the conflict resolution machinery of Adams, McGuinness and company for the mid-1990s and beyond, into the twenty-first century." He quotes Ferris, saying that "were it not for the support of the prisoners, a more serious split would have happened."[63] In fact, his leading role as an IRA prisoner intervening for the majority faction provided him with his later career as a leading Sinn Féin politician and TD.

Ferris correctly acknowledges that the political prisoners decreased the damage of the 1986 split for Sinn Féin and the IRA. The decisive role of the prisoners was known to the outside factions. Thus, the prisoners were influenced and used by factions for their own purposes. Under these circumstances, the later RSF lost the factional struggle, for they had no army, the IRA followed Adams and McGuinness. At the same time, the Continuity IRA was only a nucleus, and since the republican prisoners were organized under an army structure, no army meant no prisoners. In other words, the intention was that the prisoners influence the outcome of the factional struggle in the outside movement. The prisoners' statement issued to the RSF meeting in Kerry should influence the attending delegates in support of the majority faction. Due to this statement, the winners were those who had the support of the prisoners. Therefore, RSF has remained a marginal political organization since its foundation.

To my knowledge, the Kerry prisoners who signed the statement were all IRA prisoners not active in the Sinn Féin Cumann. In fact, the Cumann was marginalized during these years, and control over political decisions was put in the hands of the IRA staff. Seosamh Ó Mailleon remembers that the Cumann was still in existence when he was released in the spring of 1986.[64] While no records exist to show when the Cumann eventually ceased to function, Matt Treacy stresses that there was no Sinn Féin Cumann in Portlaoise when he arrived in prison in late 1989.[65] This leads to the assumption that the Cumann disbanded during the split in the republican movement. Hence, political developments that led to the IRA ceasefire in 1994, the release of the prisoners, and the signing of the Good Friday Agreement in 1998 were under the direct guidance of the IRA from then on. Political power had finally moved from Sinn Féin to the IRA military organization.

In sum, in the late 1970s, the Provisionals decided to organize the Portlaoise prisoners as Cumainn of its political wing, Sinn Féin. The formation of this Cumann was an integral part of the political self-awareness process of the Provisionals. While a Cumann had existed in Mountjoy, it ceased to exist with the transfer to Portlaoise; it was only after the conclusion of the prison protests in 1977 and the granting of most of their demands that the situation improved to the degree that allowed the Cumann to re-organize as a functional body. In 1986, most of the Sinn Féin Ard-Fheis voted to drop the policy of abstentionism from the constitution.[66] As a result, the Portlaoise Cumann ceased around the republican movement's 1986 split. The reasons for the decline and the abandoning of the Cumann remain unclear.

The debates of the Sinn Féin Cumann in Portlaoise Prison provide an exciting window into prison life and the role of prisoners in the outside republican movement.[67] Several observations can be made from the four remaining Cumann notebooks that add to our understanding of Southern republicanism during the Northern Ireland conflict. First, the prisoners' lecture program was mainly based on Irish history and Sinn Féin policy; yet during the 1980s, international topics gained more relevance. Second, these lectures and debates were led by volunteers of a small group of

Cumann members who managed to establish a monopoly on education. Third, the Cumann had strong connections with the outside
republican movement, particularly Ard-Oifig in Dublin and individual
Cumainn throughout the country. This connection resulted in drafting
letters, leaflets, policy documents, and motions to the annual Ard-Fheis
of Sinn Féin. In other words, the Portlaoise Prison Cumann played an
active part in Sinn Féin in the early to mid-1980s. Fourth, from 1982, the
Cumann meetings reflected increasing discussion on and unease with
the outside movement. This development coincided with debates on
the electoral strategy of Sinn Féin. These heated debates on elections
and the policy of abstentionism in 1982/3 significantly increased membership numbers. The overwhelming majority of the Cumann members made their support for the abstentionist policy known in various
motions over this period. Although this debate ebbed off in the later
years within the prisons, it continued outside the prison and eventually
led to the Provisional movement's split in 1986.

The previous three chapters discussed the Portlaoise Prison protests
between the spring of 1974 and the autumn of 1977, the subsequent
formation of the Sinn Féin Cumann, and the political debates that led
to the split of the republican movement in 1986. During these years,
tensions were high on the republican wing of Ireland's high-security
prison. The move from Mountjoy and the Curragh Camp to Portlaoise in November 1973 saw a dramatic deterioration of the privileges
of the prisoners in the Republic. Notably, while keeping their right to
segregation from ordinary criminal convicts, the republicans lost their
privileges of being considered political prisoners. In Northern Ireland,
the republican prisoners were granted special category status after a
hunger strike in Belfast's Crumlin Road Prison in 1972. In the Republic,
political prisoners in the Curragh Camp and Mountjoy enjoyed similar privileges. Still, when all prisoners were moved to Portlaoise, the
authorities did not immediately recognize these rights in the reopened
high-security prison. After intense negotiation, these rights were
granted, but tensions remained high. These tensions resulted in serious
riots, passive and active protests, and, finally, a series of hunger strikes.
In 1977, the prisoners were eventually granted most of their demands,
and the protests stopped.

The experience from Portlaoise was a critical period for the Provisional republican movement. The developments in the Republic, both
as a logistic hinterland for the IRA and the events in the Republic's
prisons, played a crucial role in the political and military discourse of
the movement during the Troubles. While the public campaign in support of the prisoners was marginal, the course and outcomes of these

protests had relevant implications. The IRA was a learning organization, willing to adapt its tactics to new developments; most of these
changes originated either in the prisons or in connection with prison
protests. Republicans learned from the failure of organizing a broad
campaign in support of the Portlaoise hunger strikers by setting up
the broad-front committee H-Blocks/Armagh Committee in support
of the 1980–1 hunger strikers in Northern Ireland; and so did the British government – understanding of republican imprisonment in the
Republic and, in particular, the developments within Portlaoise is vital
for the understanding of the Troubles.[68] Many developments in Portlaoise foreshadowed and informed events in the H-Blocks and other
Northern Irish prisons.

Chapter Five

"He Was Just Rhyming Off Pages of It": Internment and the Brownie Papers, 1971–1976/7

In the summer of 1969, the British army was deployed to the Northern Irish province. Initially welcomed by the Irish nationalist community, this positive perception changed quickly. House raids, curfews, and riots became part of daily life in Derry and Belfast. Both factions of the IRA, the Provisionals and the Officials, quickly reorganized after the split in 1969/70. Two years later, in the summer of 1971, they could wage an intensive campaign against the British army. The armed confrontations brought the province closer to a full state of war day by day. As a result, the internment of people suspected to be supportive of or directly involved in paramilitary activities was proposed by the Northern Ireland government and approved by the British government. And so, on 9 August 1971, the British army launched Operation Demetrius, which saw over three hundred people interned. The following days, four people were killed in riots in Belfast. Many internees were innocent, which created widespread opposition to the internment policy among nationalists and even sections of the Protestant and unionist population. That same month, 8,000 workers went on strike in Derry, and 130 councillors withdrew from district councils in Northern Ireland.[1]

The internees were held at Long Kesh, an abandoned Royal Air Force airfield near Lisburn, west of Belfast, and Magilligan, in County Derry. Initially, internees were also held on the prison ship *Maidstone* in Lough Belfast. Most of the internees were first interrogated at Ballykelly and Ballykinlar before being sent to the camps. The British army used fourteen men as guinea pigs to test various deep interrogation techniques. For several days, they were blindfolded and subjected to food and sleep deprivation, white noise, and waterboarding. These torture victims became known as the Hooded Men.[2]

One of the men held at Ballykinlar before being flown to the *Maidstone* was William Moore from Lurgan.[3] Moore was born in Gilford, Co. Down,

CIVIL AUTHORITIES (SPECIAL POWERS) ACTS

(NORTHERN IRELAND) 1922 - 1943

ORDER FOR DETENTION OF SUSPECTED PERSON

TO: THE OFFICER IN CHARGE OF THE PLACE OF DETENTION,
     IN THE "MAIDSTONE".

I, the Right Honourable Brian Faulkner, Minister of Home Affairs for

Northern Ireland, by virtue of the powers vested in me by the Civil

Authorities (Special Powers) Acts (Northern Ireland) 1922 - 1943

do hereby order and require you to receive William John (Sean) MOORE,

Bleary, Lurgan, Co Armagh.

who has been arrested under the provisions of the said Civil

Authorities (Special Powers) Acts as a person who is suspected of

acting, or having acted, or being about to act in a manner prejudicial

to the preservation of the peace or the maintenance of order,

at the place of detention in the "Maidstone" and therein to detain

him until he has been discharged by direction of the Attorney-General

or brought before a Magistrates' Court.

Dated this 10th day of August 1971.

BRIAN FAULKNER

MINISTER OF HOME AFFAIRS
FOR NORTHERN IRELAND

CIVIL AUTHORITY

Internment order for William Moore. Image courtesy of Fergal Moore.

in 1945 and used "Seán" as his first name from his early youth. He married Nuala McKerr in Lurgan in 1967. She was raised in a republican family, and soon Seán became active as well. Together with J.B. O'Hagan, he joined the Civil Rights Association in Lurgan and, through IRA veteran Art McAlinden, became involved in the republican movement. After the 1969/70 split, he joined the Provisional IRA. The newlywed Moores had moved into a bungalow in Bleary, just outside Lurgan, and daughter Dara and son Seán Óg were born in the following years. At 4:10 a.m. on Monday, 9 August 1971, about half a dozen military police officers entered the house and arrested Moore, who was taken to Pinehurst Factory in Lurgan, where the British army was billeted. A few hours later, he and his two brothers-in-law, Barry and Gerry McKerr, were brought to Ballykinlar Camp near Newcastle, Co. Down. Gerry McKerr was to become one of the fourteen Hooded Men who were taken to a secret interrogation centre.

The treatment of Moore and the other men in Ballykinlar was also harsh. Moore testified before the court that the internees were ordered to do exercises until they fainted: "There were men collapsing all around me and moaning and screaming." Then, for hours, Moore had to undergo the same exercises: "Hands up above your head, hands out in front of you, hands behind your head and put your head between your stretched legs." In between these exercises, prisoners were taken for interrogation by two plainclothesmen: "I emphasize that all the time these exercises were going on, you had to look straight ahead of you, and your eyes had to look up at the ceiling. Continuously the Military Police kept walking around, checking if we were looking at the ceiling.… Then when I went to put my head down between my legs with arms behind my head, there was a crack in my head, and I went unconscious." After two days, Moore and several others were flown by helicopter to the HMS *Maidstone*, docked in Lough Belfast. In summer 1969, the ship was used as an emergency billet for the British army, and 120 men were interned there from August 1971 to April 1972. Among them was Seán Keenan, the chairman of the Derry Citizens Defence Association who became the Provisional IRA officer-commanding on the ship. Moore was assigned as his second in command. After seventeen days, however, Moore was among the first to be released.

Moore was well connected within the IRA. Before internment, he was the officer-commanding of the small but particularly active unit in North Armagh. He worked closely with IRA leader Seán MacStiofáin. The Provisionals decided to use Moore's case to take civil action and sue the British Ministry of Defence and the chief constable of the RUC. In an interview with me in 2015, Moore explained that this was a "test case" to get internment declared unlawful.[4]

On 19 February 1972, the *Times* of London reported that Judge Rory Conaghan at Armagh County Court had awarded Moore £300, the maximum compensation possible, for wrongful arrest, detention, and assault. The judge was particularly critical of the oppressive circumstances in which Moore was held, calling them "deliberate, unlawful, and harsh." Commenting upon the army personnel called by the defence, the judge concluded that "all three are telling lies about this matter." Two days later, the *Times* wrote that the case "brought into question the legal status of the Stormont's Government internment policy." A "source close to the Stormont Cabinet" commented that the judge's decision was "potentially disastrous." In the days after the ruling, the Stormont government feared that hundreds of internees could demand compensation before the court. On the other hand, human rights lawyers hoped that the part of the ruling that stressed it was unlawful not to inform Moore beforehand that he would be held for more than forty-eight hours would become case law. However, the immediate fears of the Northern Irish and British governments were unjustified. While Moore won his civil action, the ambitious IRA attempt to rule internment unlawful failed.[5]

Internment continued until December 1975. About 3,000 men and a few dozen women were interned during these five years. Some of them were held in the camps until the 1980s, while those arrested and charged after this date were imprisoned in the newly opened H-Blocks, also on the site of the former Maze airfield. Paradoxically, internees who were granted de facto political status by recognizing their military structure were, after 1 March 1976, only separated by a fence, a wall, and a few yards from their comrades in the H-Blocks. The latter belonged to the same political and paramilitary organization but had been stripped of all their rights after being categorized as ordinary decent criminals by the British government. The internment camp Long Kesh stayed open until 1988 when the remaining internees agreed to be moved to the H-Blocks.

In the internment camp, internees were held in newly constructed Nissen huts. Groups of four Nissen huts were surrounded by barbed wire, giving the camp the unofficial name the "Cages of Long Kesh." Initially, republicans and loyalists were housed together. This practice changed with the introduction of direct rule in Northern Ireland in March 1972, when the British government assigned internees to cages according to their political affiliation. At that time, the loyalist prisoners belonged to the UDA and UVF, while republican factions present in the camp were the Provisional IRA and Official IRA. Two years later, the OIRA split. Thus, members of a newly founded third republican group, the Irish National Liberation Army (INLA), joined the camp in 1974/5. The internees could associate freely and wear their own clothes.

The military hierarchy was maintained and recognized by the camp authorities. Thus, only the elected O/Cs contacted the prison officers directly.

Life in the cages was strictly organized. Lectures, Irish classes, drills, commemorations, and sports competitions occupied the prisoners' time in those early days of the camp. Planning for escapes was another vital task to keep morale high. All these activities established a distinct sense of prison culture, including, for instance, the role of older republicans in the camp.[6] Among the internees were older republicans that had experienced imprisonment and internment during every previous decade. Thus, these republican veterans taught the new and younger internees how to adapt to life in prison and gave them their first republican and political education; introduced them to Irish history, culture, and language; and arranged military classes, military drills, and reading groups. Thereby, they truly turned Long Kesh, as they had at Frongoch fifty years earlier, into a "University of Revolution."

Michael Donnelly was among the first men interned in August 1971. The Derry citizen was one of the Hooded Men, those Irish nationalists tortured by the British army in the early days of internment. After his arrest, Donnelly was first held at the Magilligan internment camp in County Derry. Later, he had also a short spell in the Crumlin Road prison in Belfast before being ultimately transferred to Long Kesh. He remembers his arrival at Long Kesh:

> It was not too bad in there [in Crumlin Road], but when we went to the Long Kesh internment camp, it was a bit different. You were under the control of the British army. It was pretty brutal. They had dogs and all that outside the huts, and people were getting buttoned. Under those conditions, the huts were … [pause]. I remember at one time there were 120 in a hut, whereas the Brits were claiming that there were only 20. [laughing] So they were literally about zero inches between the beds. And because there were so many people in it, it always seemed that it was raining because of the condensation. I used to think the roof was leaking, but it was actually condensation, you know, so many people.[7]

The two factors, the overcrowding and the constant tensions between the British army and the internees, featured my interview partners' early memories. While Michael Donnelly was a member of the Provisional republican movement, John Nixon from County Armagh was a member of the Official IRA when he was interned. He recounts similar experiences to Donnelly's: "I went into what was called the Cages of Long Kesh, the compounds. There were these cages with forty by forty yards wide, long and Nissen huts, you seen all the images. And I came into compound 21, that was the Official IRA. There was nothing but trouble since the day I arrived in the jail because there were total conflicts all the time between the administration and the prisoners."[8]

Despite this overcrowding and the tensions, the internees could organize their day independently. Those who were members of paramilitary organizations, either republican or loyalist, set up a military structure recognized by the British army; other republicans organized themselves in the political organization Sinn Féin and set up Cumainn, similar to the Sinn Féin Cumann in Portlaoise. Yet, the internment policy also resulted in the arrest of political activists unaffiliated with any republican or loyalist groups and even civilians. Again, Donnelly remembers:

We tried to run it [Long Kesh] under our own rules. We pretty well did. We didn't make people get up or run it along monitor lines, but we had a staff, and it was all more for the benefit of the people rather to try to control them. We had a minimum time when everyone had to get up, that was around eight [o'clock in the morning]. If you were in as a member of the [Provisional] IRA, you kind of accepted that you were a prisoner of war. But there were also people who were not in the IRA, and they had a very different time to understand why they were in there and why they were being brutalized. So, we had to make a compromise in that way. So, they could lie in bed, but at eleven, they had to get up and walk around, do something, you know. It was very liberal the regime that we introduced. And again, we had advice from older people that had been in jail, someone getting back to the twenties. There was a fella called Liam Mulholland; he spent altogether eighteen years in there. These kinds of people showed you how to run the place, and we got good advice. But basically, it was never boring. We tried to get libraries in there. When the Brits raided, they ripped apart the books and urinated on them. That seemed to be their reason to raid the place.[9]

The British and the Northern Irish governments recognized the military structures in the internment camps and prisons during these early years of the conflict, following a successful hunger strike of Belfast republican Billy McKee at the Crumlin Road prison. McKee's hunger strike, in early summer 1972, secured the recognition of special category status and, thereby, the power to operate a military structure and maintain discipline in the prisons and camps. Moreover, it also meant the internees and prisoners had a legal and moral foundation for their own understanding as prisoners with PoW status. This understanding shaped the prisoners' lives in the four years after the introduction of internment in Northern Ireland.

Séanna Walsh is an Irish republican who grew up in the nationalist enclave Short Strand in East Belfast. In 1973, he was arrested at the
age of sixteen and sent to Long Kesh. He spent three years in the camp
before being released, rearrested, and charged again three months later.
This time he was sent to the H-Blocks. After the hunger strikes in 1981,
he became officer-in-command of the PIRA prisoners. He was later
released from the H-Blocks but was arrested once again. He spent his
third prison term at Crumlin Road, becoming O/C of the republican
prisoners. In July 2005, he appeared on video, reading out a statement
from the PIRA Army Council announcing the end of its armed campaign. He remembers life in Long Kesh as follows:

> Whenever I went into jail in 1973, IRA prisoners had achieved political status
> as a result of a hunger strike in May and June 1972 by the men in Crumlin
> Road Jail and the women in Armagh prison. So, the IRA prisoners had won
> the right to political status. Whenever I went into Long Kesh, Long Kesh
> was very much a prisoner of war camp, very, very clearly. [It was] exactly
> as you would imagine, having seen the films *The Great Escape* and *Stalag17*
> and all of that. It basically meant that prisoners had the freedom of the jail
> from, you know, the prison warders opened the doors at seven o'clock in
> the morning and closed them at nine o'clock at night, and it was up to the
> prisoners how they organized their day. One of the things that I decided
> to do at a very early stage, and I really only thought about these things in
> depth later – two things – I decided to make sure that I was fit, keep myself
> fit, and to keep myself well versed in global affairs, current affairs, and to
> prepare myself to go back on the streets and become re-involved with the
> struggle against the British. I was very focused on that. In the cages of Long
> Kesh, when we had political status, we had access to the formal education
> that the prison system offered…. All of that was available. But what was of
> more interest to me was the informal jail education. The education that we
> offered and provided through discussions, debates, and study groups. And
> that was all about preparing people for re-entering in the struggle.[10]

While most of my interviewees stress the positive effects of the
military structure – they were all members of paramilitary organizations during their internment – there are also a few critical voices, like
Kevin Trainor. Trainor is from Armagh City, a rural town in the south of
Northern Ireland. He became politicized by the civil rights movement,
left-wing organizations like the People's Democracy, and, consequently,
initially joined the Official IRA. Together with his unit, he later switched
to the PIRA. Since he was from Armagh City, he spent the first week following his arrest in HMP Armagh before being transferred to Crumlin

Road prison. From there, he was brought to Long Kesh in 1972. He remembers that compared to Crumlin Road prison, life in Long Kesh had "more structure with O/C and drills and marching. There were more people in there, and I suppose it was because of that. But we, the country fellas, were not into that kind of thing. We didn't see each other as soldiers. That was a Belfast thing. We just thought the marching and all that is just nonsense."[11] Rather than marching and drilling, Trainor had a great appetite for reading. He shared this habit with a large group of other internees. It was this habit, above all, that was to shape the political subjectivity of these men.

Apart from military drills, planning escapes, and producing handicrafts for the prisoners' dependents fund, most of the day was spent reading and discussing. Trainor was an ardent reader in Long Kesh. He enthusiastically remembers how he developed a passion for John Steinbeck in the camp:

> I tell you what I fucking read! It was a great discovery to me: John Steinbeck. There was a book with some silly looking cover, and I just thought: I'll read it. And I started reading it, and I thought that was fucking great, and so I read every single book by John Steinbeck. I had heard his name before, but I thought it was just a cowboy sort of a book, Western, pulp fiction, that's what the cover looked like, and I thought, I fucking read this book, and so I discovered Steinbeck. Everything else I already knew beforehand. I read Joyce and all the Irish authors, Yeats but also some American stuff too.... The book by Steinbeck was just lying around, somebody had it, and I took it, and I thought: Well, I am not reading that today. But then I just started reading it when I was just bored. Today, I don't even remember which one it was, but in the end, I read all books by Steinbeck.[12]

Another internee, Danny Morrison from Andersonstown in West Belfast, talks about reading the Walter Macken trilogy.[13] Macken was an Irish writer. His trilogy, including *Seek the Fair Land* (1959), *The Silent People* (1962), and *The Scorching Wind* (1964), deals with earlier periods in the struggle for Irish freedom, namely, Cromwell's invasion of Ireland; the famine of the 1840s; and the Easter Rising and subsequent Tan War and Civil War.[14] Yet while several internees like Trainor and Morrison remember reading literature and fiction, the focus of the internees was always on political and historical literature. Morrison explains: "In Long Kesh, there were many, many books, not just Irish history books. Books on Che Guevara, who was killed only five years earlier, and there were books on Frantz Fanon, books on the Mexican Revolution, books on South America, South Africa, on the Middle East. And there were some prisoners who also subscribed to left-wing magazines that came from London; I think it was the *Red Mole*. Amongst sections of the prisoners, there was a lot of discussions about politics."[15]

These books, as Morrison explains, were sent in by friends, supporters, solidarity movements, and Irish migrants in England. By receiving books and newspapers from anti-imperialist solidarity groups, the internees came under the influence of socialist and internationalist thinking. Yet not all Provisional republicans agreed with the left-wing newspapers sent from England, considering that the split with the "communist" Officials was still fresh in their minds. For example, Dáithí Ó Búitigh is originally from Woodvale, in Belfast, and had joined the Wolfe Tone Society in Dublin in 1967. One year later, he joined Sinn Féin. Back in Belfast in 1971, he became an organizer for the PIRA youth movement Na Fianna Éireann and was interned for five years in 1972: "We got some newsletter in with some socialist and communist stuff in it, and the O/C was not happy about it, so we lost it, we just accidentally lost it. [laughing] We had our own censorship, like porn magazines, we didn't allow porn magazines in."[16] The establishment of libraries in the various cages was part of a political and historical education program set up by the republican movement in the camps. This informal self-education focused initially on three pillars: the Irish language, Irish history and politics, and military education for IRA members. It was organized around lectures given by older, experienced republicans to educate the young, inexperienced internees, some of them still in their teens. Thereby, an early camp culture developed that was influenced by the older generation who had experienced internment and imprisonment in previous decades.

Jimmy Kavanagh is from Wexford in the south of Ireland. He joined the PIRA in the early 1970s and became active in Belfast. As a result of this activism, he was interned in Long Kesh in late 1973. He remembers the high number of teenagers among the internees: "There were an awful lot of young people in there at that time. I was eighteen, and I was one of the oldest people in the hut I was in. You had what they called at that time schoolboy internees. Young boys were taken out of school at the age of fifteen or sixteen and interned, and I would have been in with a few of them."[17] Michael Donnelly also stresses the importance of teaching the young internees: "We had various Irish classes and talks on politics and there were some young people [of] only fourteen years of age interned as well, so, of course, and we had school teachers among ourselves and so we made it compulsory for the fourteen-year-olds to go to school." He explains that these lectures were "just arranged through the camp and when someone came up with a good lecture, we organized it."[18] Dáithí Ó Búitigh elaborates further on the PIRA-organized classes:

> The education courses were semi-voluntary, depending on your status. If you were in the [Irish Republican] Army, they weren't. Irish classes were voluntary; political education was not. The prisoners had to go there. That was demanded to underline our political status, but Irish classes were voluntary. They were recommended, but that's all.... Usually, the cage staff [of the IRA] discussed the classes. You had the education officer, the training officer, and they did a series of lectures on such and such, and that's how I got the history lectures.... People say nationalism came in at such and such, and socialism came in at such and such, and Irish came in at such and such. They didn't; they were all bloody there. But it developed from there.... Sometimes, the prisoners liked to go to these classes, and sometimes they didn't. When I did the lectures, I always included an open debate, sort of "Why this happened?" One example for this were the 1930s, Charlie Kerrins being executed.[19]

While Donnelly and Ó Búitigh talk about the organization of lectures and debates through the PIRA structure, Morrison was also a member of a Sinn Féin Cumann in Long Kesh. He explains the role of these Sinn Féin Cumainn in the informal education system and the organization of the Cumainn in the camp:

> There were many Sinn Féin classes in the jail, debates, and discussions, you know, for example, I remember we debated the Sunningdale arrangement that had been set up....[20] Sinn Féin also, at least once a week, would have organized a lecture, a debate, or an Irish language class, so people would learn the Irish language as well.... Many people in jail would attend the Sinn Féin meetings in jail. It was not compulsory; it was voluntary. And some of the talks would have been, for example, on republican history. These would have been given by the older men, people who would have been in jail in the forties and in the fiftiess, and they would be passing on their knowledge and, also, we were reading material and talking about it.... Each cage would have a Cumann, and whoever was in charge would have been elected, you know, chair, secretary, there was no finance officer because we didn't have money, right.... [laughing] Where we held the meetings that was in a prefabricated hut. We had the three Nissen huts where you lived, sometimes three and a half. So, three huts and then outside in the yard you had a shower block where the toilets were and across from that was a prefabricated hut which was more modern and that had an electric blow heater in it, maybe a table, eight, ten chairs. So, at the Sinn

Féin meetings, there would always be a dozen or so. Now, we had bigger meetings if something important was to be discussed, if there was a political development, that would take place in one of the huts where everybody would be brought in, and maybe a message was read out to them.[21]

Like the Cumann in Portlaoise Prison set up in the late 1970s, the Cumainn in Long Kesh played a central role in teaching Irish history, politics, and language to younger, inexperienced members. In addition, the Cumann provided the facilities and organizational space necessary for these informal classes. Thereby, the Sinn Féin Cumainn played an essential role in informal education, but they had no decisive role in the outside movement. Nonetheless, they tried to play their part as much as possible also in the wider movement. Morrison continues: "We couldn't send people to the Ard-Fheis, but we could put down motions to be discussed, and we could nominate proxies to speak on our behalf, or somebody who had just been released could appear as a recently released prisoner."[22]

John Nixon describes the informal education system taking place in the huts occupied by the Official republican movement members. The Officials, or Stickies, as they were commonly known, had a different self-identification to the Provisionals. Contrary to the Provisional republican movement, they saw themselves as Marxists rather than nationalists. This political orientation was reflected in their self-education system:

> At that time, we had our own education system, which was politically orientated, left-wing orientated, communist orientated as well, but not only socialist, and that made us different from the other people, including the unionists and the Provisionals. We always conceived an international dimension to any struggle. You know, if you are a socialist, you are an internationalist, you understand? And we learned our politics at that time; we educated ourselves. I educated myself as well, self-education was a big thing for me, and I was intelligent enough to know what to read and what not to read. So, the political education was more or less topping up what you already had learned on the streets. It gave you more depth, you understand.[23]

In this passage, Nixon establishes the dialectic of street politics and becoming a political subject in the camp. His organization, the Official IRA, would split in 1974/5. Following a ceasefire announcement in 1973, radical members formed the Irish Republican Socialist Movement (IRSP) with its military arm, the Irish National Liberation Movement (INLA). Nixon traces his decision to join the INLA back to the political education he had received in the camp. He explains: "By the time the split came, I had become a fully fledged politician, and it was a conscious decision to join the INLA. I had the political experience from jail. I had become an educated cadre." In classical Marxist terms, he says that he became a political cadre in the camp and, thus, he made a conscious decision to leave the Officials and join the radical INLA. The education system in the Official-run cages was also affected by the split. He remembers:

> We had our own education system. Every cage has its own education system, but they all talked the same language, and they were all seeing the same books except in ours there was more Mao Tse-Tung, more Marx, you know, it was very different literature. And there were lectures every week, and you had general meetings every week when people had discussions and debates, and this went on, not every day but very regularly. We had our own teachers, people who were very well educated in left-wing politics and that was all passed down.... I was a founding member of the IRSP and the INLA. The split took place shortly after the fire [the Burning of Long Kesh by the prisoners]. The first meeting inside the jail was in December 1974. And then what changed was that the educational system was much more radical, more revolutionary. And there was a more militant aspect to that as well.[24]

Nixon's political self-reflection on his role in the camp, the split of a republican organization, and the informal education of his movement played in these developments is an observation that has not insofar appeared in any narrative of a member of the Provisional republican movement. This comment assumes that Official republicans have a deeper political understanding – an observation that I also made when interviewing members of the IRSP in Derry throughout 2014 about their pre-internment political education.

In addition to the informal education organized by the internees, formal education was offered by the camp administration. One of the internees who had an early interest in this formal education was Danny Morrison: "Prior to the arrest, I was studying A-level history and A-level English. When I arrived in Long Kesh, I started to study English literature again, and I sat my exam in English literature in summer 1973 in Long Kesh."[25] The formal education run by outside teachers and Open University lecturers was not part of the camp regime from the very start. Instead, the authorities only allowed external teachers when newspapers highlighted the lack of education facilities in the internment camps, as Michael Donnelly remembers.[26] Both republican and loyalist prisoners welcomed this development and made use of the new facilities and opportunities for education. Nonetheless, it remained an issue of tension. When the Open University courses were introduced, all internees who subscribed were moved into one cage. That was cage 20. Dáithí Ó Búitigh was also moved into this hut and remembered that tension arose due to a public statement by the British government about these courses:

> What happened there was that we set it up ourselves, we established the contact [with the Open University]. We did everything ourselves, allowed lecturers in and the next thing, at about a year and a half later, the prison staff said to the media: "Oh, we are doing this and that, and we are setting Open University courses up." Once they did that, that was a complete breach of the agreement – even with the Open University, which I found out afterwards. So, we said: Right, that's it, finished.… The agreement was that they were never to use it for their own purpose. And the Open University agreement said that as well that it was not to be used, but they wouldn't take it.… The courses had been introduced in 1973, [or] 1974, and the agreement was that it was never to be used for British propaganda purposes.… The prison authorities issued a statement saying that it was for rehabilitation purposes and that was a breach of the actual agreement. So, we stopped the courses a year and a half afterwards, that was in '75, '76.[27]

Ó Búitigh and other internees stress that the Open University courses were introduced on the internees' initiative and with the agreement – between camp authorities, internees, and the Open University – that no side would use the courses for propaganda purposes. However, the Provisional republican internees considered the camp authorities and the British government to breach this agreement and, thus, refused to cooperate on this matter. Consequently, the courses were stopped for republicans, whereas loyalists continued attending the Open University classes. Although Ó Búitigh's account cannot be verified, it shows the importance of informal and formal education for the republican internees, which made education a constant source of tension within the camps. Before moving on to the next section of this chapter, I want to conclude with a lengthy excerpt of the interview with Séanna Walsh that reveals his understanding of the importance of informal education in his own process of becoming a political subject in the camp:

> We organized it ourselves. We took the organization of it among ourselves. The idea behind [it was that] a cursory understanding of Irish history was no longer sufficient. We had to do a more in-depth study, that's what I believed, and that was what I became involved in studying Irish history. We put together a library of must-reads. You know, when people found themselves in prison: read this one, read that one. As well as Irish republican history and Irish republican politics, we also studied anti-imperialist

struggles across the world, [and] anti-colonial war. That would have been very important to us.

We would have had three must-reads. [This was] my top priority when guys came into jail from outside, and I said: Look, this is my recommended reading list. Three top priorities! One would have been *Liam Mellows and the Irish Revolution*, which was by Desmond Greaves and which gave a really good understanding of, from a radical republican, socialist perspective, of the events leading up from 1916 to the Tan War and then the Civil War and what happened after the Civil War with partition. So that was a half-decent book in terms of Ireland. We also read, that would have been a book on top of my list, Frantz Fanon, *The Wretched of the Earth*, which is about the anti-imperialist struggle in Algeria and the understanding that brought about the colonialized, the way the imperialists colonialized not just the wealth of the country; they also colonialized the minds of the occupants. And the third one was, strangely enough, a book called *The Soledad Brother*, which was by a guy called George Jackson.... The thing about it is that the beauty of this is his political awareness. How he developed an understanding of why he was in jail, and he became politicized by the fact that he was in jail. I find that very interesting, and it was always a good sort of opener for debate, particularly with guys newly coming into the prison if you could get them interested in that. Those would have been my particular three.

But we had libraries full of books. We had *Ireland Her Own* by T. A. Jackson, which was a favourite we would have used. We used Paulo Freire, the Brazilian, *The Pedagogy of the Oppressed*. That would have been the political education as well as that we would have studied Giáp, General Giáp in Vietnam and his take on guerrilla warfare. And we would have studied guerrilla warfare in Cuba, the likes of Castro and Guevara and all that. And you would have studied Gramsci and all the contemporary stuff that would have been out there at that time, which would not only help to bring about an independent Ireland but a new type of political system in Ireland as well. Because one of the things that were very important for me from an early stage was that we would have no wish to become part of an independent Ireland if it was simply an extension of the political culture of the twenty-six counties into the North.[28]

In this extended excerpt, Séanna Walsh is keen to put forward his understanding of the purpose that the informal political and historical education had for the newly arriving internees and, ultimately, for the whole republican movement. Accordingly, he recapitulates these events four decades after they occurred. Walsh tells them not from the position of an internee in Long Kesh but from the position of a narrator who has

embraced the conflict transformation process and the decommissioning of the PIRA. In fact, he retrospectively places developments that
occurred in later years, during the last phase of internment and more
so, from 1983 onwards in the H-Blocks, at the heart of confinement – in
so doing, he makes the passage particularly interesting.

Walsh first stressed that the desire to study Irish history and politics
came from the prisoners themselves and that these prisoners created
reading lists. However, the use of systematic reading lists is undocu-
mented in the camps, and the collected oral and written documents suggest that it only came into being in the H-Blocks after 1983. Before that
period, lectures, discussions, and individual reading were widespread
but unsystematic. He then discusses what he calls his three "must-
reads." At his arrest and subsequent internment in Long Kesh, Walsh
was still a young, inexperienced, and politically less-educated republican activist. As he explains at the outset, he was only sixteen when he
first went to prison. Nonetheless, Walsh presents himself as a well-read,
politically and historically educated internee in the later course of the
interview. In fact, the three books he mentions foreshadow the topics
of Irish republican self-education at a later stage. At the same time, he
projects his encounters with these works in the early internment period.

The three must-reads reflect the three areas of informal education of
Irish republicans. The first book is taken from the corpus of Irish republican history. The era of the Irish revolution from 1913 to 1923 is covered
by a biography of Liam Mellows, one of those figures from the Irish
republican pantheon. The Liam Mellows books include the areas of
Irish history and nationalism. The second book places the Irish republican struggle within the anti-imperialist struggles of the era and the
intellectual influences emerging in the post-1968 period. Frantz Fanon's
writings in this list mark the departure of the Irish republican thinking from Irish nationalism to international anti-imperialism. The third
book, George Jackson's prison writings, place Irish republican internees and prisoners within the struggle of political prisoners suffering
injustice worldwide, beginning in the early 1970s. The republican prisoners learned that their perceived injustice was not unique, and they
had potential allies in other parts of the world. This internationalization
was an essential step in the political subjectification of Irish republicans
because it contradicted the then dominant notion among Irish nationalists of the Irish as the "most oppressed people ever."

By outlining these three areas of study, Walsh introduces the three
pillars of republican self-education in the post-1983 period. In this
phase, international solidarity became a focus of republican terminology; Vietnam and Cuba are mentioned in this excerpt. He also talks

Education hut in the yard of cage/compound. The photo was taken on 8
September 2004. Image courtesy of Laurence McKeown.

about Nelson Mandela and South Africa at other stages in the interview. Yet, he becomes most explicit on that aspect when talking about
Paulo Freire. His theories became definitive for the prisoners. Freire,
a Brazilian educator and philosopher who was a leading advocate of
critical pedagogy, is best known for his book *Pedagogy of the Oppressed*.
In this book, he argues that education should empower the oppressed
so that they become equipped with the knowledge they can use to
free themselves. In his writings on education, he emphasizes that the
education of the oppressed should serve the purpose of enabling them
to overcome their plight. As will be seen in the following chapter, Irish
republicans like Laurence McKeown and Anthony McIntyre studied
Freire's writings and designed political and historical classes following his ideas.[29] Walsh thus justifies retrospectively the direction the
movement was taking from the mid-1970s onwards by assigning it
to the early internment-period developments that unfolded only in
the 1980s. In reality, the recruits coming into the camps determined
the later direction of the movement. This development was indeed
reflected in the camp culture, as we shall see in the following section.

The years 1974 and 1975 saw a new group of republicans arrive at the camps. The first internees included a higher proportion of older, experienced republicans who brought with them the experience of the previous imprisonment. As the conflict turned into a full-fledged war, the generational composition of the republican movement changed. Following the outbreak of the conflict in July 1969, events like the introduction of internment in August 1971 and Bloody Sunday in Derry in January 1972 brought recruits into the IRA. As discussed in the first chapter, unlike the older republicans, these recruits were not from republican family backgrounds and had little or no political or historical education. Yet, the IRA needed more members to wage war against the British army and security forces. This new composition of IRA members was soon reflected in the camps as more and more of these recruits were arrested. With the arrival of these recruits, life in the camps started to change. Not all the older republicans were enthusiastic about the new situation. Michael Donnelly recalls:

> At one stage, that was an earlier stage; there were quite a lot of older people in there. That made quite a difference. It was easier to talk to them, and there was education. But as time went on, there came a big influence of younger people, so it became a bit more bodily. It was very difficult – then – to live in the huts with 100, [or] 119 people. It was all designed to break you along the way, constant Brit raids. So, we countered this by digging tunnels and trying to escape. The cage I was in, Cage 5, was close to the edge of the camp, so that's where all the tunnels were.[30]

He continues:

> You didn't need discipline before, but you certainly needed a lot of discipline afterwards. You had certain people coming in, criminal elements, that wouldn't have been allowed in before. Certainly, after '74, they were allowed in. When they came into jail, they certainly didn't hold the same views as the rest of us would. And then started the petty thieving of other prisoners and stuff like that. All started from there, antagonism and fighting, and it started to break down a bit. So, the army, the IRA in Long Kesh, had to install more discipline because of that. The attitudes were very different.[31]

Dáithí Ó Búitígh has similar recollections as Donnelly: "A lot of the things that happened – there were people in jail that had different viewpoints; they were not brought up in a republican background. They were talked into viewpoints, not that I would disagree with these viewpoints, but you were dogmatic, you were censoring free thought, and that is not what we were supposed to be doing."[32]

Donnelly and Ó Búitígh are critical of the direction the Provisional republican movement took from the late 1970s and mainly the mid-1980s. Therefore, they saw recruits as a threat to the movement. But not all the younger members were the same. Gerry Adams was one of these younger members who rose through the ranks of the republican movement in the early 1970s and eventually ended up in Long Kesh. Adams came from an established republican family in Ballymurphy, a nationalist neighbourhood in West Belfast. From 1983 until 2018, he was to be president of Sinn Féin. Adams and a group of younger Belfast republicans interned in Long Kesh showed a keen interest in political education from the very start. Donnelly, who is today a harsh critic of Adams and Sinn Féin, remembers some of Gerry Adams's lectures in the camp: "He [Gerry Adams] would come along and stick a note on the door saying that he would give a lecture and it was all about Marxism, sections of 'Das Kapital.' But he didn't know what he was talking about. He was just rhyming off pages of it. Myself and Sean McDermott and Oliver Kelly decided we would ask meaning-less questions at the end of it and all taken again from Marx, you know. I don't remember the exact questions, but they were all made up anyways, but it didn't bother Adams. He answered in the same meaningless way."[33]

Adams and his group of mainly Belfast republicans were engaged in political debates in their hut, Cage 11. Anthony McIntyre had joined the Official republican youth movement (Official) Na Fianna Éireann at age sixteen in 1973. After a short spell with the Officials in Belfast, he joined the Provisionals and, shortly afterwards, was arrested and imprisoned for eighteen months. When he was eighteen, he was again arrested and sentenced and spent the next seventeen years in prison, first in Long Kesh and later as one of the Blanketmen in the H-Blocks. In the internment camp, he also spent some time in Cage 11. In prison, McIntyre developed into an influential republican thinker, becoming educational officer at one stage in the 1980s. How-ever, he also turned into one of the loudest critics of the Provisional leadership on the outside. While still in prison, he left the IRA in the late 1980s and pursued an Open University education. Following his release, he embarked on a PhD at Queen's University Belfast, formed the Republican Writers' Group, published the *Fourthwrite* magazine, and later the magazine *Blanket* to promote debate within republican-ism.[34] Due to his public opposition of Sinn Féin, he was forced out of Belfast and today lives in Drogheda, Co. Louth, where he publishes

the blog *The Pensive Quill*.[35] Despite his criticism of Gerry Adams and
the leadership of Sinn Féin around him, he remembers the impact
Cage 11 had on him:

> We spent most of the time wrecking the place when we were young.…
> Although, when I got to Cage 11 and [when I arrived there], I thought
> I was highly politicized. I came there after Adams left. Adams was in
> charge of Cage 11 for some time, and after he left Cage 11, the cage car-
> ried on and for a while the tradition they thought he had created for
> them, which was an extensive library and plenty of political discus-
> sions, plenty of debate, watching documentaries, making sure there was
> something on TV, a documentary or a news program, had priority. There
> were all these documentaries about Communism and Chile, Cambodia,
> Khmer Rouge, Vietnam, and they all were reading General Giap, Che
> Guevara, [and] discussing strategy. I thought they loved it. There was a
> lot of talk. Some of these people were very committed, and they wanted
> to learn more, and Adams held a strong IRA commitment in there. And
> they held a strong anti-leadership position in there. They thought that
> the [Southern based] leadership should be overthrown, and they were
> talking left-wing.[36]

While they were willing to discuss new political ideas early, it was not
until the failed IRA ceasefire, from 9 February 1975 to 23 January 1976,
that they publicly stressed the need for a new direction of the Provisional republican movement. Then, from August 1975 onwards, republican prisoners started to send letters and comments to the Northern
republican paper *Republican News*, openly engaging in political debates
outside the camps and prisons. Again, this was a new development.
Before this date, republican internees and prisoners had only used their
letters to newspapers to highlight the conditions in the camps and prisons, not to engage in the political debates of the movement outside, as
Danny Morrison remembers:

> It was more education than deciding political strategy because when you
> are inside, you are really, you know, you can't really appreciate properly
> what is going on on the outside. So, we wouldn't have been involved in
> designing strategy. We might have been involved in proposing ideas, etc.,
> but mostly it would have been education and publicity. So, for example, a
> number of people would have been nominated to write statements about
> what was going on. Say, for example, if there was a British army raid
> and they were very rough, and some people got their arms broken or
> their nose broken, or their tooth broken or a black eye. We would have a

number of people writing to the Irish media [about] what was going on, so basically publicity/propaganda. They raided the cages every two to three weeks, so there were always incidents. There was always a grievance that could be publicized and also, of course, encourage sympathy on the outside.[37]

With the failed truce in the mid-1970s, younger Northern republicans questioned the role of the older Southern leadership of the movement, and it was the internees in Long Kesh who first made these critical discussions public. The so-called Brownie Papers were their vehicle for spreading new ideas within the wider republican movement outside the camps. The Brownie Papers were short writings smuggled out of the cages of Long Kesh between 15 August 1975 and 19 February 1977. Gerry Adams wrote about his experience as a political prisoner under the pseudonym "Brownie" in these articles. The essays appeared first as a regular column in the *Republican News*, a newspaper affiliated with the Provisional republican movement in Belfast. While the Brownie essays focused on the internment experience, they also discussed the strategy of the republican movement, most famously in Brownie's article on active abstentionism. In this article, published in the *Republican News* on 18 October 1975, Adams ignites debate on the Sinn Féin strategy of abstaining from taking seats in the parliaments in Dublin, Belfast, and London. This question had already split the republican movement in 1969/70 and became a factor in another split in 1986. The Brownie Papers were the first political writings of Gerry Adams. Some were later republished in his book *Cage Eleven*.[38] Adams was not the first internee to publish a regular column in an Irish newspaper held in Long Kesh. Des O'Hagan, a member of the Official IRA, had a column in the *Irish Times* after his internment in August 1971. His columns were later published as a book – *Letters from Long Kesh*.[39] Still, Adams was the first Provisional republican to write a regular column, thereby introducing a new role of the IRA prisoners within their movement. In his analyses of the Brownie Papers, Lachlan Whalen writes, "There is a long tradition of republican prison writing appearing in newspapers, in many ways this is fitting, as jail literature at times shows common ground with journalism. Often, both are more concerned with the immediate, with the here-and-now, than traditional literature generally is, not just in terms of the events occurring outside the prison, but, to an even greater degree, also the events that surrounded the prison writers themselves." He stresses that it is "a warning beacon to readers outside jail walls."[40] The Brownie Papers were intended as a warning beacon to the outside supporters and the Southern republican leadership.[41]

While the Brownie Papers are often portrayed as the sole political thought of Gerry Adams, they, in fact, reflect the debates among the younger generation of Northern republicans who had joined the PIRA after the outbreak of the conflict. Thus, they were a collective intellectual endeavour to which Gerry Adams gave voice using the Brownie pseudonym. My interview partner Dáithí Ó Búitigh claims to be one of those involved in the production of the Brownie Papers. He rejects the claim that the later Sinn Féin spokesperson Richard McAuley, interned in Long Kesh with Gerry Adams, was the author of the Brownie Papers, as has occasionally been claimed.[42] He recalls:

> Oh yeah, Gerry Adams, it was not Richard McAuley. I typed every one of them.… I was the only other one to see them. He wrote them, and I typed them. He wrote them on paper, and he sent them over to me, and I typed them up because I was just asked to type them up. I was the only one to type them up. It was a lot of waffle. – To me, there was nothing in them worth discussing, it was only his personal viewpoint, but I put a few things in when I thought he got it completely wrong, I changed it. [laughing] Whether he noticed it or not, I don't know. Most of the quotes he used, I put in, and Richard McAuley's, staff [member of the IRA in Long Kesh] as PRO. I typed that as well and clearing his grammar. I typed both articles, and I know who wrote which.[43]

Ó Búitigh, today a harsh opponent of Sinn Féin, is biased in his comments about Gerry Adams and thus neglects the input of others in the development of the ideas expressed in the Brownie Papers. He stresses that the articles solely reflect Adams's personal point of view. However, he acknowledges that Richard McAuley indeed wrote some articles and that he typed them. When asked why he typed these articles if he disagreed with their content, he answers: "I had nothing better to do, so I typed them. It also kept me updated with what he was thinking. I could see what way he was thinking. I included some changes, and he didn't notice them, but they were mostly corrections of his Irish and grammar. His grammar was not the best, and his Irish was terrible. Honestly, he has very poor Irish."[44] Based on the interviews and the existing literature, I would instead argue that the articles, while not reflecting the views of the whole prisoner population, at least reflected the views of the internees in Cage 11. These prisoners were already a tightly bound group that was to become one of the most influential sections of the Provisional republican movement. Among the republicans in Cage 11 were Richard McAuley, Ivor Bell, Gerry Kelly, and Brendan Hughes. Robert W. White writes that this young generation of republicans "were involved in discussions that would have a huge effect on the IRA and Sinn Féin."[45] They truly reflected the views of the new generation of Northern republicans that climbed the ranks of the IRA and Sinn Féin in the late 1970s and 1980s, eventually successfully sidelining the Southern leadership until they spilt at the Ard-Fheis in 1986.

Ó Búitigh contradicts his own claim that Adams alone was responsible for the articles when he mentions that both Richard McAuley and he himself had an input in the preparation of the Brownie Papers. Furthermore, a chain of people was needed to smuggle the articles out of the camp. Then, the pieces had to be typed and edited again for publication in the *Republican News*. That also implies that at least some people on the paper's editorial board sympathized with some of the content; otherwise, they would not have been printed. Robert W. White suggests that ex-internee Danny Morrison, then the newly appointed editor of the *Republican News*, asked Adams to write a column for the paper.[46] In other words, while the intellectual input of Gerry Adams dominated, a group of people was needed to get the papers published – from the initial discussion to the writing, typing, smuggling, editing, and printing, thus making the Brownie Papers a collective endeavour of a specific section of the Provisional republican movement at that time.

Finally, a comment on the testimony of Dáithí Ó Búitigh. I cannot verify his story. However, then Ard Chomhairle[47] member Lita Ní Cathmhaoil from Dublin and former Blanketman Anthony McIntyre independently corroborated his pre-interment biographical account. Ó Búitigh was active in the republican movement in Belfast; he was indeed one of the city's organizers of the republican youth organization Na Fianna Éireann, and accounts mention the existence of at least one typewriter in Long Kesh. Hence, all the parts of the puzzle are there. These pieces might not be enough to verify his story, but, at the same time, there is also nothing to suggest that Ó Búitigh invented it. Therefore, I think this is at least enough to warrant telling his story. Future generations of historians might have different and more credible sources to judge his account.

Not only were the politics of the republican movement debated in the prisons, but the PIRA also set itself on a path of reorganization from the mid- to late 1970s on. The strategy was called the "long war," and it included the reorganization of the PIRA into a cell system. Gerard Hodgins is a former IRA prisoner from Belfast; he had joined the republican youth movement Na Fianna Éireann when he was "14 or 15." In May 1976, when he was only sixteen, Hodgins was arrested and spent six months on remand in the Crumlin Road prison. After his sentence, he was transferred to the H-Blocks and imprisoned for another fourteen years. Today, Hodgins lives in West Belfast, where I met him for our interview. He is strongly opposed to the politics of Gerry Adams and Sinn Féin. In fact, he told me that he was going to a rally led by republicans opposed to Sinn Féin, the 1916 Societies, in Dublin the following Saturday. Nonetheless, he also attributes the change in politics to Adams and the prisoners in Cage 11 due to the failed ceasefire in 1975. He explains:

> It was the "long war." Because, believe it or not, in the early '70s, we came that close to [getting] defeated. By 1974, '75, we were on our ropes. Honestly, the British had run us into the ground, they had a prolonged ceasefire, and at that time, they were ramping up for the criminalization policy, getting us into the H-blocks, the Ulsterisation and all that.... The rebuilding of the movement came from sort of within Long Kesh. If you were inside, you don't have the whole world on your shoulders, so if you are a thinker, you have time to think and develop strategies, and that's what they have done. They recognized that the war was not going to change; it was going to be a long war. You had to rethink your structure, you know, at that time the IRA was almost just like the British army, it had battalions, brigades, companies, you know, too large, too many people who could hear and learn too ... many things. So, we scaled down, they were talking, we go down into cells. Well, it wasn't actually cells. It was squads, and [we] dug in for a long war, but we also had to include propaganda because, at that time, the propaganda that was coming out of the movement was brilliant. They had a magazine that was called IRIS.... But that's where most of the change came from, from within the prisons. Prisons can have a close link with the organization outside, although it has to be said that the organization outside was always in supreme control, and when you are in an army, you always support your officers.[48]

Hodgins links the political and military changes to the situation that developed after the ceasefire and stresses that the debates originated within Long Kesh. However, when specifically asked who started these debates, he attributes it to Cage 11, saying: "I would say it was a collection of people close to Adams who were in the jail in the '70s or in Cage 11 with him. They were thinking roughly the same way. They were thinking more internationalist and sort of left-wing and saw a need of developing a political base. That would have been growing amongst us."[49]

Hodgins stresses the influence the debates in Cage 11 had on other prisoners and contributed a change in the attitude towards education, and prison life in general, to the group of Belfast republicans in Cage 11:

> I wouldn't really say that we used our time wisely in those days. There was
> no encouragement to get involved in any sort of education. At that time,
> the IRA was just coming into the era when it was becoming more of a liberation movement in terms of respecting people. Up until this, the IRA was
> very macho, very militaristic. It was like a reflection of the British army,
> regiments, regulations, rules, classifying people in derogatory ways if they
> had broken in the barracks [during interrogation].… A lot of shite, you
> know. But then Brendan Hughes, Ivor Bell, and Gerry Adams, they rose
> to positions within the IRA where they could develop a more revolutionary strategy – and that strategy also entailed treating people as comrades
> and encouraging their political skills and go into your history and don't be
> afraid to articulate a republican position. So, from that time on, the attitude
> of the IRA towards education would have changed, especially in jail.[50]

To conclude, the Brownie Papers were a watershed moment for the Provisional republican movement and the role of the prison population within the movement. For the first time since the outbreak of the conflict in 1968, republican internees and prisoners became political subjects who used their position as political prisoners to influence outside developments. This development marked a new approach, and from then on, this newly acquired influence would be used in every strategic debate of the movement, from the discussions surrounding abstentionism that led to the split in 1986 to the peace process in the 1990s.

The PIRA is often described as a "'traditional' hierarchical terrorist group,"[51] characterized by "pyramidal, hierarchical, organizational structures";[52] however, prison life in the Long Kesh and Magilligan internment camps in the early years of internment paints a different picture of republican internees. While a military structure existed in the camps, prison life, and internee-led education in particular, was much more flexible and less hierarchical than the Provisional IRA inside and outside the prisons following the organization's restructuring in the late 1970s. In a reassessment of the "old terrorism" versus "new terrorism" binary, Anthony Field writes that "the Provisional IRA was far from a unified, hierarchical group with an effective chain of command. Instead, it was a highly-fragmented organization, with intermittent lines of communication and competing centres of power."[53] These observations are reflected in the testimonies of former prisoners and internees during the early years of the conflict.

Chapter Six

Marxist Esperanto and Socialism in Cell 26: Reading, Thinking, and Writing in the H-Blocks, 1983–1989

In 1976, the British government opened the newly built H-Blocks at HMP Maze and phased out special category status. The new high-security prison was opened literally on the other side of a fence from the Long Kesh internment camp. From then on, all incoming republican and loyalist prisoners were treated as ordinary prisoners, while their comrades on the other side of the fence continued to enjoy special privileges. This situation led prisoners to protest about their treatment as "ordinary" prisoners, resulting in the blanket and no-wash protests and eventually in two series of hunger strikes in 1980 and 1981, which led to the deaths of ten republicans, until most of their demands were ultimately met in 1982/3. The following decade saw a relaxation of the prison regime and the development of an informal education program by the IRA and Sinn Féin members in the prisons. Debates on the long-term future of the struggle and the role that electoral and parliamentary politics would play also marked those years. These debates became increasingly leftist. It was, thus, no surprise that the fall of the Berlin Wall came as a shock for many prisoners. The end of the Soviet Union marked a dramatic shift of the prisoners' rhetoric and education from radical socialism to left-wing anti-imperialism and, due to the peace process gaining momentum, to pragmatism. In 2000, two years after signing the Good Friday Agreement, also referred to as the Belfast Agreement, HMP Maze and its H-Blocks were finally closed. The prisoners who signed the terms of the agreement were released; those opposed to the conflict transformation have remained at HMP Maghaberry, Co. Antrim.

The criminalization policy was among the three new policies introduced by the British government in the wake of the failed ceasefire of 1975. While we encountered the consequences of the collapsed ceasefire within the internment camp population in the previous chapter, the newly introduced criminalization policy would have far-reaching and immediate implications for newly arriving prisoners. The criminalization policy meant that republican prisoners sentenced after 1 March 1976 were not granted political status; instead, they were treated as so-called ordinary-decent criminals, in contrast to political prisoners, and held in the newly built H-Blocks, rather than the Long Kesh internment camp. The other two policies were: normalization, i.e., creating the impression that Northern Ireland was not war-torn but was a normal society, and Ulsterization, i.e., reducing the British presence on the streets in favour of increased use of the local police, the RUC, that gradually stepped into the place of the British army in the province. The British army did, of course, not leave the process, but did less policing.

Both criminalization and the opening of the H-Blocks were causes of resistance among Irish republicans. On the one hand, by criminalizing their prisoners, Irish republicans interpreted the new British policy as criminalizing their whole struggle and, thus, delegitimizing the right of national self-determination by the Irish people. On the other hand, the H-Block system constituted a modern form of the Panopticon by introducing total control over its inmates. Irish republicans resisted both. Hence, in resisting, they strove for the re-legitimization of their struggle while, at the same time, reclaiming control of their space, body, and time in prison. While republicans protested this new policy all over Northern Ireland, the prisons that turned into battlegrounds for political status were the newly built H-Blocks and, later, the women's prison HMP Armagh.

The H-Blocks were the eight new prison blocks built at the site of the Long Kesh internment camp; their arrangement resembled the letter H, hence their name. Unlike Long Kesh, the prisoners held in the H-Blocks were not kept in groups but were isolated in cells. The prison warders occupied the central control room. From this position, they could observe and enter all four wings and both yards of the H-Blocks. Thereby, they exercised not only total control over prisoners but also eliminated the military system of the IRA that had shaped the daily routine of prisoners in the internment camps. The new system was marked by prison uniforms, prison work, and several punitive conditions. By keeping each prisoner isolated and treating them as criminals, the prison administration introduced a system that included punishment if the prisoners resisted and rewards if they conformed to the new reality. Michel Foucault did not, of course, discuss the H-Blocks, but the system he described in *Discipline and Punishment* was, indeed, very close to it.

The so-called blanket protest started in the H-Blocks on 14 September 1976 when a young Belfast man called Kieran Nugent arrived at the prison after conviction by a non-jury Diplock court. He had been sentenced to three years' imprisonment. Upon arrival, he was told to take off his clothes and put on a prison uniform. Nugent refused, and his reported words made it into Irish republican mythology: "If you want me to wear that, you'll have to nail it to my back." For that, Nugent was thrown into a cell with nothing but a blanket to cover him, thus, making him the first "Blanketman." Over the following weeks and months, Nugent would be joined by increasing numbers of republican prisoners. By Christmas 1976, about four dozen prisoners were "on the blanket," as it was called.[1]

Laurence McKeown also joined the blanket protest when imprisoned in the H-Blocks. He explains that, initially, republicans thought the protest would be over in a few months, as they believed the British government would revoke their decision to remove special category status. But, as McKeown explains, these hopes faded as the protest dragged on:

> By the time I was sentenced, there were about one hundred prisoners on the protest.... At its height, there would have been like four hundred prisoners on it. It developed into a no-wash protest. I didn't wash for three years, from 1978 until 1981. So, when I was sentenced in April, there already was, as I said, about a hundred prisoners on it, basically you were taken from remand court or remand prison in Belfast to Long Kesh to the H-Blocks. You were told about prison gear. You said: "No, I'm not going to." My experience was I was taken into what was the reception area of the H-Block, it was H-Block 2, it's called the "circle area" even though it's a rectangle, so it's part of the terminology. We had already heard at that time a lot of reports of brutality as people were going down to the prison because, obviously, the prison authorities were trying to dissuade people from going on the protest. I was told to strip and put my clothes into a brown bag, and I stripped down to my underpants, and it's bizarre because you're in the middle of this square and there are other activities going on around you, there are prison guards and orderlies going back and forward, there's the governor going about, and you're standing in the middle of this stripped down to your underpants, and then somebody said: "Group," and a group of them gathered round, and I thought there was going to be a lot of physical abuse. But there wasn't, and somebody said: "We said strip. Get the fucking heap off." So, I ended up totally naked in the middle of this circle. And probably thinking back, it was done to degrade you or humiliate you or whatever in some way.[2]

From the moment new prisoners arrived, the warders established an atmosphere of intimidation that was supposed to break the individual and make him conform. For example, forcing protesting prisoners to strip naked and then "introducing" them to the prison in what

McKeown calls the "circle," was designed to establish a strict hierarchy and impose the message that the new prisoners were alone and helpless. John Nixon has similar memories of the H-Blocks. Having been imprisoned in the internment camp before, he thus had an experience of both regimes: "The H-Blocks were a different experience…. In the H-Blocks, it was a regime that was designed and engineered to break you in spirit, to make you conform to prison rule regulation and most importantly, to criminalize you and to criminalize your whole cause, your belief and principles. So, that had been resisted, and unfortunately for us who were in the H-Blocks, the British government decided to try to break you. So, a lot of beatings when you came in."[3]

He also explains the "prison introduction," which McKeown calls "the circle":

It's like an initiation. It is called "prison introduction," and you meet the governor, you meet all the screws. They are waiting there to meet you, and they are not in a great mood. From the very start, they want to give you a test of what is gonna come. So, it was a reception, that's what you gonna call it. It's like a reception in the hotel, but the screws are waiting for you, not the hotel manager or a nice looking – you understand? You went through the main entrance of the H-Blocks and straight into, it was actually a square, not a circle, and you were told to strip down, completely naked and there were three screws standing on one side and three screws on the other side and so on, very intimating situation, very frightful. You constantly think: "They fucking kill you." They didn't actually kill you, but they wanted to tell you, especially to people who came from the cages [of Long Kesh] like myself, they wanted to make it very, very clear that this is not the fucking cages anymore, and you were a criminal. Some of these screws actually worked in the compounds, in the cages with us. Money was a big attraction for them, and they had no problems carrying out beatings or carrying out psychological pressure. They were total mercenaries. Twenty-nine screws lost their lives, that shouldn't have happened, but a lot of things shouldn't have happened.[4]

The brutality did not stop after this first inaugural phase; instead, the physical force came to be used systematically by the prison warders to break the republicans, both physically and mentally, as Noel Cassidy, a republican from County Monaghan who was in the H-Blocks between 1977 and February 1981, recalls. When he arrived there, he was almost thirty years of age, making him one of the oldest prisoners:

We probably had the youngest Blanketman, Ciaran McGillicuddy, out of Strabane. They used to give him awful abuse. I think the hardest part of the blanket was hearing him being taken out of his cell at night and beaten, so we did. That was the hardest part, hearing other people being beaten. All of us got beaten, so we did. You got more than a few laps, especially when Narrow Water[5] happened. A lot of the screws were ex-Paras, and they came into the cells – every single cell. You could hear them coming down the wings, so you could. You could hear them going in, and you could hear the screams and the thumps, and you knew it was going to be your turn very shortly. There was nothing you could do about it. Two people in a cell and maybe half a dozen, maybe eight of them, and them coming in with their boots.[6]

Cassidy shows the helplessness of the prisoners against the prison regime by mentioning the imbalance between prisoners and warders during these beatings. This imbalance is underscored by the fact the prison warders had "boots" on, while the prisoners were "naked," highlighting the vulnerability of the protesting prisoners:

We were all locked up twenty-four hours a day, seven days a week, every day of the month, for years. You cannot do anything to defend you; you were naked.… That led us to be almost five years on the blanket, all the mess on the wall, all the beatings and I was brought to what was called the punishment block, and I was kept there for three months, and it was against the Geneva Convention.… They were denying us food, not completely but cutting down the rations.… So every day was the same, we put our mess on the walls, you were always vulnerable, and you were always hungry. It was a six by nine cell, and you had a cellmate, very little room, six by nine, and you had your mattress, no beds, just a mattress on the ground, a piece of sponge and three blankets each. If you had a pillow, you were lucky.[7]

The conditions in the H-Blocks for those on the blanket protest were particularly harsh, as these testimonies show us. The protesting prisoners were held in strict solitary confinement, twenty-four hours a day, seven days a week. In later years, two prisoners were held in one cell as a result of overcrowding. Prisoners who joined the protest lost fourteen days of remission and fourteen days of all privileges, including family visits and letters. The only time they left their cells was once a week for Mass and on the way to washrooms and visits and during searches of their cells. These brief spells outside the cells were also the only opportunity to see and communicate with other prisoners. Gerard Hodgins recalls:

I remember the screws tried to isolate us, first one at a wing and so on but in April 1977, it was not practical anymore to isolate us because there were so many. It was very brutal when you were isolated; they would come in and beat you and smack you and fucking all that. So, the numbers were building, and they created an H-Block specifically for the Blanketmen, us, who refused to wear the uniform. The first time we had any communication with each other was after five or six months into the protest. And for two days there was just talking, talking, you know, exchanging stories, gossip. We settled in there; we started to develop our interest in education around this time because some of the men who had been with us had been in the cages with political status in '73, '74, '75, and some of them had been in Cage 11. That was this cage with Adams, Ivor Bell, Brendan Hughes. So, they were able to generate discussion and get us thinking, and I was encouraged all the way through the blanket to get on, and the rest is just history, I suppose.[8]

The prison administration ordered the prisoners to wear prison uniforms on their way to the washrooms instead of towels as they did up until this point, in a further attempt to isolate and break the prisoners. This policy led to a further escalation of the situation. Warders regularly beat prisoners in the washrooms and during searches. Consequently, the prisoners refused to leave their cells to use the bathrooms. The move introduced the no-wash protest, also called the dirty protest. The prisoners were now forced to carry out all toilet functions in their cells; to keep the floor clean and dry – prisoners had no furniture, only a sponge mattress to sleep on the floor – they smeared their excrement on the walls. In later years, republican women also embarked on that form of protest. The no-wash protest lasted until the hunger strikes in 1980 and 1981. Over three hundred men were on the blanket protest between September 1976 and the October 1980 hunger strikes. At this stage, republican women in Armagh Gaol had also joined the protest.[9]

When the protesting prisoners were all moved into their own prison area, their lives started to change. While still under the same conditions, their physical separation was ended and, thereby, their isolation. Sharing the cell with one other protesting prisoner gave them security. While still covered only with a blanket, the word "naked" disappeared from the narratives. The move into a separate prison area also allowed them to communicate with each other – and with that communication came education, as Gerard Hodgins remembers. Again, the republicans who were previously held in Cage 11 of the Long Kesh internment camp led the political debates and developments in this new environment.

Communication in Irish became possible by shouting from cells or along the heating pipes that linked the cells. Thus, the learning of Irish – by shouting lessons from one door to another, for books and all learning materials were forbidden for protesting prisoners – was, on the one hand, a tool for "secured" communication, and on the other hand, it was another form of resistance to the British prison system. Seanna Walsh remembers: "One thing we did was to put an emphasis on ... teaching the Irish language as another form of resistance – that we were able to teach hundreds of guys who had no knowledge of the Irish language to give them a good basic conversational level of Irish where the majority of guys would have understood basic conversations in Irish."[10]

The establishment of Irish classes for the protesting prisoners sparked further debates and lectures in other areas, initially mainly historical topics. Still, soon the prisoners discussed all kinds of political subjects. Anthony McIntyre, who was also in Cage 11 before he was sent to the H-Blocks after his second arrest, remembers: "When we went into the H-Blocks, we would discuss things at the door on the blanket protest, only because we had nothing else to do, and we loved political discussion and debate, and lecturers would come down from the cages, and we would do them out the door, and we discussed some, we discussed everything. We discussed abortion, communism, Marxism, socialism, republicanism, right-wing republicanism, Left-wing republicanism, Irish history, women's rights, abortion, religion; we have done an awful lot of that because of the thirst for knowledge."[11]

By shouting from cell door to cell door, the prisoners communicated, learned Irish, discussed the development of the protest, and resisted the prison regime. One Derry republican who was imprisoned from 1976 to 1897 arrived in the H-Blocks from Crumlin Road prison on 8 July 1987 and remembered: "As part of this punishment, the screws tried to enforce a strict silence in the wings, so, of course, that was the first thing that we challenged. Whenever possible, we would talk to each other at the cell window and even from cell door to cell door. Of course, the screw would threaten us for not keeping quiet, but it became a cat and mouse game and a sign of our defiance that we would no longer be silent."[12]

In this situation, the prisoners decided that all discussions, lectures, and classes would be held at night. The day shift of the prison warders on the republican wings ended at 8:30 p.m., leaving only a night guard consisting of one or two prison officers in the control room of each H-Block. "That was when the blanket prisoners really came alive. We organized sing-songs, storytelling and even the odd quiz to keep morale up," remembers the same Derry republican.[13] So, while the days meant brutality, cell searches, wing shift, strip searches, and beatings, the nights were characterized by talking, discussing, lecturing, and learning. Keeping occupied with whatever exercises and debates possible was necessary for the prisoners to cope with the situation, as Gerard Hodgins explains, because for him, "'90 per cent of the time was just boring." The prison officers aimed at crushing all interaction between the prisoners during the daytime and, in that way, maintaining isolation and breaking the prisoners mentally. Hodgins explains: "It was silent. You wake up, and you lie there. The only book, the only sort of literature you had, was the Bible. So out of boredom, you know, I am an absolute expert on the Bible because I just had nothing else to read.... Most of the time, you would lie in silence, having your own thoughts. You would not lie down in defeat; you were lying in defence."[14]

Lying in defence, rather than in defeat, meant, for Hodgins, that the prisoners not only listened carefully to what was happening outside their doors to be prepared when the prison officers entered their cells, which usually resulted in fierce hand-to-hand fighting, but also preserved their mental dignity. As Hodgins recalls:

> We were talking among ourselves and having debates, singing songs, and, you know, organizing as many things as possible to keep people focused and occupy their minds rather than just sleeping in there. That helps keep you going, you know, because we are talking about four or five years of lying, you know, basically in shit. It was a hard time!... At night-time, there was the quietness on the wing, and that's when we got alive, having whatever discussions, passing Tobacco around, doing whatever we had to do. Night-time was our time!... We were trying to keep things going that helped to survive in the belly of the beast.[15]

Tommy McKearney was one of the prisoners who gave history lectures in the H-Blocks by shouting from door to door:

> At that stage, as much as to relieve the boredom, people started to do different types of education. Some of it was to learn the Irish language, some even began to learn the words of songs to sing, but a lot of us chatted about what are we doing, where are we going, how are we going to get there, where have we succeeded, where have we failed? That was a political analysis of what took us into it, what led us to be serving such lengthy sentences. One of the first things we started to do was to look at Irish history and not in the purely anecdotal way but to go back and look at the origins of the conflict in Ireland. And we didn't have any books, so for the most part, the Irish Republican Army was overwhelmingly working-class, rural working-class, urban working class. There was not; we didn't have what other groups have, we didn't have a big number of any teachers, we didn't have any lecturers, we didn't have any academics among our ranks.

We were very much of the manual working class or the small farmers. And I happen to be falling into a role, almost by accident, that I had studied history at school, at the secondary level. I had far from comprehensive knowledge, but I had an acquaintance with it, which many others didn't have. So, I was able to deliver stories on periods of Irish history. I would not particularly like to have to – if, for some reason, those talks for some reasons would have been recorded or if they were transcribed, I wouldn't particularly like to give them to academic historians.… [laughing] So, that was the first introduction of a new structured education.… I would stand in the evening whenever the majority of prison officers went off duty on the wing, and it fell silent. I would stand at the door and trying my best I could do to pitch my voice from the chink in the door along the wing for people to listen to it. So, that's how it was done.[16]

As McKearney explains, the first structured educational lectures on the blanket protest were short, chronologically ordered on aspects of Irish history. That ignited the interest of fellow prisoners for other lectures. The difference between these lectures and the previous lectures in the Long Kesh internment camp was that in the H-Blocks, the prisoners attempted to provide lectures in a broader context and addressed the topics chronologically, from the time of the Anglo-Norman invasion of Ireland in the twelfth century until the twentieth century. Thereby they provided a comprehensive history of Ireland to other inmates – as much as possible under the conditions of protest, isolation, violence, and lack of any reading or teaching materials. McKearney mentions that among the prisoners was a willingness to understand why they served these "lengthy sentences." Therefore, they began "to examine the progress of the republican movement, Sinn Féin, where we succeeded, where we had failed, where we were failing to make an impact and in that sense, what was first deemed necessary was a better understanding of Irish History." However, they insisted that this Irish history be taught systematically and "not just the anecdotes of previous years." By mentioning the "anecdotes of previous years," he dismissed the lectures of older republicans in the Long Kesh internment camp, who told unsystematic stories of their previous experiences in the republican movement and their imprisonment in past decades. This criticism also occurred in Cage 11 and was fostered by the debates in the H-Blocks and the introduction of longer sentences by the British government. Another aspect McKearney stresses is the lack of higher education among republicans and its members' rural and working-class social backgrounds. At the same time, McKearney sums it up using Marxist terminology that reflects his own political views. In other words, the historical self-education of protesting prisoners made the republican prisoners self-aware and, thereby, they grew collectively into political thinkers and political subjects. Laurence McKeown reflects on this aspect of discussions as a way of self-education for the Blanketmen:

> You know, you suddenly discover just from doing dialogue with people, because that's all we had was discussions, we didn't have this academic reading. So, therefore, the only thing you had was discussing ideas, but what I suddenly realized was that you had these opinions that you never had really sat down and consciously thought out. You just thought this. And then when someone challenged you and said: "Well, why do you think that?" And it could be about anything, colonialism, racism, sectarianism, issues like divorce, abortion, you name it. You suddenly realized: "Yeah, I have these opinions, but I never had any time, I never sat down and thought: What am I thinking and maybe there's a contradiction between what I think there, what I think here. Maybe there's a contradiction between my republican politics." And then there is the challenging of all republicanism itself. So, that period became one of the most educational, and it really influenced what happened in the jail after the hunger strike because by then; I think people had developed a critical approach and critical also of republicanism and critical of republican structures, which then, I think, led on to the formation of, well, if we're critical of the old what is it that we want the shift to be the new?[17]

In the winter of 1979, the protesting prisoners and authorities had reached a stalemate. After more than three years on the blanket, the prison administration knew they could not beat the prisoners. At the same time, despite a regular influx of new prisoners, more and more left the blanket and no-wash protests because they could not cope with the solitary confinement, squalor, beatings, and cold any longer. Eventually, the prisoners decided to end this deadlock by embarking on hunger strikes in 1980. On 27 October 1980, seven prisoners, led by their O/C Brendan Hughes from Belfast, began a hunger strike. When Hughes embarked on his hunger strike, he made Bobby Sands from Belfast O/C of the prisoners. On 1 December, three female prisoners joined the hunger strike in HMP Armagh, and on 15 December, twenty-three other male prisoners joined the hunger strike. When the hunger strike of the seven men began on 27 October, all other republican prisoners suspended their blanket protest. All focus should be on the hunger strikes. After fifty-three days, Brendan Hughes believed that a document was in a place that would grant the prisoners their main demands, namely, civilian clothes, free association, and exemption from prison work. That

Bobby Sands's cell in the H-Block prison hospital.
This photo of the cell where IRA prisoner Bobby Sands died during the
hunger strike for political status in the H-Blocks of Maze was taken by
Laurence McKeown on 8 September 2004, four years after the prison's closure.

would have satisfied the prisoners' demands. Furthermore, one hunger striker, Seán McKenna, was on the brink of death, so Hughes called off the hunger strike on 18 December. However, the document the prisoners eventually received fell well short of what they expected; the prisoners agreed that a second hunger strike was their only option.

The second hunger strike started on 1 March. This time, the republican prisoners used another tactic: Not all hunger strikers would go on hunger strikes simultaneously, but instead one prisoner every fortnight. The first prisoner to begin the hunger strike was Bobby Sands himself. Francis Hughes joined him on 15 March and Raymond McCreesh and Patsy O'Hara on 22 March. One day after Bobby Sands began his hunger strike, the Blanketmen finally ended their protest – although it had already been suspended during the hunger strikes in the autumn of 1980. The second hunger strike was only called off on 3 October 1981. In the months between May and August, ten hunger strikers died. Seven were members of the Provisional IRA, and three were members of the INLA.

The hunger strikes generated unprecedented support for the prisoners and the republican movement. On 9 April, Bobby Sands was elected to the Westminster Parliament in the Fermanagh/South Tyrone by-elections. Less than one month later, he died. One hundred thousand people attended his funeral in Belfast on 7 May 1981. In June 1981, two other H-Blocks prisoners were elected to the Irish parliament in Dublin. The hunger strikes changed the prisoners' lives, but they also set the Provisional republican movement on track to embrace electoral strategy and support for the peace process. Thereby, the hunger strikes not only significantly influenced the course of the Northern Ireland conflict; they changed Ireland forever.

The British authorities gradually granted the prisoners' demands following the hunger strikes. As a result, life inside the H-Blocks began to change: the republicans had de facto achieved political status. By 1983, living on the wings was incomparable with the situation only two years earlier. Among other things, educational facilities, libraries, and Open University courses were introduced. In addition to formal education, prisoners developed a system of informal jail education. Following a riot in October 1982 that loyalists initiated, segregation between republican and loyalist prisoners was introduced. By early 1983, Provisional republicans occupied fifteen of the twenty-eight wings within the H-Blocks, while the different loyalist factions occupied six. The segregation remained in place until the prison's closure in 2000 and provided republicans with further opportunities for structured debates, lectures, and educational classes during those years.

After the hunger strikes, the republican prisoners had a great interest in debates and books. For many years, protesting prisoners could only communicate through their doors, with their cellmate, or during Sunday Mass; furthermore, all books but the Bible were banned. After the end of the protest, these restrictions were dropped, and prisoners could associate with each other and receive parcels, books, and letters. Anthony McIntyre remembers that "there was an explosion, an intellectual thirst, and many pursued it, and we pursued it in many ways; one was the Open University, one was the reading within the prison, one the education lectures, nothing was compulsory for the most part."[18] Also, Gerard Hodgins says:

When we came out of the hunger strike in 1981, it was a massive, massive emphasis put on education, do it through the prison regime, the formal education classes. We also structured our own education, which would have been a revolutionary education, the history of the IRA, the struggle and all that stuff. If anybody would have tried to be macho or make little of somebody who wanted to learn, [he would] quickly be shut down. That attitude was just totally out of the window; you don't laugh at people. I was about twenty-three years of age by this time of my life, and it was the first time I realized how many people actually went through the full formal education system [in the schools in Northern Ireland] and came out of it and couldn't write their name, couldn't read.[19]

Thus, the prisoners used the Open University classes from the very beginning. It was the first time, and possibly the only chance in their life, that republicans from working-class backgrounds had the time and resources to study for all kinds of degrees. Many republicans studied undergraduate degrees in prison throughout the years, some of them like Anthony McIntyre, Laurence McKeown, Declan Moen, Ella O'Dwyer, or Féilim Ó hAdhmaill later successfully continued with PhD projects. Before developing their own courses, republicans used the Open University materials for their political studies. Hodgins remembers:

At that time, we had just started with Open University classes. But there was one course that was called "State and Society,"[20] and some of the literature dealt with Ireland and the IRA and the opposition to the government, and that was brilliant because that was an academic source you had that came from the [British] government, but nevertheless, it was reflecting a bit of republican ethos, and you could use that stuff to get some more people into that. And at that particular time, because I remember Sunday morning, BBC 2 used to have programs that went with the Open University, and we were all watching this because "State and Society" were talking about the IRA. There was this odd footage of the '40s and the IRA dressed up and all their camps and that stuff and doing the bombing lectures.… It helps to regenerate the people's interest and get people to read a book.[21]

But very soon, the republicans started to arrange their own classes, their own books, wrote their own educational material, and eventually organized a well-thought-out, detailed reading and course program. Laurence McKeown oversaw the education program for the prisoners in the 1980s. He explains that "the type of education program that we had within the jail … was very much influenced by Paulo Freire's book, *Pedagogy of the Oppressed*, which we could smuggle into jail in 1982, and a very extensive program of education within the jail in terms of politics, world politics, guerrilla armies, whatever, as well as academic education."[22] Paulo Freire was born on 19 September 1921 in the northeast of Brazil. He graduated with a PhD from the University of Recife in 1959. Two years later, he became the Department of Cultural Extension director at his alma mater. At Recife, he was involved in educational projects dealing with mass illiteracy. During those years, Freire developed and practised his radically democratic pedagogy. Freire's method was not just about teaching literacy; he also understood education as a process of politicization. Nevertheless, Freire was convinced that educating the masses would eventually lead to liberation from the oppressor. Having been forced into exile by the military dictatorship in 1964, he moved to Chile, where he wrote his most influential book, the Portuguese best seller *Pedagogy of the Oppressed*. It was first published in English in 1970 and is now a Penguin Modern Classic.[23] The end of the protests saw an increased interest in education and left-wing literature, and Freire combined both, which explains his popularity among the prisoners and influence over them. Gerard Hodgins explains:

> Because intelligent people rose to the leadership of the [republican] movement and they realized that education can be a tool of liberation and emancipation. One of the people we were encouraged to read was Paulo Freire, the *Pedagogy of the Oppressed*, a very difficult book to understand, very complicated language, very complex, precise but what a book. We enjoyed it. The thing I liked [was] when he talks about revolution. We believed in the revolution; we were convinced that we gonna win and change politics for the better.[24]

In 1991, the prisoner Féilim O'Hagan published a collection of writings from republican prisoners under *Reflections on the Culture of Resistance in Long Kesh*. There he also writes about the influence of Freire on the prisoners in the early 1980s:

> Through the period of intense debate in the few years after the Blanket, thoughts turned to the development of a structured education programme for the camp. Some of us had stumbled upon the writings of Brazilian educationalist Paulo Freire and, in particular, his book *Pedagogy of the Oppressed*. We discovered that we were unknowingly already implementing some of his ideas about education, and this discovery had a powerful and encouraging effect on us. His approach to education, in which the active learning process is rooted in the student's own experience of the world, and she/he is not just a passive recipient of what others define as knowledge, related very closely to what we ourselves had discovered to be the best approach.
>
> Education is the dynamo of the culture of our wings. It was through reading Freire's theories and from an examination of our own practical experience that we came to identify the term "education" as encompassing all

aspects of our everyday life, a radically different concept from that gained through formal schooling, which dictates a rigid separation between academic subjects and the rest of life. In relating it to our everyday life, we are often made to feel uncomfortable because education, in its true sense, necessarily challenges old assumptions.[25]

Both McKeown and O'Hagan mention that the structure of the prisoners' lives changed after the Blanket protests. The prisoners understood themselves as a collective and stressed that the hierarchy in prison became more horizontal. Nonetheless, the military structure of the PIRA remained intact, and within this structure, the new position of educational officer was introduced. The introduction of this new role reflected the stronger concentration on structured education. Yet, it also meant that the educational classes remained under the control of the PIRA prison staff. Another aspect that is mentioned is the challenge of "old assumptions." As in Cage 11, the prisoners became the initiators of discussions in the outside movement through their debates, readings, and writings. The prisoners started to embrace radical left-wing ideas and discuss parliamentarian politics. Both Marxism and taking seats in parliaments were taboos for the Provisionals until then, for both areas were associated with the Officials, who had split from the Provisionals in 1969/70. Thereby, the prisoners became leaders of political change.

The 1980s were marked by radical left-wing thinking among the prisoners. Over the years, the educational classes became more radical, as reflected by the introduction of Marxist terminology and reading material and more internationalist, which meant that a greater focus was put on other anti-imperialist struggles. Danny Morrison explains this sudden interest in Marxist literature by the circumstances the prisoners found themselves in. He says that the prisoners started to look for answers for the situation they found themselves in during the blanket protest and why the war turned into the "long war." These were challenging questions because republicans had anticipated a rapid victory and British withdrawal in the early 1970s. Under those circumstances, the prisoners got access to the prison library and books that solidarity groups and friends sent them. Many of these books were Marxist or leftist literature, and the prisoners were initially enthusiastic about the content of these writings because they thought Marxism could be the answer to all their problems. As Morrison explains: "When the prisoners eventually get their own clothes and are allowed out of their cells, in my opinion, because they lived in such an atmosphere, there was a huge tendency towards ultra-leftism. You know, Marxism, Communism. A lot of positions were, in my opinion, not based on reality and because I was Director of Publicity [of the republican prisoners] and I was also communicating with many of the prisoners, I had the task of speaking to them and causing an offence and annoying them."[26]

This left-wing attitude was not reflective of the supporters and members of the Provisionals outside the prisons, but originated in the camps and prisons. Asked if this ultra-leftism was echoed on the outside, Morrison replies: "I would say it was disproportionally higher among the prison population than on the outside. Of course, on the outside, there were all those debates, especially because the armed struggle was going on longer than anybody expected, and the IRA had to amend its strategy and expectations. For example, from 1977, they were talking about the 'long war,' so if you get arrested, you will be in jail for a long, long time, you will be serving your time. There was not an amnesty just around the corner."[27]

Since there was no "amnesty around," prisoners used their time in prison to look for answers to how the struggle could be developed under this new scenario and what Provisionals wanted to see after a British withdrawal – the answers were, again, supposedly found in Marxism. Laurence McKeown held the newly introduced position of educational officer in the H-Blocks. During his interview, he explained his rationale for how he approached the preparation of the classes:

> I think then also as we looked further into our education it was about – and I've had this discussion with people who had a different experience of say the Soviet Union, but obviously we looked very much to Marxist groups, whether it was in Mozambique or Angola, Cuba, the Soviet Union. I was studying Marxism which was really the opposite of what republicans in the early stages would have done. In fact, they weren't allowed to study Marxism. But for us it was, we had a saying: A concrete analysis of a concrete situation – as opposed to the old attitude of republicanism which was very simplistic, very principled, idealistic – not really thought out – so, I suppose in a sense our whole approach in the period after the hunger strike was that things have to be very methodically and objectively thought out – Okay if I'm going to do this what's that going to lead on to? What's going to be the implications? So why do this? Am I supposed to do this – so developing that very critical thinking?[28]

Since a new generation of post-1969 recruits joined the Provisionals and ended up in the prisons, many who joined the protest in the H-Blocks received their first political education through the lectures. When they ended the protests and gained literature access, many prisoners read their first political work, and many were attracted by socialism and Marxism. Yet, without structured introductions to Marxism and political theory, they developed different understandings of socialism. Thus, different schools of thought emerged in the prisons. These different schools of thought would reflect a debate that started to develop in the outside movement as well. At the Sinn Féin Ard-Fheis in 1981, Danny Morrison made a speech that indicated the willingness of the majority of Belfast republicans to embrace the widespread support the Provisionals enjoyed in the aftermath of the hunger strikes by contesting elections. Electoral victories were used to push for a new strategy that Morrison called "the Armalite and the Ballot box" at the Ard-Fheis in 1981. In a historic speech, he said: "Who here really believes that we can win the war through the ballot box? But will anyone here object if, with a ballot paper in this hand, and an Armalite in this hand, we take power in Ireland?" These few words were to become the political program of the republican movement, and it was this path aimed at combining electoral politics and armed struggle that opened the discussions for abandoning abstentionism and taking seats in the parliament in Dublin. Chapter four has seen similar debates on abstentionism leading up to the republican split in 1986 in Portlaoise Prison.[29] However, the lines of conflict were different in the H-Blocks for two reasons: First, in the H-Blocks, there was a much higher presence of post-1969 recruits who were less orthodox than their Southern comrades. Second, there was a greater interest in socialism and a more pragmatic approach to the republican program among these recruits than among the more conservative nationalists in the Republic of Ireland.

Today, Tommy McKearney is a committed Marxist, a writer – his last book is a history of the PIRA – and a regular contributor to the Communist Party of Ireland's newspaper *Socialist Voice*. Hence, he interprets the different approaches and factions developing among the prisoners from his political point of view. This philosophical interpretation must be considered when reading the following lengthy excerpt from my interview with him. McKearney characterizes three strands of political thought in the prisons. Other interview partners, like Anthony McIntyre, Laurence McKeown, and Danny Morrison, provide a similar portrait of the prisoners at that time. However, McKearney's analysis is most profound and, therefore, I will quote it in full:

> From my point of view, there were three schools of thought that emerged from the long discussion that had started after the 1975 ceasefire and came to a definitive point with the hunger strikes and the mass movement on the streets.… One was that we just keep on going the way we are going. We stay out of electoral politics; we stay out of parliamentary participation;

we just keep going with a campaign of shooting. The other position was that we should engage across the board in the electoral campaign and that it would be necessary to progress the electoral campaign that we engage, that we take our seats in the parliament in Dublin and in the parliament in the North [in Stormont in Belfast]. That is the policy that became known as the "Armalite and the Ballot box." And then a third position, which was by far a minority position and that was a position that I was advocating that it wasn't – that we just continue shooting, I said that just isn't, that just doesn't have a purpose whatsoever, I mean we just can't keep repeating what we have been doing, it's not gonna make a difference. The Armalite and the Ballot box, I said, there is an inherent contradiction in this because if you want to play a role in parliament, you would not be allowed to progress in parliament if you have an armed campaign. You can't argue for parliamentary constitutional reform while you have an armed wing to bring down the constitution. You may think you can do it, but in practice, you can't do it because you gonna be caught. You are not gonna make any progress. You gonna be exposed, and sooner or later, if it is just to get the votes, you have to make a decision, either you go for votes, or you keep on shooting. And my criticism wasn't necessarily that we gonna make an end to the armed campaign.[30]

The first school of thought McKearney describes is represented by the older republicans that had their support base in the Republic of Ireland and rural areas. These republicans are usually associated with the pre-1969 recruits. They came from a staunch republican background, often urban lower-middle class, and farmers from rural areas. Politically, they are ardent supporters of abstentionism while supporting internationalism and anti-imperialist socialism. They had a natural distaste for communism, Soviet-style socialism, and Marxism. Their socialism, instead, orientates towards Third World socialism and the Non-Aligned Movement. On national matters, they advocate federalism, neutrality from the EEC and NATO, and a Schumacher-like[31] economic model. This model follows the idea that smaller entities are more comfortable coordinating and, therefore, more productive than the central organization of the economy. This policy was associated with the early leaders of the Provisionals, such as IRA man Dáithí Ó Conaill; the first president of Provisional Sinn Féin, Ruairí Ó Brádaigh, who stepped down in 1983 when Sinn Féin dropped the federal *Éire Nua* policy that was the republican policy program since the early 1970s; and his brother Seán, the first editor of the republican newspaper *An Phoblacht*. Ó Conaill was one of the architects of the Provisional policy of *Éire Nua*, a program that outlined a federal, democratic structure of a future United Irish Republic;

Seán Ó Brádaigh was a follower of French-style republicanism, Swiss-style neutrality, and federalism; and his brother Ruairí was an advocate of abstentionism. Ruairí is also the author of *Dílseacht*, a historical overview of the IRA's claim that their Army Council is the de facto Government of Ireland. These people split from Sinn Féin after dropping abstentionism in Dublin at the Ard-Fheis in 1986. They formed Republican Sinn Féin, the first "dissident" republican organization to emerge – a term and historical interpretation rejected by RSF itself.

The second school of thought that McKearney mentions is the group of post-1969 recruits who had their support base among the recruits from mainly urban Irish nationalist areas in Northern Ireland. The public figures of this group were primarily made up of the ex-internees who developed new ideas criticizing the Southern-based leadership while being held together in Cage 11 of Long Kesh. I discussed the emergence of this group in the previous chapter. Following the mass support for the Anti-H-Block/Armagh Committee, the popular group in support of the protesting prisoners during the late 1970s and the hunger strikes in 1980/1, and the victories of several republicans in local and national elections during this time, these people advocated a new approach for the republican movement. As Morrison's speech at the Ard-Fheis in 1981 signalled, the armed struggle should be combined with electoral policy. Since this new approach was incompatible with the political views of the older leadership, the latter had to be politically disarmed by dropping the *Éire Nua* policy at the Ard-Fheis of 1983.

The third group is a minor faction, as McKearney himself acknowledges by saying it "was by far a minority position." Indeed, this communist position was advocated by a section of the republican prisoners in HMP Maze, headed by McKearney himself. The supporters of this position were a small but not insignificant number of prisoners and a small group of supporters, mainly relatives, outside. They criticized the position of the two leading factions in the debate. On the one hand, they criticized the pro-abstentionist camp as being too militarily stubborn and continuously doomed to repeat past mistakes; on the other hand, they argued that the combination of armed struggle and parliamentary politics as advocated by the anti-abstentionist position was unworkable and, at some stage, either the armed struggle or parliamentary politics would have to be dropped because there was no way to advance in parliament while keeping a paramilitary wing. However, McKearney's faction did not reject the armed struggle but defended the right to wage an armed campaign against the imperialist oppressor, as it was called, by the Irish people. Instead of taking the electoral road, McKearney's group suggested organizing broad-based support for republicanism in a militant, semi-syndicalist trade union struggle, thereby provoking a popular uprising in Northern Ireland that the IRA would militarily support.[32] As the factional struggle intensified, this group split from the Provisionals and formed the League of Communist Republicans (LCR). The LCR was a small and short-lived group of prisoners. Following their departure from the Provisionals, these prisoners were transferred into a separate wing in the newly built HMP Maghaberry, only a small distance from HMP Maze. Since the group was primarily confined to the jail, it soon disintegrated.[33] Despite its size, the group held a relevant position in prison during the factional struggle in the Provisionals, for it, in part, showed the heterogeneity of and lively debates among the prison population; equally important, the existence of an organized group of "dissident" prisoners provided a support network for other dissenting prisoners who did not support either of the two leading factions, such as Anthony McIntyre.

All these factions promoted different approaches towards political education in Long Kesh. Although dominant during the internment period, the first school of thought had largely disappeared in the Northern prisons; it continued to be the dominant faction in Portlaoise. The second school of thought was split between people who advocated a socialist approach and those who advocated a more pragmatic approach. While the first approach was dominant during the 1980s, the second approach became dominant during the conflict transformation process during the 1990s. McKearney, instead, promoted classical Marxist literature as the basis for political education. He remembers that in the 1980s, he argued that "we need to define a socialist position. We need to look at the class-based struggle; we need talking in terms of examining the works of Karl Marx. We need to look at a qualitatively different position."[34] In his opinion, only militant trade unionism combined with national self-determination was the way forward for the republican movement. Still, the politically illiterate prisoners from working-class backgrounds had to be educated about such a class analysis, McKearney explains: "Based on my [own] and other analyses, we are talking here of class analyses as much as national self-determination, and on that basis that we would advocate a qualitatively different situation. And to do that, we had to educate. That was where the education came from.... We needed to say why we need a new militant trade union. You have to teach people the class struggle!"[35] Anthony McIntyre promoted a different approach; he was an advocate of the so-called pragmatic education; he remembers: "Tommy McKearney, in the mid-80s, was trying to organize a Marxist education, and we were trying to organize what we called a 'pragmatic education.' Tommy's was highly political.

Ours, the pragmatic education, was highly different. What we were trying to do was getting people to come to terms with the experience in
jail and work from the bottom up, [but we] didn't preclude Marxism."[36]

So, while the "pragmatic education" was less-orthodox Marxism, it
was still dominated by socialism: "Then we moved on to something
they called 'the process' in the jail. They were trying to recruit cadres,
and people like Spike Murray began to push a more left-wing education based on Marxism, but it became a wee bit too selective for me
because they were starting to exclude people from it because they were
only bringing in this revolutionary here and there and I said that I don't
fancy that."[37]

As informal education became increasingly structured, the prisoners introduced a more left-wing terminology. However, the difference
between the leftist pragmatic approach and McKearney's orthodox
Marxist approach was that the first group focused on modern literature usually associated with "new left" approaches and anti-imperialist
theory; these were authors and revolutionaries like Antonio Gramsci,
Che Guevara, General Giap, Mao Tse-Tung, Frantz Fanon, and Jean-
Paul Sartre. McKearney instead focused on the Marxist "classics," i.e.
the philosophical and economic writings of Karl Marx, Friedrich Engels,
and Vladimir Lenin.

Various forms of teaching and learning methods were introduced to
educate the prisoners, such as the discussions held in small groups of
four prisoners in the yard, as McIntyre tells: "The education took place
in the yard, and we had what we called 'the two-by-two's,' when two
men tasked with education would sit down with two other men, and
they would sit and have a discussion about their views on this and that.
It was a wee bit like 'the party,' you know. In hindsight, I would say that
there was an enormous pressure on the group."[38]

The prisoners particularly enjoyed these small group discussions
because they received intensive tutoring that helped them when reading political literature for the first time, but they were guided through
the reading by peers from a similar social and generational background.
McKearney stresses this aspect:

> There is something else that often happens in working-class communities
> that working-class people are very aware of their educational, academic
> inadequacies. That is not universal, but there are many working-class peo-
> ple who regret that they don't have a better understanding, a better edu-
> cation. They find in a normal course of events, when they are out in the
> wider world, that they either don't have the time or they can't afford to
> dedicate the time because they are working, or they are unemployed and

don't have the resources to attend even if they are offered opportunities. But academia is something that can intimidate working people. It's not always user-friendly in terms of working-class people who feel education-ally inadequate to turn up for a course to sit in with academics, to listen to teachers teaching.… What a lot of our people found was that they were not dealing with academics. They felt that they were talking to their own, and it was much easier to sit and talk to me or some of the others because we were simply just their pals from the next cell. We were their comrades, their friends.[39]

Another form was the study group:

There were study groups, and the study groups were around books. Paul Sweezy done a book on *Socialism*, and we were studying that, and some-times people were concentrating on [James Connolly's] *Labour in Irish His-tory*. Then I used to take study groups myself. If people wanted to discuss socialism or communism or Marxism, I would take some study groups. And at one point, we developed a study program on Irish history in the prison. It was eventually published by the Sinn Féin publisher. It was called *Questions of History*, and I had written the most of that. And that was an attempt to bring Marxist analyses to the education in the jail based on Irish history.[40]

The booklet *Questions of History*, a historical introduction to Irish his-tory since the Anglo-Norman conquest in the late twelfth century, was compiled by the staff members of the IRA in prison. Later, the booklet was smuggled out of jail and published by Sinn Féin in Dublin. The preface explains:

An attempt is made to illustrate, to some degree, the role of both capital and labour in the development of Irish society and the class conflict they inevitably engender. The colour scheme involved is to try to throw up more clearly central themes and relevant points which need to be debated and discussed, not merely read or listened to. The mainstream of the paper is written in black, red is used for generative themes and special empha-sis, green represents direct quotations, each of which has been carefully selected and inserted with the purpose of articulating an important point, blue is used for "problem-posing" questions. Each "generative" theme is designed to produce a reflection on the part of the participants. Prob-lem posing questions should be discussed at length, and from constant familiarisation with them, it is hoped to develop a critical and inquisitive approach to all study.[41]

This introduction reflects the James Connolly school of socialist republicanism combined with national struggle and class politics. The terminology indeed echoes Connolly's widely read historical essays. The booklet's content is a clear example of "pragmatic education" in practice, with its anti-imperialist and socialist touch that was starkly different from McKearney's orthodox Marxism. Furthermore, the comprehensive and sophisticated system of questions proves that a great emphasis was put on learning by discussing and not on the individual reading of the learning material. This excerpt best reflects the use of a Freirean learning philosophy inside the Maze. The growing influence of the prisoners among the broader movement was then reflected in a note by the editors of the booklet that says:

> This book had been published by the Educational Department of Sinn Féin for the purpose of promoting political discussion, the views and ideas in the book are those of the prisoners. It is a valuable historical document as well as a practical educational tool. The prisoners are using our history as a vehicle for influencing our present and future. In doing so, they are letting us see the ideas and values that motivate them as well as the spirit that says everyone has a part to play in the Irish revolution, whether with a rifle or a pen. The book should be used – as they intended – as a source of material for discussion.[42]

The book's editors echo the prisoners' approach and aim to promote the discussions of Irish history and literature to collectively establish new ideas from the prison population to their outside supporters. Thus, as in the 1970s with the publication of the Brownie articles, the prisoners once again become the initiators of debate picked up by the broader republican movement outside the prison walls.

However, the prisoners not only held discussions in smaller or bigger groups, but lectures were also the third form of political education – as was the case during internment in the 1970s. To hold lectures, the prisoners needed space. As McIntyre remembers: "Cell 26 was a double cell, and as things went on, we turned it into a library and a small TV room, so people could sit and have discussions in Cell 26. I remember Seamus Kearney saying to me one day about Cell 26 that: "Socialism now exists in two places of the world, in Albania and in cell 26.'"[43] In the late 1980s, the prisoners used this double cell for lectures and established their own library. That the republican prisoners could themselves decide to use one double cell as a lecture hall and library underlines how much life inside the H-Blocks had changed in less than a decade. Only six years earlier, republican prisoners were locked up naked in these cells, with no furniture or heating, and smeared their excrement on the walls to keep the floors dry.

The organization of education reflected the conditions the prisoners found in the H-Blocks. In the 1970s, their day was marked by resistance; thus, political education was only possible by shouting from door to door during the night. In the 1980s, the prison regime gradually relaxed, and the republicans gained segregation from non-republican inmates and free association on the wings. A Derry republican arrived in the H-Blocks in 1986, less than five years after the hunger strikes. His memories differ remarkably from those prisoners in the early years of the H-Blocks, reflecting the relaxed prison regime that was already in place for over three years. He recalls: "On arrival at H2, I was greeted by fellow republican prisoners and shown to my cell. I was instructed about the running of the wing, who the O/C was and what time the cells were locked and unlocked. Although the prison guards had the keys, the men effectively ran the wing. The screws would unlock the cell doors at 8:00 a.m. so you could have access to the wing. There was no regime enforced on the men."[44]

The same prisoner also remembers the importance of education among the republican prisoners and mentions that: "Men were always encouraged to get involved in education. Classes were delivered by our comrades covering Irish, Irish history, politics, and other subjects." While all these memories suggest a relaxed time of collective debate and decision-making in the H-Blocks, these events unfolded under a cloud of a fierce factional struggle among the Provisionals. The various outside factions understood the moral power of republican prisoners for rank-and-file activists. Since the Belfast leadership around Gerry Adams rose into top positions of both the military and the political wings of the movement, they could influence the IRA staff in the H-Blocks. They thereby successfully used the prisoners to copper-fasten their anti-abstentionist position. The Portlaoise prisoners were staunch supporters of maintaining abstentionism, but in Northern Ireland, the majority supported the dropping of abstentionism. Even prisoners who later became harsh critics of the Adams leadership, like Gerard Hodgins, acknowledge this. He says that abstentionism, "Would have been discussed, but the prison would have been largely what Adams was doing because most of the prison firmly believed that what he was doing at that time was building up a revolutionary movement. That was what we were thinking. The bulk of the movement believed that. People are generally sheep, and nice words can easily lead them. We were guilty of naivety."[45]

Yet, it was not only naivety but also outside influence on the prisoners – and the political education classes – that turned out to be the best way to influence the political thinking of the prisoners. Those who did not conform got sidelined, as McKearney remembers: "The changing plates that underlay the IRA were taking it towards a parliamentary, exclusively parliamentary position. Their main focus was against the old militarists, but they were also undermining those who were against the electoral position [like me and the LCR]. So, I was getting pushed, and others who were advocating a fairly conventional Marxist position were getting pushed to the side and sidelined and marginalized."[46]

McKearney is convinced that the republican prisoners were too radical for the outside leadership in the 1980s. The Northern group around Adams and McGuinness pushed for the end of abstentionism and for taking seats in the parliament in Dublin, while the prisoners talked of the socialist revolution. Consequently, the outside leadership started to influence and channel these radical positions towards social-democratic positions by controlling the educational program. McKearney says: "They brought together a number of republican intellectuals, the likes of Pat McKeown, Laurence [McKeown], Sid Walsh. You know, bright and clever people, educated people, and they laid out a program, suggested readings, lectures on history, reflections on the current situation. But which effectively was accommodating the Sinn Féin's leadership position, flexibility. At best, [it was] left-socialism but probably more centre social-democracy. Bit by bit, the party could accommodate itself in a free market environment, and it is prioritized to get into office and not socialist transformation. And their [educational] program accommodated that."[47]

Anthony McIntyre shares different experiences of the influence of the outside movement on the prisoners through selected members of the IRA staff in the H-Blocks. For McIntyre, the break came with replacing the educational officer Spike Murray with Laurence McKeown. McIntyre relates that:

> Laurence took over, and I noticed that from that point on, they were more interested in an education program that reflected the needs of the [outside] leadership while Spike Murray wasn't pushing an education program that was reflecting the needs of the leadership…. The [new] educational program was tailored to suit the ideological outlook of the Adams leadership. Spike would have been pushing a program which I felt was Marxist and critical of the leadership, and I noticed when I wrote a document called "the Whitaker strategy"[48] as part of the history program, and they said it was questioning Gerry Adams' commitment to socialism and they wanted it to be suppressed.[49]

Dissenting voices among the prisoners, like McIntyre or the group of Marxists around McKearney, were suppressed, marginalized, and isolated. As a result, the majority leader could lessen the damage caused by the 1986 split, despite the departure of eighty to one hundred prisoners out of four hundred prisoners in Northern Ireland left after the 1986 split.[50] Indeed, none of them joined the newly formed RSF party. Thus, these developments inside the prison went almost unnoticed by the outside supporters. To ensure that this remained the case, the republican movement controlled the flow of information coming out of the prisons. Prisoners held influential roles among the nationalist community in Northern Ireland, and they were a broad constituency. Thus, prisoners were encouraged to write letters to influence their friends and families in the run-up to the 1986 split and afterwards, but as McKearney explains:

> The word comes from the Pope to the Bishops, the Bishops tell the Priests, and the Priests tell the faithful what to believe, and it works that way. So, the prisoners were responding; these were not spontaneous positions. These were no positions of creative enlightenment where prisoners decided: "My goodness, I write a letter!" Word was coming in from the leadership what to write. Occasionally there was a prisoner writing what the leadership didn't want. There is never any totality in any of these events, but, by and large, that was what was happening. But most of these guys fell into line. They were not in dispute. They had not been beaten up to do it.[51]

McKearney's line of argumentation mirrors Gerard Hodgins's comments. Hodgins, who was not a follower of McKearney's LCR, also says that the outside leadership had control over the letters the prisoners wrote for newspapers and magazines: "There was a PRO. The PRO would deal with the media. If you wanted to write a letter yourself, you could do that, but the only thing they asked was to send it to the centre. The centre, you know, is where the POW Office is, where all the comms go, where they come from, so they can have a read first. You were supposed to send it to the centre, but I know that I sometimes sent it to the office and they never appeared in the papers, so fuck it."[52]

As Hodgins explains, the prisoners had a PRO who oversaw the public communications of the prisoners. The PRO was part of the IRA staff in prison. During the hunger strikes, the PROs were, for example, Brendan "Bik" McFarlane and Richard O'Rawe; at a later stage, it was Danny Morrison. While the prisoners could also write letters or articles themselves, all written material, called communiqués, that left the prison had to go through the Prisoners Department of Sinn Féin in Belfast, which Hodgins calls the "POW Office" in "the centre," i.e., the Sinn Féin Belfast office. Thus, the Prisoners Department had the power to censor letters opposed to the majority line of Sinn Féin. As a result, several letters might have disappeared in the office in Belfast. Still, one cannot deny the fact that most prisoners, both in the Republic and Northern Ireland, followed the new anti-abstentionist policy of Sinn Féin, as did Hodgins:

> In 1986, most people followed Adams because there were rumours that we gonna have a Tet offensive like the Vietnamese, and there were rumours that a lot of gear was coming in. We hadn't actually got it yet; we hadn't got the Libyan gear. It was not there for use, but the plan was supposed to be that when the Eksund was coming – the one that was caught – the gear would come North immediately and have it, and we just shoot, attack everything and sustain it for as long as possible. We accepted [we would] have a lot of casualties because it was gonna be a different kind of warfare, but we were up for it. That was why Adams could carry the whole movement. He was promising, on the one hand, we were driving them out because we finally had the international connections and the gear, and that's how he carried them. Even I voted for abandoning the abstentionism because I saw it as a political obstacle.[53]

In the 1980s, the Provisionals re-established the close links they previously held in the early 1970s with the Libyan regime of Muammar Gaddafi. Gaddafi provided the IRA with plastic mortar Semtex, millions of US dollars and various kinds of arms, including its first RPG-7 rocket-propelled grenade launchers. One of the ships from Libya to Ireland was the *Eksund*, intercepted off the French coast. Nonetheless, the Provisionals were well-equipped by Gaddafi in the mid-1980s, and many republicans thought that a broad offensive like the Tet Offensive by the North Vietnamese forces that decided the Vietnam War would also be possible for the IRA in Northern Ireland. Many republicans naively thought that military victory was on the horizon, and with the electoral support that had grown since the hunger strikes, the British army could be driven from the North, the island finally reunited, and their own Irish "Cuba" established off the coast of Britain. Unfortunately, the prisoners' hopes were soon crushed by another international event: the fall of the Berlin Wall.

Chapter Seven

"It's Only When You Look Back …": The Fall of the Berlin Wall and the Peace Process in the 1990s

The fall of the Berlin Wall was a dramatic event for the republican prisoners and is mentioned in several interviews. The events in Berlin were broadcast worldwide, and the prisoners were allowed to watch the news on TV in the evenings. Over the previous seven to eight years, the prisoners had developed their own interpretation of socialism and the events in Berlin, the fall of the Soviet Union, and what they considered the defeat of their newly found international allies, made no sense to them. Danny Morrison says, "I do think when the [Berlin] Wall came down in Germany in 1989, a lot of them got their eyes opened, and there was a move away from this purist ideological approach to a more pragmatic form of politics."[1] Yet, how did it come to this rapid disillusionment of the same men who only months earlier had finally established "Socialism in cell 26"? Tommy McKearney gives two main reasons for this development. The first was that the political education, while heavily loaded with socialist terminology, only introduced a fashionable version of Third Worldism unsuitable for the Irish situation and, thus, the republicans were only introduced to radical terms but never reached a profound understanding of socialism and Marxism:

> I had been pushing for the study of conventional, orthodox … Marxist classics, the [Communist] Manifesto, 18th Brumaire, the Civil War in France, the State and Revolution, Lenin's works, Marx's works. I said: Let's just work on that, and let's just set aside the more fashionable pieces! Leave for the time being Che and Fidel. We were getting into a different world here because they are testing unique problems. Problems unique to Cuba, problems unique to Vietnam. You can be aware of Che and Fidel, be aware of Giap and Hồ Chí Minh but let's look at the classics because, after that, that's what you need to build into an Irish answer. We are not going to the Sierra Madre mountains because they are in Cuba, and we are

not going to have a "long march" (referring to Mao's long march in China; DR) because, in Ireland, you can march from one side to another. We are not marching from South China to the North, you know, let's be realistic and look at the basics, and that is class struggle, it's the role of the state, it's imperialism, it's finance.[2]

The second reason was a certain peer pressure to go to as many educational classes as possible, not because the individual prisoner was interested in them but because it was fashionable to pretend to be involved in education. Anthony McIntyre previously referred to it as "party" behaviour, comparing it with the state party's role in the GDR. Similarly, McKearney explains that "there was a certain amount of peer pressure to appear [to the educational classes], peer pressure to subscribe to it which I think happened when people talk about the Marxist-Leninist education program at that time. It was fashionable! There was peer pressure to appear to be a radical!"[3] While Hodgins, McKearney, and McIntyre all became critics of the new political line of the Provisionals, even one of the architects of the new policy, Danny Morrison, acknowledged that the educational classes in the late 1980s merely served a self-fulfilling prophecy:

> Amongst the cynics, there was a feeling, I think, the more classes you went to, the better you were thought of as a republican. That was the type of culture there was. So, I mean, you know, a friend of mine who was a real cynic, I remember when I arrived and ended up in H-Blocks with him, that was his second time in jail, he had been on the blanket before, doing twenty or twenty-five years and he was joking, and he says: "You know, have you been to the Coronation Street *rang*[4] yet?" Coronation Street was a BBC soap, so he was letting on that we even got a *rang* that discussed Coronation Street.[5]

Under those circumstances, the radical rhetoric of the prisoners, also reflected in the prison magazines and letters, lost all meaning. As a result, prisoners went to more and more classes, but their political understanding stagnated, and thus international developments hit them hard and confused them. Thus, Anthony McIntyre echoes Morrison's assumption that the republican prisoners were not socialist but only radicals who used amalgams of left-wing rhetoric, a phenomenon he describes as "Marxist Esperanto."[6]

The Berlin Wall had fallen and removed the illusion of a socialist future from the prisoners. At the same time, the conflict in Northern Ireland started to transform, and the peace process gained momentum.

The prisoners were looking for new guidance and a new ideology to understand the world in this situation. Once again, like the fall of the Berlin Wall, it was an international event that had a lasting impact on the political views of the republican prisoners. Only months after the collapse of the GDR, on 11 February 1990, ANC leader Nelson Mandela was released from prison.

Mandela was, in many ways, a role model for republican prisoners in Ireland. He was a freedom fighter, and he fought injustice and discrimination. Indeed, on behalf of Black Africans, he contested a similar social, cultural, and political oppression experienced by the Catholics in Northern Ireland. But, most importantly, he had served a lengthy prison sentence – like most of the republican prisoners who had been sentenced after 1976. For many prisoners, an end to the conflict and a release from prison appeared possible by following Mandela's example. Yet, following Mandela's example meant accepting compromises for most Provisional prisoners, and preparing prisoners for these compromises after years of waiting for an Irish Tet Offensive meant unchaining the educational classes from radical Marxist rhetoric.

Seanna Walsh talks about the years 1989 and 1990 in the H-Blocks, which were marked by news about the fall of the Berlin Wall and the release of Nelson Mandela:

> One of the things that I remember [is] I was arrested in October, [or] November 1988, and I would have been on remand in Crumlin Road jail for about fourteen months, which meant that I was in Crumlin Road jail when the wall came down. And it was in February of the following year that I was sentenced and brought up to Long Kesh. One of the things that happened with the fall of the Berlin Wall, first of all, people didn't see it coming; no one saw it coming.… And, therefore, whenever things started moving, the first thing that struck me was: Fuck! Nobody seen this coming, and when things start moving in politics, they can move very quickly.… It also brought a sense of reality to the republican prisoners. To an extent, there was an unrealistic expectation about how we can bring about political change in Ireland.… But then, in February 1990, Mandela got released, and once Mandela got released, you understood that this was the end of Apartheid, and that was the end of the South African regime. And this regime, which seemed so monolithic and impervious to political change, was simply gone in a year or two after the release of Mandela. So, while the wall had a deflating impact upon aspects of a certain section of the republican prisoners, the release of Mandela and the collapse of the South African regime gave a lot of people hope that things can change, and they can change utterly in a very short time.[7]

Walsh also mentions the impact the fall of the Berlin Wall had on him and how the event took him by surprise. Amid all this political and personal confusion, Mandela was released from prison. So, while one potential ally – the Soviet Bloc – was gone, another future partner gained the attention of the republican prisoners, which was anti-imperialism. The educational program within the H-Blocks was soon triggered to suit the new political direction. The revolutionary socialist rhetoric and reading materials were substituted with pragmatic anti-imperialism in line with the ANC policy in South Africa and the PLO policy that led to the Oslo Accords. As Walsh remarks, the release of Mandela was the turning point in South African history that brought the apartheid regime to its knees. Following that logic, the release of the republican prisoners would usher in a new era marked by British military disengagement from the island.

At the same time, the peace process was set on track. In January 1988, SDLP leader John Hume and Sinn Féin president Gerry Adams held the first series of [initially] secret meetings. Danny Morrison remembers:

> There were a lot of things happening. The first [loyalist] ceasefire took place in 1991, for the first time in sixteen years, there was the rumour coming up that Gerry Adams and John Hume were meeting, that was the Hume-Adams-Talks, there was the Downing Street declaration, there was the run-up to the [IRA] ceasefire. So, there were lots of things to discuss, and my role in proposing what we should discuss was to be pragmatic. Because, in my opinion, once we had a ceasefire, we gonna be compromising. So, some of the discussion we had was what was acceptable, what would be unacceptable, and I remember I annoyed a few people by turning around saying I thought there is gonna be another [Northern Ireland] assembly and we probably have to take our seats. And that annoyed some people who couldn't think about that. They just laughed. And some of them didn't come to terms with it when it happened. Some of them came with us, some of them had left. One, in particular, is in éirígí[8] now, one ex-prisoners who strongly rejected to what I was saying at that time.

The Northern Irish Peace Process was a period of conflict transformation that started with the talks of the SDLP leader John Hume and the president of Sinn Féin Gerry Adams on 11 January 1988 and lasted until the decommissioning of (supposedly) all weapons by the IRA on 26 September 2005. The process can be subdivided into three phases. The first phase ran from 1988 until the IRA and loyalist ceasefire in 1994. The second phase ran from the truce until the Belfast Agreement on Good Friday 1998. Finally, the third phase marked the agreement's implementation until the decommissioning of the IRA in 2005.

The first phase started with a meeting of the two leaders of the nationalist parties in Northern Ireland, John Hume of the SDLP and Gerry Adams of Sinn Féin. The meeting was the first in a series of meetings between the two politicians between 1988 and 1993. Following the first round of these meetings, members from four Northern Ireland parties, the Alliance Party, the SDLP, the Ulster Unionist Party, and the Democratic Unionist Party, met in Duisburg, West Germany, on 14 October 1988. Sinn Féin was still excluded from these talks. Nonetheless, Gerry Adams announced in a speech on 5 March 1989 that he sought a "non-armed political movement to work for self-determination" of Ireland. Then, on 3 November 1989, the then secretary of state for Northern Ireland, Peter Brooke, admitted that the IRA could not be defeated militarily, and he also said he could not rule out talks with Sinn Féin if there were an end to violence. April 1991 then brought the first ceasefire by the Combined Loyalist Military Command (CLMC), an umbrella structure of the leading loyalist paramilitary organizations. The truce lasted until 4 July of the same year. The IRA followed with a three-day ceasefire over Christmas 1992. In April 1993, John Hume and Gerry Adams held another series of meetings. The talks resulted in the issuing of two joint statements. The second statement was issued on 25 September 1993 and outlined the Hume/Adams Initiative, which "aimed at the creation of a peace process." The IRA welcomed this announcement in a statement released on 4 October. During these weeks, the British government and Sinn Féin held secret talks. On 28 November, both sides confirmed that they were in contact. The developments eventually resulted in the Downing Street Declaration issued by John Major, then British prime minister, and Albert Reynolds, then Irish prime minister, on 15 December. The Downing Street Declaration affirmed both the right of the people of Ireland to self-determination and that Northern Ireland would be transferred to the Republic from the United Kingdom only if a majority of its population was in favour of such a move. As part of the perspective of the so-called Irish dimension, it also included the principle of consent that the people of the island of Ireland had the exclusive right to solve the issues between Northern Ireland and the Republic by mutual consent. These ideas eventually made their way into the 1998 Belfast Agreement. In 1994, the United States entered the Northern Irish peace process when Bill Clinton, then US president, ordered Gerry Adams to be given a visa to enter the United States. In April, the IRA called another three-day ceasefire, and secret talks between the then secretary of state for Northern Ireland, Patrick Mayhew; Michael Ancram, a minister at the Northern Ireland Office; and Gerry Adams were held in Derry on 16 August. As a result, the IRA announced a "complete cessation of military activities" from 31 August 1994. On 13 October, the Combined Loyalist Military Command followed the IRA's lead and declared a ceasefire. This ceasefire marked the end of the first phase of the peace process.

The second phase started with the ceasefire announcement of the significant paramilitary groups in Northern Ireland. However, the peace talks faced obstacles. Republicans expected substantial negotiations following the ceasefire announcement of the IRA. Instead, on 7 March 1995, Patrick Mayhew laid down special conditions before Sinn Féin could enter official talks. These conditions became known as the "Washington 3." They essentially meant that the IRA had to decommission before Sinn Féin could enter negotiations. This request led to a deadlock of the process, and US Senator George Mitchell was asked to report on the issue. On 24 January 1996, the Mitchell Report on arms decommissioning was published in Belfast. However, factions of the IRA disagreed with the report, and on 2 February, the IRA ended its ceasefire with a bomb in London. Another bomb detonated in Manchester on 15 June, destroying significant parts of the city centre. Nonetheless, Sinn Féin received a record vote of 15.5 per cent at the Northern Ireland Forum elections on 30 May 1996. Despite the IRA bombings in England, opposition within the republican movement grew. On the one hand, internal opposition emerged with the foundation of the 32 County Sovereignty Committee (32CSC) in 1996, headed by Bobby Sands's sister Bernadette and included Omagh Sinn Féin Councillor Francis Mackey. Within the IRA, a hardline faction grouped around Quartermaster Mickey McKevitt that later became known as the Real IRA. On the other hand, external opposition emerged with the bombing of Kilyhelvin Hotel in Enniskillen, Co. Fermanagh, by the 1986-founded Continuity IRA, linked to the RSF party. The deadlock in the peace process was only broken when a Labour government was elected to office in England in April 1997. On 20 July 1997, the IRA renewed their ceasefire, while the 32CSC formally split from Sinn Féin, forming the 32 County Sovereignty Movement. In September, Sinn Féin signed the Mitchell Principles outlined in the January 1996 report, and all involved parties to the talks eventually signed the Belfast Agreement on Good Friday, 10 April 1998. Section 10 of the Good Friday Agreement deals with prisoners. The section reads:

1. Both Governments will put in place mechanisms to provide for an accelerated programme for the release of prisoners, including

transferred prisoners convicted of scheduled offences in Northern Ireland or, in the case of those sentenced outside Northern Ireland, similar offences (referred to hereafter as qualifying prisoners). Any such arrangements will protect the rights of individual prisoners under national and international law.

2. Prisoners affiliated to organisations which have not established or are not maintaining a complete and unequivocal ceasefire will not benefit from the arrangements. The situation in this regard will be kept under review.

3. Both Governments will complete a review process within a fixed time frame and set prospective release dates for all qualifying prisoners. The review process would provide for the advance of the release dates of qualifying prisoners while allowing account to be taken of the seriousness of the offences for which the person was convicted and the need to protect the community. In addition, the intention would be that should the circumstances allow it, any qualifying prisoners who remained in custody two years after the commencement of the scheme would be released at that point.

4. The Governments will seek to enact the appropriate legislation to give effect to these arrangements by the end of June 1998.

5. The Governments continue to recognise the importance of measures to facilitate the reintegration of prisoners into the community by providing support both prior to and after release, including assistance directed towards availing of employment opportunities, re-training and/or re-skilling, and further education.[9]

The agreement was endorsed by the people of Ireland in two separate referenda in the Republic and Northern Ireland on 22 May. On 2 December 1999, unionists and Sinn Féin entered a Northern Irish Executive and devolution of powers from Westminster in London to the new local parliament of Northern Ireland at Stormont in Belfast.

The signing and implementation of the Good Friday Agreement marked the beginning of the final phase of the conflict transformation process. Despite various setbacks and suspensions of the Executive, the process remained intact. As part of the peace process, HMP Maze was closed, and all paramilitary prisoners, both republican and loyalist, who signed up to the terms of the 1998 agreement were released. The last seventy-six prisoners were released from HMP Maze on 28 July 2000. This release brought the number of prisoners released under the Good Friday Agreement to 428 in total. In addition, the Independent International Commission on Decommissioning (IICD) was set up, and the IRA began decommissioning its weapons on 23 October 2001. Four years later, on 26 September 2005, the IICD reported that the IRA had decommissioned all its weapons. In 2007, 2009, and 2010, loyalist paramilitary groups UFF, UVF, and UDA followed and decommissioned their weapons. Finally, on 8 February 2010, the IICD announced that even the two smaller republican groups, the Official republican movement, a split from the Official IRA, and the INLA, as well as the loyalist faction South East Antrim UDA, had handed over their arms.

During these two decades, the support of the political prisoners for the process was crucial. Indeed, the conflict could not have been transformed, nor the compromises sold to the republican and loyalist supporters, without the backing of the prisoners. An episode in early 1998 illustrates that the role of the prisoners was not only crucial for the republican actors but also among loyalists. On 27 December 1997, the Irish National Liberation Army killed the leader of the loyalist splinter group LVF Billy Wright inside the H-Blocks. Three INLA prisoners had climbed the roof of the H-Blocks and entered the loyalist area where they shot Wright with a smuggled gun. On 3 January, following the killing, the loyalist prisoners in Maze voted to withdraw their support for the peace process. They took this position to express their opposition to the handling of the process by the British government and argued that the republicans were granted overly broad concessions. As a result, Marjorie (Mo) Mowlam, then secretary of state for Northern Ireland, announced that she would go into the prison to meet representatives of UDA and UFF prisoners in an attempt to change their decision and regain their support for the peace process. While the DUP described the decision by Mowlam as "madness," the UUP welcomed it. Two days later, the meeting took place, and Mowlam convinced the prisoners to change their position. In a statement, the UDA and UFF prisoners reaffirmed their support for the peace process. These events, which unfolded during the first ten days of January 1998, a crucial period for the peace process, illustrate the importance of the prisoners because even the secretary of state for Northern Ireland, the highest representative of the British government in Northern Ireland, willingly arranged a meeting with members of proscribed paramilitary organizations inside a high-security prison because she knew the stance of the Loyalist prisoners threatened the success of the peace process.

Gerard Hodgins remembers that most prisoners were supportive of the peace process and that the prisoners played a role in "building a dialogue":

> My personal view at that time was to argue for a ceasefire because we were stagnating, and we were not going nowhere; there was a stalemate.

It was getting tougher, it [was] getting harder to move, we were disrupted more often and the physical support movement what you always need, civilian people that support you, all that was getting much, much harder to access. Probably up until then, when somebody had gear in the house, and they were coming up, they were getting alright sentences if caught, but that all changed, and they started handing out heavy prison sentences for doing that, and you could end up with twenty-five years for not making much of an impact. Also, the war towards the end was becoming dirtier and dirtier, and I have no doubt that the British intelligence [had their hands] in it, and there were terrible civilian victims. I don't know. I didn't feel comfortable with [the way the war was going]. I didn't become a pacifist in any way, but I was just becoming convinced that we were not getting to defeat them militarily.[10]

This statement reflects the weariness of war and imprisonment felt by Hodgins in the 1990s, and his assessment is a far cry from his earlier hopes of an IRA Tet Offensive. Although most of the prisoners were supportive of the process, the changes were still enormous: ceasefire, parliamentarism, sharing government with unionists, decommissioning, and, ultimately, giving up on the prospects of a united Ireland. The prisoners needed to be assured that they supported the right thing. Seanna Walsh says:

During the negotiations, the IRA prisoners would have been very much informed. The prisoners would have been visited by the [outside] leadership. The republican leadership would have been brought in [the H-Blocks] to discuss the political project and what we would do with the political project. At one stage, in the running up to the Good Friday Agreement, the republican leadership on the outside negotiated with the British to bring in a very high-level delegation of the [South African] ANC. They were brought into Long Kesh, and about 150 IRA prisoners were brought into the gym, and we were given the opportunity to listen and to discuss the evolution of a peace process and how we could move from armed struggle into the achievement of our political objectives without furthering the course of the armed struggle. That was very important for us. But the other side was that we felt that we had a role to reassure our visitors and our relatives and our families that the objectives that we went to prison for, that these objectives could be achieved through this new unarmed strategy that the movement was pursuing.[11]

Walsh describes the dual process of winning the support of the prisoners for the peace process by the outside leadership and then using the prisoners to influence their own families and friends on the outside. In that way, the outside leadership could indirectly increase the support for the peace process among their rank-and-file members. The British government understood these mechanisms, and since they were pursuing the same goal as the Provisional leadership, namely, the cementing of the peace process, they relaxed the prison regime. On the one hand, British politicians and republican activists were allowed into the prison to speak with loyalist and republican prisoners; on the other hand, representatives of other former armed movements who pursued a political path like the ANC were allowed access to the prisons. Another strategy was to let individual prisoners out on parole earlier and more often so they could contact their leadership outside the prisons directly and get information to their imprisoned comrades. By so doing, the prison authorities could control the flow of information coming into the prison, but they could also ensure that only prisoners supportive of the peace process were granted parole and met the outside republican leadership. As Danny Morrison explains:

> The prisoners were exactly told what was going on at any stage of time.... Also, more prisoners qualified for parole, the Brits let them out, and they could hold conversations privately. You didn't have to worry that it was bugged, in the jail, you always had to be careful. We always had to be in the back of our mind that the cell was bugged.... So, prisoners came out on parole, learned what was going on, what the latest was and went back in again sometimes as ambassadors of the situation and in this way, the vast majority of the prisoners stayed on board.[12]

While both the British government and the republican leadership kept the prisoners "on board" during the peace process, Morrison knows full well that the prisoners were being exploited and were not kept fully informed during this process:

> Everyone wants to know everything 100 per cent, and sometimes prisoners would complain that they were only told 60 per cent. But, if you are in negotiations, as the leadership was, you have to be very careful that the British government would think that its position was less than it was demanding. So, you always play your cards close to your chest and often, it meant that prisoners felt that they had been excluded, so were the volunteers on the ground. They were not always told everything either because the whole point of leadership is to lead, and in our case, we were moving from a revolutionary situation to a much more contemporary situation, you know, where you come from the position of fundamentality,

you know, the Brits have to get out, there has to be an amnesty, a united Ireland, you have to modify those, and you have to achieve what you can achieve and maximize your achievements.[13]

The outside leadership developed tight control over the flow of information that the prisoners received, as well as among the prisoners. Thus, prisoners already critical of the leadership argued that prisoners had, in fact, no theoretical input in the peace process. Tommy McKearney contends that the outside leadership made the decisions, namely, the Army Council of the IRA, and the role of prisoners was to confirm these decisions to the republican base. As Treacy, a former Portlaoise prisoner, said, "Prisoners were merely pawns in the game." McKearney explains: "Frankly, they didn't have any role. The IRA is not guided by any concept of democracy. Decisions were taken on a leadership level and fed down through the movement and at that stage, what happens is a question of persuading the movement to endorse the leadership. It wasn't and still isn't a question of the wider body arriving at a conclusion and then instructing the leadership. It is certainly the other way around. The army council was taking a decision. That's what it was at that time."[14]

Anthony McIntyre explains what mechanisms were used inside the prison to achieve the situation described by McKearney:

> People say that the prisoners were in favour of it. Well, the leadership in the jail was handpicked to ensure that there was no dissent. That, when they went for a peace process, the prisoners would go for a peace process. The leadership goes for a peace process; the prisoners go for a peace process. If the leadership went for singing the fucking Sash[15] on the Shankill Road,[16] the prisoners back them singing the Sash on the Shankill Road. That's how it was done. That was an organization that would marginalize you, that would make you feel the enormous pressure of the group. There would have been strategies of marginalization and replacement and make it very hard for you. I remember particularly after Tommy McKearney, and his people went off to Maghaberry and had their own wing. There was only me and Seamus Kearney for a while who were still dissenting. And then other people got into the jail from Tyrone and stuff, and it got better.[17]

He continues to describe the marginalization of dissenting voices:

> Through the IRA structure, command, and control structure, those who didn't hold the line were not allowed to be on the [IRA] staff; they were marginalized. They were not ostracized. Some people were, you

know, bad feeling, you were subject to [a] whispering campaign, that
you were anti-IRA. They used to call you things like "Contra," "contra-
revolutionary," and all these things. They were trying to undermine you
socially. They didn't beat you up or anything, and they wouldn't have
kicked you in the football pitch, you know, and if you were short of cigarettes, they give you one, but they were just making sure that you felt
uncomfortable. You were never inside; you were always made to feel that
you were an outsider.[18]

A combination of leadership manoeuvres described by Danny Morrison, physical and mental tiredness as mentioned by Gerard Hodgins,
and marginalization as outlined by Tommy McKearney and Anthony
McIntyre led to the support of the republican prisoners of the peace
process. Finally, as part of the peace process, the prison authorities recognized the IRA command structure in the H-Blocks in 1994. From then
on, they liaised with the IRA O/C on all matters relating to the running
of the prison. Hence, this level of influence and recognition exceeded
what political prisoners had in the cages of the Long Kesh internment
camp under special category status. Almost thirteen years after the
hunger strikes had ended, the republican prisoners had achieved full
recognition as political prisoners, even though it was a gesture of good-
will during the conflict transformation by the British government. The
same year, an Irish-language wing had been introduced, like the one
in Portlaoise Prison in the 1980s. The Gaeltacht wing was known as
Gaeltacht na Fuiscoige (Gaeltacht of the Lark). By gaining these concessions to the political prisoners, the British government aimed to secure
the peace process – a strategy that ultimately worked for both sides; the
peace process was achieved, and the prisoners were released.

The previous three chapters described the political self-educational
classes of the republican prisoners in the H-Blocks of HMP Maze
between 1976 and 2000. I analysed three distinct phases during these
twenty-four years. The first phase ran from the opening of the H-Blocks
in 1976 until the end of the hunger strikes in the autumn of 1981 and
was marked by isolation, prison protests, and physical resistance. Political education was mainly centred around Irish nationalism and history.
The second phase ran from the gradual regranting of special category
status in 1982/3 until the fall of the Berlin Wall. It was marked by a thirst
for political debate and literature by the prisoners, the establishment of
structured political education classes, and discussions on abstentionism and parliamentarism. During this phase, the political education
was marked by Marxist rhetoric and socialist literature – the lack of
profound analysis of the national and international situation combined

Gates to exercise yard H-Block 4. The photo was taken on 8 September 2004.
Image courtesy of Laurence McKeown.

with radical rhetoric was cynically referred to by Danny Morrison as "Marxist Esperanto." The third phase ran from the fall of the Berlin Wall and the release of Nelson Mandela from prison in 1989/90 until the closure of the H-Blocks in July 2000. A turn to pragmatic education marked this phase, influenced by national liberation movements moving from armed struggle to parliamentary politics, such as the ANC in South Africa and PLO in Palestine. The purpose of political education during this period was to foster the peace process.

During these three distinct periods, political education was in a dialectical relationship with both outside and inside developments. In other words, in the 1970s, with the lack of any reading material during the protests, the prisoners could only spread existing knowledge among their comrades. In contrast, in the 1980s and 1990s, they made full use of the study material provided to them by the Open University, books they received from friends or sympathizers in England, and newspapers and current affairs magazines in later years. As part of this process of political self-awareness, the self-understanding of their own role within the republican struggle evolved. Seanna Walsh explains that "in the '70s, during that whole period [of internment], we would have been preparing people to get out on the streets and become involved again in the armed struggle. After the hunger strikes and that whole period, another field of struggle opened, and that was the whole area of political struggle and in terms of politics."[19] In the 1970s, the internees served short sentences and prepared themselves for the immediate return to armed struggle, but in the 1980s, the prisoners faced a long war and lengthy sentences, and they understood that they would not return to armed struggle immediately. To put it in the words of the leader of the 1981 hunger strikes, they learned that they had another part to play.[20] Laurence McKeown also stresses the difference between the purpose of political education in the 1970s and afterwards: "Let's say, the imprisonment in the early 1970s – this was when IRA prisoners would have been very …, and certainly, their command staff would have been very conservative, very right-wing, very Catholic and that's the reflection of the community and the IRA at that time, whereas in later years very much more left – studying Marxism, very much more collective leadership, very much more de-structuring of command structures."[21]

While the political education reflected a turn to left-wing literature and understanding of the prisoners, in the end it served the purpose of facilitating the shift of the Provisionals from armed struggle to parliamentarism. Instead of building a united democratic socialist republic, they entered the local government in a coalition with their unionist opponents in Belfast – on a still divided island. Despite the revolutionary sentiments and Marxist Esperanto in the H-Blocks, it was only because of the support of the prisoners that this process was successful, and thus Gerard Hodgins looks back and asks himself: "It's only when you look back, you recognise this in hindsight. You look back, and you say to yourself: How the fuck did I not notice?"[22]

An Irish Century of Camps

With *Learning behind Bars*, I provide the first comparative analysis of Irish republican prisoners on both sides of the Irish border and a long-term examination of Irish republican prisoners over three decades of the Northern Ireland conflict.

The book, moreover, places the prisoners' minds at the centre of research, while the literature over the past three decades since the end of the high-profile hunger strikes has overwhelmingly focused on the prisoners' bodies. The prisoners' minds developed in the interplay of political education and resistance. Depending on the prison regime, the republicans sometimes had unrestricted access to education and free association, as in the 1990s, and sometimes had no access to reading material and lived in almost total isolation, as during the blanket protests in the late 1970s. This ebb and flow meant that their political education was not a linear process.

My study also shows that political prisoners can be leaders of conflict transformation processes. Contrary to Michel Foucault, who described prisons as institutions designed to create docile citizens by marginalizing their inmates, I argue that convicted members of self-described "national liberation movements" can instead be leaders of political change outside the prison walls. While Foucault's assumption is valid for criminal prisoners without political beliefs, the high-profile examples of Abdullah Ocalan in Turkey, Arnaldo Otegi in the Basque Country/Spain, Nelson Mandela in South Africa, and Gerry Adams in Northern Ireland show that prisoners incarcerated for membership of national liberation movements and broad social movements are not on the margins of society. Instead, these prisoners listed above were all leaders of political change during the conflict transformation process in their countries.[1]

During the Northern Ireland conflict, prisoners started a critical debate in the camps and prisons. The Provisional IRA prisoners used their authority to criticize the leadership of the Provisionals for the failed truce of 1975/6, thereby igniting a debate in the wider republican movement outside the prisons by smuggling statements and articles out of the prisons. The articles became known as the Brownie Papers. Following their release from prison, this group of prisoners used their status as well-known former prisoners to reach influential positions in their movement and, from these positions, they supported the conflict transformation process.

By using original interview data with thirty-four former republican prisoners, I first explained how the internment camps and prisons provided an environment for critical thinking; second, I showed how prisoners then used their position to initiate critical debates outside the prisons that eventually led to the acceptance of the peace process by the republican movement. The prisoners were the true leaders of a debate that, although it twice turned into factional struggles and splits in 1986 and 1996/7, ultimately transformed the Provisional republican movement from a militant nationalist movement determined to establish the United Socialist Republic in the mid-1970s to a movement that supported the Good Friday Agreement in 1998 and today embraces parliamentary politics. In sum, by using Irish republican prisoners during the Northern Ireland conflict as a case study, I illustrate, on the one hand, how political prisoners can be leaders of political change and, on the other hand, that we must distinguish political prisoners from Foucault's concept of criminal prisoners.

As with most historical research projects, this book analyses a case study based on a well-defined methodological and theoretical framework. Therefore, it provides material for further research on aspects that remain untouched by this study. Among them are the political education of Irish republican prisoners in England and abroad, in North America and Europe. These prisoners served their time under entirely different circumstances than those in Ireland; due to their smaller numbers, they were often not separated from ordinary criminal prisoners and had no network of republican prisoners around them. Two other groups of Irish republican prisoners that remain untouched by this book are the republican women in HMP Armagh and the imprisoned members of republican groups who were opposed to the Good Friday Agreement. Other strands of future research are the inclusion of more archival and written material by the republican prisoners, as started by Lachlan Whalen; the experience of the prison warders; or the political education of the loyalist prisoners in Long Kesh, which Connal Parr has touched on in *Inventing the Myth*.[2] The latter topic would open an exciting field of comparative analysis. Apart from comparing Irish republicans with other political prisoners in Northern Ireland, valuable topics for comparison could also be found outside Ireland by comparing Irish republicans with former prisoners' experiences of other national liberation movements; imprisoned radicalized Islamist terrorists; or criminal prisoners that have pursued education while serving their sentences.

By comparing different incarceration systems in both Irish states, I negate the often-invented discontinuity from camps to prisons. I argue that the prisons are in a linear continuity with the internment camps in Ireland. This link becomes visible through my long-term approach to the topic. Rather than focusing on a certain period of the Northern Ireland conflict, I wrote an oral history of Irish republicans during all three decades of the conflict. In other words, recent developments in Northern Ireland can only be understood if a historical approach to Social Movement and Terrorism Studies is adopted. The developments from camps to prisons reflects the adaptation of the British state policy to the changing use of political violence in Ireland. Understanding the treatment of radical prisoners in a historical context helps us understand the state responses to and the rationale of terrorism and political violence actors in Western Europe today.

The current wave of terrorism in Europe is not a new phenomenon. While the actors' motivations, ideologies, tactics, and outcomes differ from the past, terrorism and political violence have been regular occurrences throughout the twentieth century. Charles Townshend traced the origins back to the terrorism of Russian revolutionaries and anarchists in the nineteenth century.[3] Recent research by Lisa Stampnitzky and Andrew Silke provide literature for an understanding of the emergence and development of the field of Terrorism Studies since the 1960s.[4] Nonetheless, Silke argues that there is a tendency in terrorism research to assume that it started with 11 September.[5] As early as 2000, Martha Crenshaw argued that the study of terrorism is inherently event driven.[6] Thus, Richard English, in his latest book, stresses that the study of terrorism "requires a historically grounded answer."[7] In the past few years, such a historical approach to Terrorism Studies and Social Movements Studies has been used by renowned scholars, such as English himself, Stefan Berger, and Robert W. White.[8] Following White and Charles Tilly, I argue that we understand terrorism and political violence best if we use long-term analyses of these phenomena.[9] Hence, this book also reflects the need for a "historical turn" in studying terrorism and political violence by examining what prisoners of radical groups actually do in the camps and prisons.[10]

The research on camps has made relevant progress in previous years. In the twentieth century, the study of camps was restricted mainly to research camp systems in various countries or political systems. However, the last few years have seen academics writing global histories of camps in the long twentieth century. The edited volumes by Bettina Grainer and Alan Kramer on the "success story of camps" quickly became a standard reference for researchers, as is Christoph Jahr and Jens Thiel's edited volume on "camps before Auschwitz."[11] In addition, Dan Stone has written a short global history of concentration camps.[12] Andrea Pitzer's book also falls into this category.[13] Finally, while only touching on sport, Gregor Feindt, Anke Hilbrenner, and Dittmar Dahlmann attempt to contribute to the increasing literature on the global history of camps.[14] However, it must be noted that the only contribution discussing Ireland in all of these volumes is my chapter on sport in internment camps and prisons during the Northern Ireland conflict in the latter publication.[15]

While Ireland does not appear in these global histories of camps, the island experienced more than its fair share of camps and other forms of incarceration in the twentieth century. Stone writes that camps "encompass a multitude of realities."[16] Indeed, all these "realities" appear in twentieth-century Ireland, except for the death camps. Following the 1916 Easter Rising, Irish republicans were held in PoW camps in Wales; the later Civil War saw the mass imprisonment of Anti-Treaty republicans; during "The Emergency" in the Second World War, republicans were interned in the Curragh Military Camp, so were German PoWs; during the IRA's Operation Harvest in the 1950s and 1960s, the Irish government re-introduced internment. Finally, the eruption of the Northern Ireland conflict initially brought scores of Catholics fleeing violent pogroms over the border. They were housed in appalling conditions in Ballymullen Barracks in Tralee, Co. Kerry. During the conflict, Ireland witnessed the mass incarceration of suspected political activists on both sides of the Irish border, first by introducing internment in August 1971 and, later, in the Panopticon-like H-Blocks and the high-security prison Portlaoise, and a range of other penitentiaries. During internment, a prison ship in Lough Belfast was used to hold political activists, and some of the prisoners were tortured, being subjected to the deep interrogation techniques that the US forces later used in Abu-Ghraib. They became known as the Hooded Men. In recent years, another particularly dark chapter of forcible confinement came to the attention of the Irish public. In the twentieth century, over 30,000 women and girls were held in Magdalene Laundries, operated by the Roman Catholic Church. So-called fallen women were held there under the constant threat of physical violence, psychological abuse, and rape and were forced to work in slave-like conditions.

Ireland provides a critical case study for the evolution of camps and prison systems in the twentieth century. The multitude of camps and prisons existed in Ireland under changing political frameworks. The first camps were opened when the whole island was still a British colony. Following the independence of the Southern Irish Freestate, the new post-colonial state made full use of the colonial heritage of camps and prisons; PoW camps were set up in a neutral state during the Second World War; the re-introduction of internment in the newly constituted Republic of Ireland provides a rare example of post-1945 internment in Western liberal democracy; the Magdalene Laundries offer material for research into the Catholic Church's role in the confinement of women and children; and, finally, the developments during the Northern Ireland conflict provide an understanding of contemporary internment and mass incarceration in war-torn societies. Indeed, during the lengthy stages of the twentieth century, Giorgio Agamben's "state of exception" became a sad reality on the island of Ireland.[17] The people of Ireland experienced changing constitutional arrangements in the twentieth century; yet, all states on the island used camps and prisons to control sections of their citizens; this makes Ireland arguably a prime example for studying the "century of camps."

This book closes the link between the camps and the prisons – two institutions of incarceration and confinement that are often analysed separately. In Ireland, the prisons continued the camp policy by other means. As I have mentioned earlier, my book connects the analysis of political education from camps to prisons. Internment camps holding Irish prisoners differ from the early concentration camps of the late nineteenth century and the death camps of the twentieth century. The main difference is, of course, mortality. However, there are also several similarities between the early concentration camps in South Africa, the Philippines, and Cuba on the one hand, and the internment camps holding Irish prisoners after 1916 in Wales and the 1970s in Ireland.[18] First, both types of camps were opened as a direct response to guerrilla campaigns during a colonial conflict. Second, they were directed against a significant section of the population – in the Irish case against male Catholics suspected of Nationalist sympathies. Third, the camps served as collective punishment of the Nationalist community.[19] The internment policy was reintroduced in Northern Ireland in the summer of 1971 and formally ended in December 1975. However, the criminalization policy of Irish nationalists succeeded, and the newly built H-Blocks of HMP Maze became its centre after 1976.

We will only fully understand all these aspects of incarceration if we analyse them in a long-term historical framework. In other words, we need a *long durée* study of Irish confinement systems. Despite adopting a long-term historical approach over three decades, I could merely analyse a fraction of this system. How people lived, became political subjects in this system, and influenced political developments outside the prison walls is the topic of this book. In this way, I sought to make a modest contribution to a better understanding of Ireland's century of camps.

Interview Partners

Aoife (Cumann na mBan), Belfast, 13 February 2010.
Tim Brannigan, Belfast, 28 July 2015.
Don Brown, Derry City, 16 April 2014.
John Crawley, Monaghan Town, Co. Monaghan, 30 April 2015.
Michael Donnelly, Derry City, Co. Derry, 17 April 2017.
Eithne (Cumann na mBan), Belfast, 29 January 2010.
Gerard Foster, Belfast, 3 April 2014.
Fra Halligan, Belfast, 18 April 2014.
Vivion Hayden, Dublin, 14 April 2015 and 17 April 2015.
Dan Hoban, Newport, Co. Mayo, 15 April 2015.
Gerard Hodgins, Belfast, 28 July 2015.
Lawrence Hughes, Letterkenny, Co. Donegal, 2 September 2013.
John Hunt, Ballybunnion, Co. Kerry, 6 August 2015.
Jim Kavanagh, Wexford, Co. Wexford, 16 April 2015.
Peig King, Dublin, 13 March 2010.
Tommy McKearney, Monaghan, Co. Monaghan, 30 July 2015 and 5 August 2015.
Frank McCarron, Derry, 15 April 2014.
Laurence McKeown, Dundalk, Co. Louth, 29 July 2015, and Florence, Italy, 12 October 2016.
Matt Leen, Tralee, Co. Kerry, 19 April 2015.
Martin (Socialist Republican), Derry, 16 April 2014.
Anthony McIntyre, Drogheda, Co. Louth, 30 March 2014.
Eugene McLoone, Derry, 16 April 2017.
Martin McLoone, Derry, 17 April 2017.
Sean Moore, Monaghan. Co. Monaghan, 12 April 2017.
Danny Morrison, Belfast, 28 July 2015.
Sean Murphy, Tralee, Co. Kerry, 19 April 2015.
Gerard Murray, Belfast, 3 April 2014.
John Nixon, Armagh City, Co. Armagh, 13 April 2017.

Dáithí Ó Búitigh, Belfast, 7 April 2014.

Ruairí Ó Brádaigh, Roscommon Town, Co. Roscommon, 14 March 2010.

Tony O'Hara, Derry, 15 April 2014.

Seosamh Ó Maileoin, Tyrellspass, Co. Westmeath, 16 March 2015 and 30 April 2015.

Seán Óg Ó Mórdha, Dublin, Co. Dublin, 17 April 2015.

Seán Ó Sé, Dublin, 5 April 2014.

Offaly Republican, Co. Offaly, 2015.

Phil (Provisional Republican), Derry, 2 September 2013.

Seamus Swan, Wexford, Co. Wexford, 23 July 2015.

Kevin Trainor, Armagh City, Co. Armagh, 14 April 2017.

Malachy Trainor, Armagh City, Co. Armagh, 13 April 2017.

Matt Treacy, Dublin, 14 April 2015.

Séanna Walsh, Belfast, 29 July 2015.

Warren (Socialist Republican), Derry, 3 April 2014.

Notes

Introduction

1 Jim Gibney, "It Is Only Right to Honour the Women of the Rising," *Irish News*, 30 March 2016.

2 Martin McCleery, *Operation Demetrius and Its Aftermath: A New History of the Use of Internment without Trial in Northern Ireland 1971–75* (Manchester: Manchester University Press, 2015).

3 Neil Ferguson, "Northern Irish Ex-prisoners: The Impact of Imprisonment on Prisoners and the Peace Process in Northern Ireland," in *Prison, Terrorism and Extremism: Critical Issues in Management, Radicalisation and Reform*, ed. Andrew Silke (London: Routledge, 2014), 271.

4 In this book I discuss the informal, self-organized classes and lectures as well as the individual and collective reading of political and historical literature among Irish republican internees and prisoners during their incarceration. However, the formal prison education, such as the Open University courses undertaken by both republican and loyalist prisoners, is not part of this research project.

5 Goffman defines a total institution "as a place of residence and work where a large number of like-situated individuals cut off from the wider society for an appreciable period of time together lead an enclosed formally administered round of life" Erving Goffman, *Asylums* (Harmondsworth: Penguin, 1968), 11.

6 John Whyte, *Interpreting Northern Ireland* (Oxford: Oxford University Press, 1991). See also Bill Rolston, *Review of Literature on Republican and Loyalist Ex-prisoners* (Belfast: OFMDFM, 2011).

7 For an understanding of the changing social structure of the republican movement in the early 1970s, see Lorenzo Bosi, "Explaining Pathways to Armed Activism in the Provisional Irish Republican Army, 1969–1972," *Social Science History* 36, no. 3 (2012), 347–90; Robert W. White,

Provisional Irish Republicans: An Oral and Interpretive History (Westport, CT: Greenwood Press, 1993); Robert W. White, "Issues in the Study of Political Violence: Understanding the Motives of Participants in Small Group Political Violence," *Terrorism and Political Violence* 12, no. 1 (2000), 95–108.

8 "Interview with Jim Gibney," accessed 3 May 2022, www.pbs.org/wgbh /pages/frontline/shows/ira/inside/gibney.html.

9 The Official IRA was formed after the split within the IRA in 1970 but had announced a conditional ceasefire, allowing defence and retaliation already in May 1972. In opposition to this ceasefire, radical members formed the INLA, which is still active, although they formally decommissioned their weapons in 2010. The Continuity IRA and Real IRA are smaller groups formed in opposition to the peace process in 1986 and 1997, respectively; for an overview of the events that led to the formation of these paramilitary groups, see John F. Morrison, *Origins and Rise of Dissident Irish Republicanism: The Role and Impact of Organizational Splits* (London: Bloomsbury, 2013).

10 Richard English, *Armed Struggle: The History of the IRA* (Oxford: Oxford University Press, 2003); John F. Morrison, "A Time to Think, A Time to Talk: Irish Republican Priosners in the Northern Irish Peace Process," in *Prisons, Terrorism and Extremism: Critical Issues in Management, Radicalisation and Reform*, ed. Andrew Silke (London: Routledge, 2014), 75–86.

11 Alex P. Schmid, "Radicalisation, De-radicalisation, Counter-radicalisation: A Conceptual Discussion and Literature Review," *ICCT Research Paper* 97 (2013).

12 Cathal McManus, "Conceptualising Islamic 'Radicalisation' in Europe through 'Othering': Lessons from the Conflict in Northern Ireland," *Terrorism and Political Violence* 32, vol. 2 (2020), 325–44.

13 Luisa Passerini, *Memory and Utopia: The Primacy of Inter-subjectivity* (London: Routledge, 2014).

14 Polymeris Voglis, *Becoming a Subject: Political Prisoners during the Greek Civil War* (Oxford: Berghahn Books, 2002).

15 James Khalil, "A Guide to Interviewing Terrorists and Violent Extremists," *Studies in Conflict & Terrorism* 42, no. 4 (2019).

16 Andrew Silke, "The Impact of 9/11 on Research on Terrorism," in *Mapping Terrorism Research: State of the Art, Gaps and Future Directions*, ed. Magnus Ranstorp (London: Routledge, 2007), 77.

17 Liam Clarke and Kathryn Johnston, *Martin McGuinness: From Guns to Government* (Edinburgh: Mainstream Publishing, 2001).

18 Anthony McIntyre, "No Beret or Gloves on the Top of the Coffin," *The Pensive Quill*, 2 April 2017, http://thepensivequill.am/2017/04/no-beret -or-gloves-on-top-of-coffin.html.

19 William Murphy, *Political Imprisonment & the Irish, 1912–1921* (Oxford: Oxford University Press, 2014).

20 Peter Shirlow and Kieran McEvoy, *Beyond the Wire: Former Prisoners and Conflict Transformation in Northern Ireland* (London: Pluto Press, 2008).

21 Rod Earle and James Mehigan, *Degrees of Freedom: Prison Education at the Open University* (Bristol: Policy Press, 2019).

22 Quoted from Lorenzo Bosi, "Contextualizing the Biographical Outcomes of Provisional IRA Former Activists: A Structure-Agency Dynamic," in *Activists Forever? The Long-Term Impacts of Political Activism*, eds. Olivier Fillieule and Erik Neveu (Cambridge: Cambridge University Press, 2019), 202–20.

23 Quoted from Bosi, "Contextualizing the Biographical Outcomes of Provisional IRA Former Activists."

24 Quoted from Lorenzo Bosi, "Explaining Pathways to Armed Activism in the Provisional Irish Republican Army, 1969–1972," *Social Science History* 36, no. 3.

25 Kieran McEvoy, *Paramilitary Imprisonment in Northern Ireland: Resistance, Management, and Release* (Oxford: Oxford University Press, 2001), 227–49.

26 Quoted from Bosi, "Contextualizing the Biographical Outcomes of Provisional IRA Former Activists."

27 Quoted from Bosi, "Contextualizing the Biographical Outcomes of Provisional IRA Former Activists."

28 Ferguson, "Northern Irish Ex-prisoners."

29 Brandon Hamber, "Flying Flags of Fear: The Role of Fear in the Process of Political Transition," *Journal of Human Rights* 5, no. 1 (2006).

30 Richard English, "Left on the Shelf," *Fortnight* 388 (2000); Kirsty Scott, "Men of Letters, Men of Arms," *The Guardian*, 2 December 2000.

31 Jacqueline Dana and Seán McMonagle, "Deconstructing 'Criminalization': The Politics of Collective Education in the H-Blocks," *Journal of Prisoners on Prisons* 8, nos. 1 & 2 (1997).

32 I have published two articles on republican prisoners in Portlaoise. These two articles emerged from the same research as this book, but most of the material presented in these articles has been ommitted from the book: Dieter Reinisch, "The Fight for Political Status in Portlaoise Prison, 1973–7: Prologue the H-Blocks Struggle," *War & Society* 40, no. 2 (2021); and Dieter Reinisch, "Debating Politics during Confinement: Newly Discovered Notebooks of the Sinn Féin Portlaoise Prison Cumann, 1979–1985," *Archives* 56, no. 2 (2021).

33 John Horgan, *Divided We Stand: The Strategy and Psychology of Ireland's Dissident Terrorists* (Oxford: Oxford University Press, 2012), 96.

34 Gearóid Ó Faoleán, *A Broad Church: The Provisional IRA in the Republic of Ireland 1969–1980* (Dublin: Merrion Press, 2019); Dieter Reinisch, "Teenagers

and Young Adults in Dissident Irish Republicanism: A Case Study of Na Fianna Éireann in Dublin," *Critical Studies on Terrorism* 13, no. 4 (2020).

35 Paul Gill and John Horgan, "Who Were the Volunteers? The Shifting Sociological and Operational Profile of 1240 Provisional Irish Republican Army Members," *Terrorism and Political Violence* 25, no. 3 (2013).

36 Reinisch, "Portlaoise Prison."

37 Mary Rogan, *Prison Policy in Ireland: Politics, Penal-Welfarism and Political Imprisonment* (London: Routledge, 2011); Mike Tomlinson, "Imprisoned Ireland," in *Western European Penal Systems: A Critical Anatomy*, eds. Vincenzo Ruggiero, Mick Ryan, and Joe Sim (London: Sage, 1995); Mark Finnane and Ian O'Donnell, "Crime and Punishment," *The Cambridge Social History of Modern Ireland* (Cambridge: Cambridge University Press, 2017).

38 Brian Campbell, Laurence McKeown, and Felim O'Hagan, *Nor Meekly Serve My Time: The H-block Struggle, 1976–1981* (Belfast: Beyond the Pale Publications, 1998); Laurence McKeown, *Out of Time: Irish Republican Prisoners, Long Kesh, 1972–2000* (Belfast: Beyond the Pale, 2001); Richard O'Rawe, *Blanketmen: An Untold Story of the H-block Hunger Strike* (Dublin: New Island, 2005); Deaglán Ó'Mocháin, "Criminalization and the Post Hunger Strike Resistance of IRA Prisoners in the H-Blocks of Long Kesh" (PhD diss., Queen's University, 2011).

39 Rogan, *Prison Policy in Ireland*, 16.

40 Brian Hanley, *The Impact of the Troubles on the Republic of Ireland, 1968–79: Boiling Volcano?* (Manchester: Manchester University Press, 2018); Patrick Mulroe, *Bombs, Bullets and the Border: Ireland's Frontier: Irish Security Policy, 1969–1978* (Dublin: Irish Academic Press, 2017); Ó Faoleán, *A Broad Church*.

41 William Murphy, "Justice and Uncertainty," *Irish Economic and Social History* 47 (2020).

42 Luisa Passerini, "Utopia and Desire," *Thesis Eleven* 68, no. 1 (2002).

43 The term "long war" would normally refer to the Provisional IRA's armed campaign after the reorganization of the IRA in the late 1970s; the relevant departure signalled by Jimmy Drumm's speech at Bodenstown in 1977. In essence it meant that younger figures in the paramilitary leadership moved away from the clearly defined tactic of short armed campaigns against the British presence in Ireland towards an understanding of a long-lasting guerrilla war that could take up to two or three decades; see Brendan O'Brien, *The Long War: The IRA and Sinn Féin* (New York: Syracuse University Press, 1999).

44 Voglis, "Becoming a Subject," 12–15.

45 Jana Sawicki, "Feminism, Foucault and 'Subjects' of Power and Freedom," in *The Later Foucault*, ed. Jeremy Moss (London: Sage, 1998).

46 Michael Foucault, *Discipline and Punish: The Birth of the Prison* (London: Allen Lane, 1977).

47 I discuss this aspect in relation to my research about Irish republican women in the following article in more detailed: Dieter Reinisch, "'Is Austria a Catholic Country?': Trust and Intersubjectivity in Post-conflict Northern Ireland," *Oral History Review* 48, no. 2 (2021).

48 Alexander Bogner and Wolfgang Menz, "Das theoriegenerierende Experteninterview: Erkenntnisinteresse, Wissensformen, Interaktion," in *Das Experteninterview. Theorie, Methode, Anwendungen*, eds. Alexander Bogner, Beate Littig, and Wolfgang Menz (Wiesbaden: VS-Verlag für Sozialwissenschaften, 2005), 62–3.

49 Yvonne McKenna, "Sisterhood? Exploring Power Relations in the Collection of Oral History," *Oral History* 31, no. 1 (2003): 68.

50 Joanne McEvoy, "Elite Interviewing in a Divided Society: Lessons from Northern Ireland," *Politics* 26, no. 3 (2006): 185.

51 Name changed in accordance with consent form.

52 Field notes of interview with Eithne, 29 January 2010, Belfast.

53 Field notes of interview with Aoife, 13 February 2010, Belfast.

54 McKenna, "Sisterhood?," 67.

55 Kathleen M. Blee, *Women of the Klan: Racism and Gender in the 1920s* (Los Angeles: University of California, 2008), 5.

56 McEvoy, "Elite Interviewing in a Divided Society," 184.

57 Claire Mitchell, "Behind the Ethnic Marker: Religion and Social Identification in Northern Ireland," *Sociology of Religion* 66, no. 1 (2005): 8.

58 Ben Crewe, "Not Looking Hard Enough: Masculinity, Emotion, and Prison Research," *Qualitative Inquiry* 20, no. 4 (2014): 394.

59 Paul Arthur, "Elite Studies in a Paranocracy: The Northern Ireland Case," in *Research Methods for Elite Studies*, eds. George Moyser and Margaret Wagstaffe (London: Allen & Unwin, 1987).

60 Other oral history studies with Irish republicans were conducted by Jack Hepworth and Marisa McGlinchey at a UK university at the same time as my research, and both had different experiences during the field research: Jack Hepworth, *"The Age-Old Struggle": Irish Republicanism from the Battle of the Bogside to the Belfast Agreement, 1969–1998* (Liverpool: Liverpool University Press, 2021); Marisa McGlinchey, *Unfinished Business: The Politics of "Dissident" Irish Republicanism* (Manchester: Manchester University Press, 2019).

1 The Irish Prison Arena: Republican Prisoners and the Northern Ireland Conflict

1 Sean O'Mahony, *Frongoch: University of Revolution* (Dublin: FDR Teoranta, 1987).

2 John Maguire, *IRA Internments and the Irish Government: Subversives and the State, 1939–1962* (Dublin: Irish Academic Press, 2008).

3 Seán McConville, *Irish Political Prisoners, 1920–1962: Pilgrimage of Desolation* (London: Routledge, 2014).

4 Dieter Reinisch, "Teenagers and Young Adults in Dissident Irish Republicanism: A Case Study of Na Fianna Éireann in Dublin," *Critical Studies on Terrorism* 13, no. 4 (2020).

5 Joanne McEvoy, *The Politics of Northern Ireland* (Edinburgh: Edinburgh University Press, 2008), 8.

6 For an introduction to the Northern Ireland Troubles, see Gordon Gillespie, *A Short History of the Troubles* (Dublin: Gill & Macmillan, 2010); Marc Mulholland, *Northern Ireland: A Very Short Introduction* (Oxford: Oxford University Press, 2003).

7 Thomas Hennessey, *The Evolution of the Troubles, 1970–72* (Dublin: Irish Academic Press, 2007); Thomas Hennessey, *Northern Ireland: The Origins of the Troubles* (Dublin: Gill & Macmillan, 2005).

8 Huw Bennett, "Detention and Interrogation In Northern Ireland 1969–1975," in *Prisoners in War*, ed. Sibylle Scheipers (Oxford: Oxford University Press, 2010).

9 McCleery, *Operation Demetrius and Its Aftermath*.

10 Huw Bennett, "'Smoke without Fire'? Allegations against the British Army in Northern Ireland, 1972–5," *Twentieth Century British History* 24, no. 2 (2013).

11 Samantha Anne Caesar, "Captive or Criminal?: Reappraising the Legal Status of IRA Prisoners at the Height of the Troubles under International Law," *Duke Journal of Comparative & International Law* 27, no. 2 (2017).

12 McKeown, *Out of Time*.

13 Caesar, "Captive or Criminal?"

14 Campbell, McKeown, and O'Hagan, *Nor Meekly Serve My Time*.

15 The figures are discussed, among other studies, in these publications: Patrick Joseph Bishop and Eamonn Mallie, *The Provisional IRA* (London: Corgi Books, 1994), 12; Kevin Toolis, *Rebel Hearts: Journeys within the IRA's Soul* (London: Picador, 1997), 151; Brendan O'Leary, "IRA: Irish Republican Army (Óglaigh na hÉireann)," in *Terror, Insurgency and the State: Ending Protracted Conflicts*, eds. Marianne Heiberg, Brendan O'Leary, and John Tirman (Philadelphia: University of Pennsylvania Press, 2007), 209–10; Claire Mitchell, "The Limits of Legitimacy: Former Loyalist Combatants and Peace-Building in Northern Ireland," *Irish Political Studies* 23, no. 1 (2008); Kieran McEvoy, *Paramilitary Imprisonment in Northern Ireland: Resistance, Management, and Release* (Oxford: Oxford University Press, 2001), 16.

16 Shirlow and McEvoy, *Beyond the Wire*.

17 OFMDFM, *Recruiting People with Conflict-Related Convictions: Employers' Guidance* (Belfast: OFMDFM, 2007), 3.

18 O'Leary, "IRA," 210.

19 Ruth Jamieson, Peter Shirlow, and Adrian Grounds, *Ageing and Social Exclusion among Former Politically Motivated Prisoners in Northern Ireland*

(Belfast: Changing Ageing Partnership, 2010), 11. Area studies provide additional numbers: Michael Ritchie, *The Cost of Imprisonment* (Belfast: Tús Nua, 1998); Tracy Irwin, "Prison Education in Northern Ireland: Learning from our Paramilitary Past," *The Howard Journal of Criminal Justice* 42, no. 5 (2003): 472–3; Paul O'Neill, *An Loiste Uir: Prisoner/ex-Prisoners Project* (Belfast: An Loiste Uir, 1998); Brandon Hamber, *"Blocks to the Future": A Pilot Study of the Long-term Psychological Impact of the "No Wash/Blanket" Protest* (Derry: Action and Research International, 2005), 1, 111.

20 Note that of the 1,761 deaths caused by republicans since 1968, only 517 led to prison sentences. Likewise, just 421 of the 841 people killed by loyalists resulted in convictions. This leaves 1,664 deaths without anyone charged; Chris Ryder, *The Fateful Split: Catholics and the Royal Ulster Constabulary* (London: Methuen, 2004), 335.

21 Tim Pat Coogan, *The Troubles: Ireland's Ordeal 1966–1996 and the Search for Peace* (London: Random House, 1996), 126.

22 Scheipers, "Introduction: Prisoners in War," 7.

23 Bennett, "Detention and Interrogation."

24 Caesar, "Captive or Criminal?," 326.

25 Niall Gilmartin and Margaret M. Scull, "Republican Women and Catholic Church Responses to the Strip Searching of Female Prisoners in Northern Ireland, 1982–92," *Women's History Review* (2021), DOI: 10.1080/09612025.2021.1958455.

26 Clive Walker, "Irish Republican Prisoners. Political Detainees, Prisoners of War or Common Criminals?" *The Irish Jurist* 24 (new series), no. 2 (1984): 199.

27 Liam O'Ruairc deals with this problem in a comment for *The Pensive Quill*: Liam O'Ruairc, "Common Criminals or Political Law-Breakers?" *The Pensive Quill*, accessed 3 May 2022, http://thepensivequill.am/2010/08 /common-criminals-or-political-law.html.

28 "Political Category Status" in Northern Ireland meant that persons convicted and sentenced to more than nine months' imprisonment for so-called scheduled offences had a regime free of work, and prison duties and were recognized as a group.

29 In Portlaoise Prison, the republican prisoners wear their own clothes and associate at times. Prison work is also defined in broad terms at Portlaoise, and it gives implicit recognition to the command structure of republican paramilitary organizations.

30 Walker, "Irish Republican Prisoners," 225.

31 Caesar, "Captive or Criminal?," 348.

32 Andrew Silke, "Terrorists, Extremists and Prison: An Introduction to the Critical Issues," in *Prisons, Terrorism and Extremism: Critical Issues in Managment, Radicalisation and Reform*, ed. Andrew Silke (London: Routledge, 2014), 4.

33 Silke, "Terrorists, Extremists and Prison," 5.

34 Shirlow et al., *Abandoning Historical Conflict*.

35 Irwin, "Prison Education in Northern Ireland," 472.

36 Diego Gambetta and Steffen Hertog, *Engineers of Jihad: The Curious Connection Between Violent Extremism and Education* (Princeton, NJ: Princeton University Press, 2016), 100–27.

37 Dieter Reinisch, "Corporeality, Militant Performance, and the Northern Irish Prisons Protests, 1971–1983," In *Performing Memory: Corporeality, Visuality, and Mobility after 1968*, edited by Luisa Passerini and Dieter Reinisch. New York: Berghahn, forthcoming.

38 John F. Morrison, "Fighting Talk: The Statements of 'The IRA/New IRA.'" *Terrorism and Political Violence* 28, no. 3 (2016): 605.

39 OFMDFM, "Recruiting People with Conflict-Related Convictions," 3.

40 Féilim Ó hÁdhmaill, *Equal Citizenship for a New Society? An Analysis of Training and Employment Opportunities for Republican Ex-prisoners in Belfast* (Belfast: Coiste na nIarChimí, 2001), 19–20.

41 O'Neill, *An Loiste Uir*.

42 Ó hÁdhmaill, *Equal Citizenship for a New Society*.

43 Ritchie, *The Cost of Imprisonment*.

44 Laurence McKeown, "'Casualties of War' or 'Agents of Change': Irish Republican Prisoners, Maze/Long Kesh Prison, 1972–2000," in *Political Ideology in Ireland: From the Enlightenment to the Present*, eds. Olivier Coquelin, Patrick Galliou, and Thierry Robin (Newcastle: Cambridge Scholars Publishing, 2009), 276.

45 Interview with Anthony McIntyre, Drogheda, Co. Louth, 30 March 2014.

46 Interview with Gerard Hodgins, Belfast, 28 July 2015.

47 Ibid.

48 Kevin Rooney, "Education: A Panacea for Our Sectarian Ills?," in *Peace or War? Understanding the Peace Process in Northern Ireland*, eds. Chris Gilligan and Jon Tonge (Aldershot: Ashgate, 1997), 120.

49 Interview with Gerard Murray, Belfast, 3 April 2014.

50 Interview with Peig King, Dublin, 13 March 2010.

51 In this context, Ard-Fheis is the Irish term for the Annual General Meeting of Irish Republican political organizations, such as Sinn Féin or the IRSP.

52 Interview with Fra Halligan, Belfast, 18 April 2014.

53 Fáilte Cluain Eois, *Their Prisons, Our Stories* (Monaghan: Fáilte Cluain Eois Books, 2015), 122.

54 Eois, *Their Prisons, Our Stories*, 125.

55 *Éire Nua*, or "New Ireland," is a political program that was adopted by the Provisional Republican Movement in early 1972. It outlines their vision of a federal democratic 32 Counties Republic. It was widely promoted by Provisional Republicans throughout the 1970s but was abandoned by the delegates of the Sinn Féin Ard-Fheis in 1983.

56 English, *Armed Struggle*, 252.
57 Lachlan Whalen, *Contemporary Irish Republican Prison Writing: Writing and Resistance* (New York: Palgrave Macmillan, 2007).
58 Ed Moloney, *A Secret History of the IRA* (New York: W.W. Norton, 2002), 150–70; Denis O'Hearn, *Nothing but an Unfinished Song: Bobby Sands, the Irish Hunger Striker Who Ignited a Generation* (New York: Nation Books, 2006), 74–85.
59 Morrison, "Fighting Talk," 606.
60 OFMDFM, "Recruiting People with Conflict-Related Convictions," 4.
61 Donnacha Ó Beacháin, "From Revolutionaries to Politicians: Deradicalization and the Irish Experience," *Radical History Review* 85, no. 1 (2003): 115.
62 Reinisch, "Corporeality, Militant Performance."
63 Adrian Grounds and Ruth Jamieson, "No Sense of an Ending: Researching the Experience of Imprisonment and Release among Republican Ex-prisoners," *Theoretical Criminology* 7, no. 3 (2003): 348.
64 Ruth Jamieson and Adrian Grounds, *No Sense of an Ending: The Effects of Long-term Imprisonment amongst Republican Prisoners and Their Families* (Monaghan: Seesyum Press, 2002).
65 Kieran McEvoy et al., "The Home Front: The Families of Politically Motivated Prisoners in Northern Ireland," *British Journal of Criminology* 39, no. 2 (1999).
66 Peter Shirlow, *The State They Are In: An Independent Evaluation* (Belfast: University of Ulster Social Exclusion Research Unit, 2001).
67 Morrison, "Fighting Talk," 605.
68 Grounds and Jamieson, "No Sense of an Ending: Researching the Experience."
69 David McKittrick, "Belfast: A City of Alienated Youth," *The Independent*, 20 June 2009.
70 Maurice Goldring, "Jours tranquilles à Belfast," *Les cahiers de médiologie* 13, no. 1 (2002).
71 Interview with Matt Treacy, Dublin, Co. Dublin, 14 April 2015.

2 "Portlaoise Is an Example for This": Portlaoise Prison Protests, 1973–1977

1 David Beresford, *Ten Men Dead* (London: Grafton Books, 1987), 131–3; Mansour Bonakdarian, "Iranian Consecration of Irish Nationalist 'Martyrs': The Islamic Republic of Iran and the 1981 Republican Prisoners' Hunger Strike in Northern Ireland," *Social History* 43, no. 3 (2018).
2 Matthews Whiting, *Sinn Féin and the IRA: From Revolution to Moderation* (Edinburgh: Edinburgh University Press, 2018).
3 Behan, "We Are All Convicted Criminals"; Wall, "Embarrassing the State."

4 Rogan, *Prison Policy in Ireland*, 146.

5 Rogan, *Prison Policy in Ireland*, 130.

6 Rogan, *Prison Policy in Ireland*, 130–54.

7 Eoin O'Sullivan and Ian O'Donnell, *Coercive Confinement in Ireland: Patients, Prisoners and Penitents* (Manchester: Manchester University Press, 2012).

8 Rogan, *Prison Policy in Ireland*, 217.

9 Shane Kilcommins et al., *Crime, Punishment and the Search for Order in Ireland* (Dublin: Institute of Public Administration, 2014).

10 Tomlinson, "Imprisoned Ireland."

11 Mark Findlay, "'Criminalization' and the Detention of 'Political Prisoners': An Irish Perspective," *Contemporary Crises* 9, no. 1 (1985), 10.

12 Dieter Reinisch, "The Fight for Political Status in Portlaoise Prison."

13 Rogan, *Prison Policy in Ireland*, 140.

14 Findlay, "Criminalization."

15 Findlay, "Criminalization"; Mark Findlay, "Organized Resistance, Terrorism, and Criminality in Ireland: The State's Construction of the Control Equation," *Crime and Social Justice* 21/22 (1984), 95–115; Feargal Francis Davis, *The History and Development of the Special Criminal Court 1922–2014* (London: Bloomsbury, 2014).

16 Rogan, *Prison Policy in Ireland*, 142.

17 Behan, "We Are All Convicted Criminals," 7.

18 John Lonergan, *The Governor* (Dublin: Penguin 2010), 115.

19 Findlay, "Criminalization," 11.

20 Thomas Hennessey, *Hunger Strike: Margaret Thatcher's Battle with the IRA* (Dublin: Irish Academic Press, 2014), 458–70.

21 Rogan, *Prison Policy in Ireland*, 138–42.

22 Brendan Hughes and Douglas Dalby, *Up Like a Bird: The Rise and Fall of an IRA Commander* (Castleisland, Republic of Ireland: Time Warp Book, 2021): 65–95.

23 Kevin Grant, "British Suffragettes and the Russian Method of Hunger Strike," *Comparative Studies in Society and History* 53, no. 1 (2011).

24 Lachlan Whalen, "'A Womanish Thing': The Price Sisters and the Gendered Dimensions of Irish Republican Hunger Strikes in England, 1973–74," *New Hibernia Review* 23, no. 2 (2019), 95–113.

25 Ian Miller, *A History of Force Feeding: Hunger Strikes, Prisons and Medical Ethics, 1909–1974* (Basingstoke: Palgrave Macmillan, 2016), 195–219.

26 Miller, *A History*, 4.

27 Miller, *A History*, 8.

28 "Opinion: Hunger-Strike," *An Phoblacht/Republican News*, 14 February 1985, 2.

29 Rogan, *Prison Policy in Ireland*, 54–73.

30 National Library of Ireland (subsequently NLI), JUS/14/603; Confidential note by Governor Portlaoise Prison.

31 Ó Faoleán, *Broad Church*, 44.
32 Interview with Seosamh Ó Maileoin, Tyrellspass, Co. Westmeath, 30 April 2015.
33 National Archive of Ireland (subsequently NAI), DFA-2012-59.1721; Department of Justice (subsequently DoJ), Demands by Prisoners. Concessions by Government, 1972–1977.
34 Ibid.
35 Behan, "We Are All Convicted Criminals," 6.
36 Note that the DoJ says in the above-cited statement that free association was available.
37 Findlay, "Criminalization," 9.
38 F. Stuart Ross, *Smashing H-Block: The Rise and Fall of the Popular Campaign against Criminalization, 1976–1982* (Liverpool: Liverpool University Press, 2011), 21.
39 NLI, Sean O'Mahony Papers, MS 44,183/1; Conditions in Ireland.
40 "IRA Men Blast Escape out of Top-Security Jail," *The Montreal Gazette*, 16 August 1974.
41 Hanley, *Boiling Volcano*, 102.
42 Ross, *Smashing H-Block*, 21.
43 Hanley, *Boiling Volcano*, 90.
44 Fáilte Cluain Eois, *Their Prisons, Our Stories*, 155–7.
45 Findlay, "Criminalization," 10.
46 Interview with Dan Hoban, Newport, Co. Mayo, 15 April 2015.
47 Hanley, *Boiling Volcano*, 102.
48 Ross, *Smashing H-Block*, 21.
49 Hanley, *Boiling Volcano*, 102.
50 Fáilte Cluain Eois, *Their Prisons, Our Stories*, 141.
51 NLI, Sean O'Mahony Papers, MS44,183/4; Hunger Strike in Port Laois and Curragh Prisons, Sinn Féin Press Release, 12 February 1975.
52 Hanley, *Boiling Volcano*, 102.
53 Interview with Hoban.
54 Interview with Hoban.
55 NLI, Sean O'Mahony Papers, MS44,183/1; End of Hungerstrike, Prisoners' Communique from Portlaoise Prison, undated.
56 "12 IRA Members Quit Prison Fast," *The Morning Record*, 17 February 1975.
57 Ibid.
58 NAI, DFA-2012-59.1721; DoJ, Demands by Prisoners. Concessions by Government, 1972–1977.
59 Interview with Vivion Hayden, Dublin, 14 April 2015.
60 NLI, Sean O'Mahony Papers, MS44,183/1; *Irish Republican Information Service*, Press Release 14 December 1975.
61 NLI, Sean O'Mahony Papers, MS44,183/1; Dáithí O'Connell and Liam Kelly letter to the Visiting Committee, Portlaoise Jail, 2 December 1975.

62 NLI, Sean O'Mahony Papers, MS44,183/1; "Republican Prisoners in Portlaoise Jail Are Demanding a Public Sworn Enquiry into the Management of Portlaoise Jail," 2 December 1975.

63 NAI, DFA-2012-59-1596; Government Information Service, 31 December 1975.

64 NLI, Sean O'Mahony Papers, MS44,183/1; Hunger Strike in Portlaoise Prison, Statement from the IRIS, 2 January 1976.

65 NLI, Sean O'Mahony Papers, MS44,183/1; Portlaoise Jail Situation, IRIS, 3 January 1976.

66 Hanley, *Boiling Volcano*, 89.

67 NLI, Sean O'Mahony Papers, MS44,183/1; Portlaoise Prison, IRIS, 28 February 1976.

68 NLI, Sean O'Mahony Papers, MS44,183/2; Eamonn McCann, "Inside Portlaoise," *Sunday World*, 20 March 1977.

69 Hanley, *Boiling Volcano*, 102.

70 Hanley, *Boiling Volcano*, 55, 108.

71 Hanley, *Boiling Volcano*.

72 NLI, Sean O'Mahony Papers, MS44,184/1; Witness statement by Patrick Casey to Fr. Piaras O'Duill, 23 April 1977.

73 Hanley, *Boiling Volcano*, 108.

74 NLI, Sean O'Mahony Papers, MS44,183/2; Pat Holmes, Inside Portlaoise, *Irish Press*, 10 November 1977.

75 NLI, Sean O'Mahony Papers, MS44,183/1; Portlaoise Hunger Strike.

76 Ross, *Smashing H-Block*, 29.

77 NUI Galway, Hardiman Library, Special Collection, Ruairí Ó Brádaigh Papers, POL28/94; Demands of the Portlaoise Hunger Strikers.

78 Fáilte Cluain Eois, *Their Prisons, Our Stories*, 162.

79 NLI, Sean O'Mahony Papers, MS44,184/1; "Jail Conditions the Real Issue, Says Ó Brádaigh," *Irish Press*, 15 April 1977.

80 Interview with Hayden.

81 NLI, Sean O'Mahony Papers, MS44,184/1; Darach McDonald, "Why the Hunger Strike Failed," *Hibernia*, 29 April 1977, 5.

82 NAI, DFA-2007-59-221; "Portlaoise Prison – Hunger Strike Threat," press statement, DoJ, 25 February 1977.

83 NLI, Sean O'Mahony Papers, MS44,184/2; "Portlaoise Pledges Must be Honoured," AP/RN, 26 April 1977, 1.

84 Ross, *Smashing H-Block*, 21, 29; However, Rogan mentions a few support groups: Rogan, *Prison Policy in Ireland*, 143–4.

85 Fáilte Cluain Eois, *Their Prisons, Our Stories*, 127.

86 Fáilte Cluain Eois, *Their Prisons, Our Stories*, 142.

87 NLI, Sean O'Mahony Papers, MS44,184/2; Statement issued from Liberty Hall, AP/RN, 26 April 1977, 1.

88　Fáilte Cluain Eois, *Their Prisons, Our Stories*, 162.

89　Hanley, *Boiling Volcano*, 110.

90　NAI, DFA-2012-59.1721; DoJ, Demands by Prisoners. Concessions by Government, 1972–1977.

91　McDonald, "Why the Hunger Strike Failed."

92　Findlay, "Criminalization," 12.

93　NAI, DFA-2007-59-221; Statement by Minister of Justice, 1977.

94　NAI, DFA-2012-59.1721; DoJ, Demands by Prisoners. Concessions by Government, 1972–1977.

95　NAI, JUS-2012-59-1721; Demands by Prisoners, Concessions by Government, 1972–1977, Liam Hourican to Taoiseach.

96　Interview with Ruairí Ó Brádaigh, Roscommon Town, Co. Roscommon, 14 March 2010.

97　PRONI NIO/12/128A Reid to Concannon, 25 July 1978; quoted in Hennessey, *Hunger Strike*, 24.

98　NAI, DFA-2012-59-1596.

99　Hennessey, *Hunger Strike*, 72.

100　Hennessey, *Hunger Strike*, 454.

101　NAI, DFA-2010-20-16; Tim Pat Coogan, "Portlaoise Example That the H Blocks Should Follow," *The Guardian*, 31 October 1980.

102　NAI, DFA-2010-20-16; "Leader: The Irish Dimension," *The Guardian*, 31 October 1980.

103　Behan, "We Are All Convicted Criminals," 13; Findlay, "Criminalization," 13.

104　Ross, *Smashing H-Block*.

105　Francis Stuart Ross, "The Prisoners' Support Campaign, Sinn Féin and the Hunger Strikes," In *Irish Republican Counterpublic: Armed Struggle and the Construction of a Radical Nationalist Community in Northern Ireland*, edited by Anne Kane and Dieter Reinisch (London: Routledge, 2023).

106　Hennessey, *Hunger Strike*, 24, 72–4, 454.

107　NAI, DFA-2012-59-1596.

108　Behan, "We Are All Convicted Criminals," 13.

109　Findlay, "Criminalization," 13.

110　Lonergan, *Govenor*, 117.

3 "No Prisoner Has the Right to Advance the Education of Another": Education in Portlaoise Prison

1　Handwritten letter by Seán Morrissey; NAI, JUS-14-603.

2　Parliamentary question to the minister for justice by John O'Connell; NAI, JUS-14-603.

3　Irish Republican Information Service, 14 December 1975; NLI, Seán O'Mahony Papers, MS 44,183/1.

4 Letter by Dáithí O`Connell, undated; NLI, Seán O'Mahony Papers, MS 44,183/1.

5 Lectures banned in Portlaoise Jail; NLI, Seán O'Mahony Papers, MS 44,183/1.

6 "A Day in the Life of a Prison Provisional," *Irish Times*, 25 April 1977, 11.

7 Pat Holmes, "Inside Portlaoise," *Irish Press*, 10 November 1977; NLI, Seán O'Mahony Papers, MS 44,183/2.

8 An Appeal to Reason and Humanity; NLI, Seán O'Mahony Papers, MS 44,183/1.

9 Fr. Piaras O'Duill, *Portlaoise Prison – Why There Was a Hunger Strike*; NLI, Seán O'Mahony Papers, MS 44,183/3.

10 Anco stands for "An Chomhairle Oiliúna"; the National Manpower Service Youth Employment Agency was a state agency in Ireland with responsibility for assisting those seeking employment. It was succeeded by Foras Áiseanna Saothair, the Training and Employment Authority and commonly known as FÁS, in January 1988.

11 Fr. Piaras O'Duill, *Denial of Educational Facilities in Portlaoise Prison*; NLI, Seán O'Mahony Papers, MS 44,183/3.

12 Interview with Seosamh Ó Maileoin, Tyrellspass, Co. Westmeath, 16 March 2015.

13 "Screws" is Hiberno-English slang for warders and prison officers.

14 Interview with Matt Leen; *Saoirse* 241, May 2007, 7.

15 The "Four Courts" is Ireland's main courts building, located on Inns Quay in Dublin, and houses the Supreme Court, the Court of Appeal, the High Court, and the Dublin Circuit Court. In 1922, it was the headquarters of the Anti-Treaty IRA forces. The bombing of the building by Pro-Treaty forces marked the beginning of the Irish Civil War that was waged in 1922 and 1923. This is what the interviewee refers to when mentioning that Dinny O'Brien was in "Four Courts."

16 Interview with Matt Leen; *Saoirse*, 7–8.

17 Interview with Dan Hoban.

18 Department of Justice, Demands by Prisoners. Concessions by Government, 1972–1977, NAI, DFA-2012-59.1721.

19 Reinisch, "Political Prisoners and the Irish Language."

20 Department of Justice, Demands by Prisoners. Concessions by Government, 1972–1977, NAI, DFA-2012-59.1721.

21 Prison Protests in Northern Ireland. Content of General Briefing Note; NAI, DFA-2012-59-1596.

22 Barrett, *Martin Ferris*, 86–7, 110–11, 170.

23 Barrett, *Martin Ferris*, 171–2.

24 Barrett, *Martin Ferris*, 172.

25 Barrett, *Martin Ferris*, 177.

26 Barrett, *Martin Ferris.*

27 Failte Cluain Eois, *Their Prisons, Our Stories*, 125.

28 Reinisch, "Debating Politics during Confinement."

29 Department of Justice, Demands by Prisoners. Concessions by Government, 1972–1977, NAI, DFA-2012-59.1721.

30 Interview with Brendan McCaffrey in Failte Cluain Eois, *Their Prisons, Our Stories*, 165.

31 Interview with Pat Treanor in Failte Cluain Eois, *Their Prisons, Our Stories*, 169.

32 Rod Earle and James Mehigan, *Degrees of Freedom: Prison Education at the Open University* (Bristol: Policy Press, 2019).

33 Interview with Seán Mulligan in "Inside Portlaoise: Interview with a Recently-Released Prisoner," *AP/RN*, 14 February 1983, 9.

34 Interview with John Carroll in Maire De Barra, "Discontent in Portlaoise," *AP/RN*, 17 June 1982, 5.

4 The Harvey/McCaughey/Smith Cumann: Sinn Féin in Portlaoise Prison, 1978–1986

1 Evans and Tonge, "From Abstentionism to Enthusiasm;" Lynn, "Tactic or Principle."

2 Ruairí Ó Brádaigh, *Dílseacht: The Story of Comdt. Gen. Tom Maguire and the Second (All-Ireland) Dáil* (Dublin: Irish Freedom Press, 1997).

3 For an analysis of the social and regional composition of the leadership of the Provisional Republican Movement, see Moloney, *A Secret History of the IRA*; White, *Provisional Irish Republicans.*

4 Sinn Féin, Constitution & Rules, Dublin, undated.

5 Harvey and McGlynn thirtieth anniversary commemoration, *An Phoblacht*, 28 August 2003.

6 Unknown, Sinn Féin. In Mountjoy + Portlaoise, private possession.

7 See Sinn Féin, *Éire Nua: The Social and Economic Programme of Sinn Féin* (Dublin: Sinn Féin, 1971).

8 Unknown, Sinn Féin. In Mountjoy + Portlaoise, private possession.

9 Unknown, Sinn Féin. In Mountjoy + Portlaoise, private possession.

10 Sinn Féin Minute Books, *Portlaoise Prison, Eanáir 1979 – Aibreán 1980*, private possession.

11 Unknown, Sinn Féin. In Mountjoy + Portlaoise, private possession.

12 National Graves Association, ed. *Belfast Graves* (Belfast: An Phoblacht, 1985), 53–6; Sinn Féin, ed. *Tírghrá: Ireland's Patriot Dead* (Dublin: Republican Publications, 2002), 165.

13 Unknown, Sinn Féin. In Mountjoy + Portlaoise, private possession.

14 Interview with Pat Treanor in Failte Cluain Eois, *Their Prisons, Our Stories*, 168–9.

15 Interview with Pat Treanor.
16 Interview with Seosamh Ó Maileoin, 30 April 2015.
17 Interview with Seosamh Ó Maileoin.
18 Interview with Jim Kavanagh, Wexford Town, Co. Wexford, 16 April 2015.
19 Interview with Jim Kavanagh.
20 Interview with Seosamh Ó Maileoin, 16 March 2015.
21 Reinisch, "The Fight for Political Status in Portlaoise Prison."
22 Interview with Matt Leen, Tralee, Co. Kerry, 19 April 2015.
23 Interview with Jim Kavanagh.
24 Interview with Seosamh Ó Maileoin, 16 March 2015.
25 Hiberno-English word for "fun."
26 Interview with Jim Kavanagh.
27 Interview with Dan Hoban.
28 Interview with Vivion Hayden, 14 April 2015.
29 Unknown, Sinn Féin. In Mountjoy + Portlaoise, private possession.
30 Interview with Seosamh Ó Maileoin, 16 March 2015.
31 Interview with John Carroll in Maire De Barra, Discontent in Portlaoise; *AP/RN*, 17 June 1982, 5.
32 Interview with Matt Leen.
33 Interview with Matt Treacy.
34 Coireall MacCurtáin is usually referred to as Cyril MacCurtain in the documents and interviews.
35 Jim Lynagh from County Tyrone is usually referred to as "S. Laighneach" in the minute books.
36 Interview with Pat Treanor in Fáilte Cluain Elois, *Their Prisons, Our Stories*, 166–71.
37 Interview with Seosamh Ó Maileoin, 16 March 2015.
38 Interview with Seosamh Ó Maileoin, 30 April 2015.
39 Interview with Matt Leen.
40 Interview with John Crawley, Monaghan Town, Co. Monaghan, 30 April 2015.
41 Interview with Matt Treacy.
42 Interview with Seosamh Ó Maileoin, 30 April 2015.
43 Interview with Seán Óg Ó Mórdha, Dublin, Co. Dublin, 17 April 2015.
44 Interview with Matt Treacy.
45 MacGiollaChríost, *Jailtacht*, 38; Whalen, *Contemporary Irish Republican Prison Writing*.
46 MacGiollaChríost, *Jailtacht*, 145.
47 MacGiollaChríost, *Jailtacht*.
48 Interview with Matt Treacy.
49 Reinisch, "Political Prisoners and the Irish Language."
50 Interview with Vivion Hayden, 14 April 2015.

51 Sinn Féin Minute Books, Portlaoise Prison, 1983/1984/1985, private possession.

52 Interview with Seosamh Ó Maileoin, 30 April 2015.

53 Interview with Vivion Hayden, 14 April 2014.

54 Interview with Vivion Hayden.

55 Interview with Jim Kavanagh.

56 Interview with Seosamh Ó Maileoin, 16 March 2015.

57 Interview with Seosamh Ó Maileoin.

58 Interview with Seosamh Ó Maileoin.

59 Interview with Jim Kavanagh.

60 Barrett, *Martin Ferris*, 181.

61 Barrett, *Martin Ferris*.

62 Barrett, *Martin Ferris*, 182–3.

63 Barrett, *Martin Ferris*, 183–4.

64 Interview with Seosamh Ó Maileoin, 16 March 2015.

65 Interview with Matt Treacy.

66 Robert W. White, *Provisional Irish Republicans*, 131–68.

67 For a detailed discussion of the Cumann minute books, see: Dieter Reinisch, "Debating Politics during Confinement."

68 Dieter Reinisch, "The Fight for Political Status in Portlaoise Prison."

5 "He Was Just Rhyming Off Pages of It": Internment and the Brownie Papers, 1971–1976/7

1 Rosa Gilbert, "No Rent, No Rates: Civil Disobedience against Internment in Northern Ireland, 1971–1974," *Studi irlandesi* 7 (2017).

2 Bennett, "Detention and Interrogation in Northern Ireland 1969–1975."

3 Dieter Reinisch, "How an Armagh Court Ruled Internment Was Unlawful in 1972," *RTÉ Brainstorm*, 5 January 2021, www.rte.ie /brainstorm/2021/0105/1187741-internment-northern-ireland -troubles-1970s-sean-moore.

4 Interview with Sean Moore, Monaghan. Co. Monaghan, 12 April 2017.

5 Reinisch, "How an Armagh Court Ruled Internment Was Unlawful."

6 Denis O'Hearn, "Repression and Solidary Cultures of Resistance: Irish Political Prisoners on Protest," *American Journal of Sociology* 115, no. 2 (2009).

7 Interview with Michael Donnelly, Derry City, Co. Derry, 17 April 2017.

8 Interview with John Nixon, Armagh City, Co. Armagh, 13 April 2017.

9 Interview with Michael Donnelly.

10 Interview with Séanna Walsh, Belfast, Co. Antrim, 29 July 2015.

11 Interview with Kevin Trainor, Armagh City, Co. Armagh, 14 April 2017.

12 Interview with Kevin Trainor.

13 Interview with Danny Morrison, Belfast, Co. Antrim, 28 July 2015.

14 Danny Morrison, "Walter Macken – Loyal Provincialist," *An Phoblacht*.

15 Interview with Danny Morrison.

16 Interview with Dáithí Ó Búitigh, Belfast, Co. Antrim, 7 April 2014.

17 Interview with Jimmy Kavanagh.

18 Interview with Michael Donnelly.

19 Interview with Dáithí Ó Búitigh.

20 The so-called Sunningdale Agreement was an attempt to establish a power-sharing Executive in Northern Ireland and a cross-border Council of Ireland. The agreement was signed in Sunningdale, Berkshire, on 9 December 1973, but Unionist opposition, violence, and a Loyalist general strike caused its collapse in May 1974.

21 Interview with Danny Morrison.

22 Interview with Danny Morrison.

23 Interview with John Nixon.

24 Interview with John Nixon.

25 Interview with Danny Morrison.

26 Interview with Michael Donnelly.

27 Interview with Dáithí Ó Búitigh.

28 Interview Séanna Walsh.

29 Interview with Anthony McInytre; Interview with Laurence McKeown, Dundalk, Co. Louth, 29 July 2015.

30 Interview with Michael Donnelly.

31 Interview with Michael Donnelly.

32 Interview with Dáithí Ó Búitigh.

33 Interview with Michael Donnelly.

34 Niall Carson and Paddy Hoey, "The Bell and the Blanket: Journals of Irish Republican Dissent," *New Hibernia Review* 16, no. 1 (2012). The archive of both magazines is available online in the Irish Republican Movement Collection: www.ulib.iupui.edu/collections/IrishRepublicanMovement.

35 Henry McDonald, "Writer Forced out of Home by IRA Threats," *The Guardian*, 1 April 2001.

36 Interview with Anthony McIntyre.

37 Interview with Danny Morrison.

38 Gerry Adams writing as Brownie, The Collected Brownie Articles; carried in *Republican News*, 16 August 1975 to 19 February 1977; P6221, NIPC, Linen Hall Library, Belfast.

39 Des O'Hagan, *Letters from Long Kesh* (Dublin: Citizen Press, 2012).

40 Whalen, *Contemporary Irish Republican Prison Writing*, 12.

41 Dieter Reinisch, "Prisoners as Leaders of Political Change: Cage 11 and the Peace Process in Northern Ireland," in *Historians on Leadership and Strategy: Case Studies From Antiquity to Modernity*, ed. Martin Gutmann (Cham: Springer, 2020).

42 Suzanne Breen, "The Tale of Brownie and the Bard," *News Letter*, 25 March 2004.

43 Interview with Dáithí Ó Búitigh.

44 Interview with Dáithí Ó Búitigh.

45 Robert W. White, *Out of the Ashes: An Oral History of the Provisional Irish Republican Movement* (Dublin: Merrion Press, 2017), 149.

46 White, *Out of the Ashes*, 135.

47 Ard Chomhairle, meaning "high council" in English, is the Irish term for the national leadership of Sinn Féin.

48 Interview with Gerard Hodgins.

49 Interview with Gerard Hodgins.

50 Interview with Gerard Hodgins.

51 Isabelle Duyvesteyn, "How New Is the New Terrorism?," *Studies in Conflict & Terrorism* 27, no. 5 (2004): 443; Doron Zimmermann, "Terrorism Transformed: The 'New Terrorism,' Impact Scalability and the Dynamic of Reciprocal Threat Perception," *Connections* 3, no. 1 (2004): 23.

52 Bruce Hoffman, "Change and Continuity in Terrorism," *Studies in Conflict and Terrorism* 24, no. 5 (2001): 417–18.

53 Antony Field, "The Hollow Hierarchy: Problems of Command and Control in the Provisional IRA," *Journal of Terrorism Research* 8, no. 3 (2017): 14.

6 Marxist Esperanto and Socialism in Cell 26: Reading, Thinking, and Writing in the H-Blocks, 1983–1989

1 White, *Out of the Ashes*, 144.

2 Reinisch, "Interview with Former Political Prisoner," 232–3.

3 Interview with John Nixon.

4 Interview with John Nixon.

5 The Warrenpoint ambush, or Narrow Water ambush, was an attack by the Provisional IRA on 27 August 1979. Eighteen British soldiers were killed and six were seriously injured, making it the deadliest attack on the British Army during the conflict.

6 Fáilte Cluain Elois, *Their Prisons, Our Stories*, 52.

7 Interview with John Nixon.

8 Interview with Gerard Hodgins.

9 Mary S. Corcoran, *Out of Order: The Political Imprisonment of Women in Northern Ireland, 1972–98* (Devon: Willan, 2006); Ciaran McLaughlin, "Memory, Place and Gender: Armagh Stories: Voices from the Gaol," *Memory Studies* (2017); Azrini Wahidin, "Menstruation as a Weapon of War: The Politics of the Bleeding Body for Women on Political Protest at Armagh Prison, Northern Ireland," *The Prison Journal* 99, no. 1 (2019), 112–31.

10 Interview with Seanna Walsh.
11 Interview with Anthony McIntyre.
12 Mickey Cooper, *The Prison Story* (Derry: Tar Abhaile, 2011), 47.
13 Cooper, *The Prison Story*.
14 Interview with Gerard Hodgins.
15 Interview with Gerard Hodgins.
16 Interview with Tommy McKearney, Monaghan Town, Co. Monaghan, 30 July 2015.
17 Reinisch, "Interview with Former Political Prisoner," 233.
18 Interview with Anthony McIntyre.
19 Interview with Gerard Hodgins.
20 The Open University course "State and Society" was taught by the Marxist sociologist Stuart Hall.
21 Interview with Gerard Hodgins.
22 Reinisch, "Interview with Former Political Prisoner," 228.
23 Dieter Reinisch, "Paulo Freire: The Brazilian Educator Who Shaped Prisoners in the Maze," *RTÉ Brainstorm*, 24 September 2021, www.rte.ie/brainstorm/2021/0924/1248713-paulo-freire-brazilian-educator-shaped-long-kesh-prisoners.
24 Interview with Gerard Hodgins.
25 Felim O'Hagan, *Reflections on the Culture of Resistance in Long Kesh* (Sinn Féin, 1991), 7–8.
26 Interview with Danny Morrison.
27 Interview with Danny Morrison.
28 Reinisch, "Interview with Former Political Prisoner," 236.
29 For a detailed analysis of the debates surrounding abstentionism in Portlaoise, see: Reinisch, "Debating Politics During Confinement."
30 Interview with Tommy McKearney, 30 July 2015.
31 Ernst Friedrich Schumacher was a German-British economist who is best known for his proposals for human-scale, decentralized, and appropriate technologies. In 1973, he published his most famous book *Small Is Beautiful: A Study of Economics As If People Mattered*.
32 Interview with Tommy McKearney, 30 July 2015.
33 Liam O'Ruairc, "The League of Communist Republicans, 1986–1991," *Fourthwrite* (2001).
34 Interview with Tommy McKearney.
35 Interview with Tommy McKearney.
36 Interview with Anthony McIntyre.
37 Interview with Anthony McIntyre.
38 Interview with Anthony McIntyre.
39 Interview with Tommy McKearney.
40 Interview with Anthony McIntyre.

41 Republican Prisoners of War, *Questions of History* (Dublin: AP/RN Print and Sinn Féin Education Department, 1987), 1.

42 Republican Prisoners of War, *Questions of History*.

43 Interview with Anthony McIntyre.

44 Fáilte Cluain Eois, *Their Prisons, Our Stories*, 82.

45 Interview with Gerard Hodgins.

46 Interview with Tommy McKearney, 5 August 2015.

47 Interview with Tommy McKearney.

48 Named after the Irish economist Thomas Kenneth Whitaker (8 December 1916–9 January 2017).

49 Interview with Anthony McIntyre.

50 O'Ruairc, "The League of Communist Republicans," 2.

51 Interview with Tommy McKearney, 30 July 2015.

52 Interview with Gerard Hodgins.

53 Interview with Gerard Hodgins.

7 "It's Only When You Look Back …": The Fall of the Berlin Wall and the Peace Process in the 1990s

1 Interview with Danny Morrison.

2 Interview with Tommy McKearney.

3 Interview with Tommy McKearney.

4 "Rang" is the Irish term for "class." It was used by the Republican prisoners for classes and lectures.

5 Interview with Danny Morrison.

6 Interview with Anthony McIntyre.

7 Interview with Seanna Walsh.

8 Éirígí is a small Republican party that split from Sinn Féin after the acceptance of the Northern Irish police force PSNI at a special Ard-Fheis in 2007.

9 Agreement reached in the multi-party negotiations (10 April 1998); http://cain.ulst.ac.uk/events/peace/docs/agreement.htm.

10 Interview with Gerard Hodgins.

11 Interview with Seanna Walsh.

12 Interview with Danny Morrison.

13 Interview with Danny Morrison.

14 Interview with Tommy McKearney.

15 The Sash is a ballad commemorating the victory of King William III in the Williamite War in Ireland in 1690–1. It is particularly popular among Unionists and Loyalists because it glorifies the victory of the Protestants over Catholics during major battles during that war such as the Siege of Derry or the Battle of the Boyne.

16 A Protestant working-class area with particularly strong support for militant Loyalism in West-Belfast.

17 Interview with Anthony McIntyre.

18 Interview with Anthony McIntyre.

19 Interview with Seanna Walsh.

20 In the prison diary Bobby Sands wrote during the first seventeen days of his hunger strike in 1981, he noted: "I have always taken a lesson from something that was told me by a sound man, that is, that everyone, Republican or otherwise, has his own particular part to play. No part is too great or too small, no one is too old or too young to do something." Bobby Sands, *Writings from Prison* (Cork: Mercier Press, 1997).

21 Reinisch, "Interview with Former Political Prisoner," 228–9.

22 Interview with Gerard Hodgins.

Conclusion: An Irish Century of Camps

1 For a detailed analysis, see: Dieter Reinisch, "Prisoners as Leaders of Political Change."

2 Connal Parr, *Inventing the Myth: Political Passions and the Ulster Protestant Imagination* (Oxford: Oxford University Press, 2017), 134–41; Whalen, *Contemporary Irish Republican Prison Writing*.

3 J. Bowyer Bell, *On Revolt: Strategies of National Liberation* (Cambridge, MA: Harvard University Press, 1976); Charles Townshend, *Terrorism: A Very Short Introduction* (Oxford: Oxford University Press, 2011).

4 Lisa Stampnitzky, *Disciplining Terror: How Experts Invented "Terrorism"* (Cambridge: Cambridge University Press, 2013); Andrew Silke and Jennifer Schmidt-Petersen, "The Golden Age? What the 100 Most Cited Articles in Terrorism Studies Tell Us," *Terrorism and Political Violence* 29, no. 4 (2017).

5 Andrew Silke, *Talking Terror* podcast, 20 September 2017, https://soundcloud.com/user-366747443/andrew-silke.

6 Martha Crenshaw, "The Psychology of Terrorism: An Agenda for the 21st Century," *Political Psychology* 21, no. 2 (2000).

7 Richard English, *Does Terrorism Work?* (Oxford: Oxford University Press, 2016), 1.

8 English, *Does Terrorism Work?*; Stefan Berger and Holger Nehring, "Introduction: Towards a Global History of Social Movements," in *The History of Social Movements in Global Perspective* (Springer, 2017); White, *Out of the Ashes*.

9 Robert W. White and Tijen Demirel-Pegg, "Social Movements and Social Movement Organizations: Recruitment, Ideology, and Splits," in *The Troubles: Northern Ireland and Theories of Social Movements*, ed. Lorenzo

Bosi and Gianluca De Fazio (Amsterdam: Amsterdam University Press, 2017). An earlier historical approach has been provided by Charles Tilly in Charles Tilly, Louise Tilly, and Richard Tilly, *The Rebellious Century, 1830–1930* (Cambridge, MA: Harvard University Press, 1975).

10 Giovanni Mario Ceci, "A 'Historical Turn' in Terrorism Studies?," *Journal of Contemporary History* 51, no. 4 (2016).

11 Bettina Greiner and Alan Kramer, eds., *Welt der Lager: Zur "Erfolgsgeschichte" einer Institution* (Berlin: DeGruyter, 2013); Christoph Jahr and Jens Thiel, eds., *Lager vor Auschwitz: Gewalt und Integration im 20. Jahrhundert* (Berlin: Metropol, 2013).

12 Dan Stone, *Concentration Camps: A Short History* (Oxford: Oxford University Press, 2017).

13 Andrea Pitzer, *One Long Night: A Global History of Concentration Camps* (Boston: Little, Brown and Company, 2017).

14 Gregor Feindt, Anke Hilbrenner, and Dittmar Dahlmann, eds., *Sport under Unexpected Circumstances: Violence, Discipline, and Leisure in Penal and Internment Camps* (Göttingen: Vandenhoeck & Ruprecht, 2018).

15 Dieter Reinisch, "Sport, Resistance, and Irish Republican Identity in Internment Camps and Prisons," in *Sport under Unexpected Circumstances: Violence, Discipline, and Leisure in Penal and Internment Camps*, ed. Gregor Feindt, Anke Hilbrenner, and Dittmar Dahlmann (Göttingen: Vandenhoeck & Ruprecht, 2018).

16 Stone, *Concentration Camps*, 122.

17 Giorgio Agamben, *State of Exception* (Chicago: University of Chicago Press, 2005).

18 John McGuffin, *Internment* (Tralee: Anvil Books, 1973).

19 Jonathan Hyslop, "The Invention of the Concentration Camp: Cuba, Southern Africa and the Philippines, 1896–1907," *South African Historical Journal* 63, no. 2 (2011).

Bibliography

Agamben, Giorgio. *State of Exception*. Chicago: University of Chicago Press, 2005.

Alexander, Michelle. *The New Jim Crow: Mass Incarceration in the Age of Colorblindness*. New York: New Press, 2012.

Aretxaga, Begoña. *Shattering Silence: Women, Nationalism and Political Subjectivity in Northern Ireland*. Princeton, NJ: Princeton University Press, 1997.

Arthur, Paul. "Elite Studies in a Paranocracy: The Northern Ireland Case." In *Research Methods for Elite Studies*, edited by George Moyser and Margaret Wagstaffe, 202–15. London: Allen & Unwin, 1987.

Barrett, J.J. *Martin Ferris: Man of Kerry*. Dingle, Republic of Ireland: Brandon, 2005.

Bauman, Zygmunt. "Das Jahrhundert Der Lager?" In *Genozid und Moderne: Band 1: Strukturen Kollektiver Gewalt Im 20. Jahrhundert*, edited by Mihran Dabag and Kristin Platt, 81–99. Wiesbaden: VS Verlag für Sozialwissenschaften, 1998.

Behan, Cormac. "'We Are All Convicted Criminals'? Prisoners, Protest and Penal Politics in the Republic of Ireland." *Journal of Social History* 52, no. 2 (2018): 501–26.

Bell, J. Bowyer. *On Revolt: Strategies of National Liberation*. Cambridge, MA: Harvard University Press, 1976.

Bennett, Huw. "Detention and Interrogation in Northern Ireland 1969–1975." In *Prisoners in War*, edited by Sibylle Scheipers, 187–203. Oxford: Oxford University Press, 2010.

– "'Smoke without Fire'? Allegations against the British Army in Northern Ireland, 1972–5." *Twentieth Century British History* 24, no. 2 (2013): 275–304.

Beresford, David. *Ten Men Dead: The Story of the 1981 Irish Hunger Strike*. London: Grafton, 1987.

Berger, Stefan, and Holger Nehring. "Introduction: Towards a Global History of Social Movements." In *The History of Social Movements in Global*

Perspective, edited by Stefan Berger and Holger Nehring, 1–35: Cham, Switzerland: Springer, 2017.

Bishop, Patrick Joseph, and Eamonn Mallie. *The Provisional IRA*. London: Corgi Books, 1994.

Blee, Kathleen M. *Women of the Klan: Racism and Gender in the 1920s*. Los Angeles: University of California, 2008.

Bogner, Alexander, and Wolfgang Menz. "Das Theoriegenerierende Experteninterview: Erkenntnisinteresse, Wissensformen, Interaktion." In *Das Experteninterview: Theorie, Methode, Anwendungen*, edited by Alexander Bogner, Beate Littig, and Wolfgang Menz, 33–70. Wiesbaden: VS-Verlag für Sozialwissenschaften, 2005.

Bonakdarian, Mansour. "Iranian Consecration of Irish Nationalist 'Martyrs': The Islamic Republic of Iran and the 1981 Republican Prisoners' Hunger Strike in Northern Ireland." *Social History* 43, no. 3: 293–331.

Bosi, Lorenzo. "Explaining Pathways to Armed Activism in the Provisional Irish Republican Army, 1969–1972." *Social Science History* 36, no. 3 (2012): 347–90.

– "Contextualizing the Biographical Outcomes of Provisional IRA Former Activists: A Structure-Agency Dynamic." In *Activists Forever? The Long-Term Impacts of Political Activism*, edited by Olivier Fillieule and Erik Neveu, 202–20. Cambridge: Cambridge University Press, 2019.

Buntman, Fran Lisa. *Robben Island and Prisoner Resistance to Apartheid*. Cambridge: Cambridge University Press, 2003.

Caesar, Samantha Anne. "Captive or Criminal?: Reappraising the Legal Status of IRA Prisoners at the Height of the Troubles under International Law." *Duke Journal of Comparative & International Law* 27, no. 2 (2017): 323–48.

Campbell, Brian, Laurence McKeown, and Felim O'Hagan. *Nor Meekly Serve My Time: The H-Block Struggle, 1976–1981*. Belfast: Beyond the Pale Publications, 1998.

Carson, Niall, and Paddy Hoey. "The Bell and the Blanket: Journals of Irish Republican Dissent." *New Hibernia Review* 16, no. 1 (2012): 75–93.

Ceci, Giovanni Mario. "A 'Historical Turn' in Terrorism Studies?" *Journal of Contemporary History* 51, no. 4 (2016): 888–96.

Clarke, Liam, and Kathryn Johnston. *Martin McGuinness: From Guns to Government*. Edinburgh: Mainstream Publishing, 2001.

Coogan, Tim Pat. *The Troubles: Ireland's Ordeal 1966–1996 and the Search for Peace*. London: Random House, 1996.

Corcoran, Mary S. *Out of Order: The Political Imprisonment of Women in Northern Ireland, 1972–98*. Devon, UK: Willan, 2006.

Crenshaw, Martha. "The Psychology of Terrorism: An Agenda for the 21st Century." *Political Psychology* 21, no. 2 (2000): 405–20.

Crewe, Ben. "Not Looking Hard Enough Masculinity, Emotion, and Prison Research." *Qualitative Inquiry* 20, no. 4 (2014): 392–403.

Dana, Jacqueline, and Seán McMonagle. "Deconstructing 'Criminalization': The Politics of Collective Education in the H-Blocks." *Journal of Prisoners on Prisons* 8, nos. 1 & 2 (1997): 418–21.

Duyvesteyn, Isabelle. "How New Is the New Terrorism?" *Studies in Conflict & Terrorism* 27, no. 5 (2004): 439–54.

Earle, Rod, and James Mehigan. *Degrees of Freedom: Prison Education at the Open University*. Bristol, UK: Policy Press, 2019.

English, Richard. "Left on the Shelf." *Fortnight* no. 388 (2000): 32–3.

– *Armed Struggle: The History of the IRA*. Oxford: Oxford University Press, 2003.

– *Does Terrorism Work?* Oxford: Oxford University Press, 2016.

Eois, Fáilte Cluain. *Their Prisons, Our Stories*. Monaghan, Republic of Ireland: Fáilte Cluain Eois Books, 2015.

Evans, Jocelyn, and Jonathan Tonge. "From Abstentionism to Enthusiasm: Sinn Féin, Nationalist Electors and Support for Devolved Power-Sharing in Northern Ireland." *Irish Political Studies* 28, no. 1 (2013): 39–57.

Feindt, Gregor, Anke Hilbrenner, and Dittmar Dahlmann, eds. *Sport under Unexpected Circumstances: Violence, Discipline, and Leisure in Penal and Internment Camps*. Göttingen: Vandenhoeck & Ruprecht, 2018.

Ferguson, Neil. "Northern Irish Ex-Prisoners: The Impact of Imprisonment on Prisoners and the Peace Process in Northern Ireland." In *Prison, Terrorism and Extremism: Critical Issues in Management, Radicalisation and Reform*, edited by Andrew Silke, 270–83. London: Routledge, 2014.

Field, Antony. "The Hollow Hierarchy: Problems of Command and Control in the Provisional IRA." *Journal of Terrorism Research* 8, no. 3 (2017): 11–23.

Findlay, Mark. "Organized Resistance, Terrorism, and Criminality in Ireland: The State's Construction of the Control Equation." *Crime and Social Justice* 21/22 (1984): 95–115.

– "'Criminalization' and the Detention of 'Political Prisoners': An Irish Perspective." *Contemporary Crises* 9, no. 1 (1985): 1–17.

Finnane, Mark, and Ian O'Donnell. "Crime and Punishment." In *The Cambridge Social History of Modern Ireland*, edited by Eugenio F. Biagini and Mary E. Daly, 363–82. Cambridge: Cambridge University Press, 2017.

Forth, Aidan. *Barbed-Wire Imperialism: Britain's Empire of Camps, 1876–1903*. Oakland: University of California Press, 2017.

Foucault, Michel. *Discipline and Punish: The Birth of the Prison*. London: Allen Lane, 1977.

Gabaccia, Donna R., and Franca Iacovetta. "Introduction." In *Borders, Conflict Zones, and Memory: Scholarly Engagements with Luisa Passerini*, edited by Donna R. Gabaccia and Franca Iacovetta, 1–20. London: Routledge, 2018.

Gambetta, Diego, and Steffen Hertog. *Engineers of Jihad: The Curious Connection between Violent Extremism and Education*. Princeton, NJ: Princeton University Press, 2016.

Gilbert, Rosa. "No Rent, No Rates: Civil Disobedience against Internment in Northern Ireland, 1971–1974." *Studi irlandesi* 7 (2017): 19–43.

Gill, Paul, and John Horgan. "Who Were the Volunteers? The Shifting Sociological and Operational Profile of 1240 Provisional Irish Republican Army Members." *Terrorism and Political Violence* 25, no. 3 (2013): 435–56.

Gillespie, Gordon. *A Short History of the Troubles*. Dublin: Gill & Macmillan, 2010.

Gilmartin, Niall ,and Margaret M. Scull. "Republican Women and Catholic Church Responses to the Strip Searching of Female Prisoners in Northern Ireland, 1982–92." *Women's History Review* (2021), DOI: 10.1080/09612025.2021.1958455.

Goffman, Erving. *Asylums*. Harmondsworth, UK: Penguin, 1968.

Goldman, Liran. "From Criminals to Terrorists: The US Experience of Prison Radicalization." In *Prisons, Terrorism, and Extremism: Critical Issues in Management, Radicalization, and Reform,* edited by Andrew Silke, 47–59. London: Routledge, 2014.

Goldring, Maurice. "Jours Tranquilles À Belfast." *Les cahiers de médiologie* 13, no. 1 (2002): 131–8.

Grant, Kevin. "British Suffragettes and the Russian Method of Hunger Strike." *Comparative Studies in Society and History* 53, no. 1 (2011): 113–43.

Greiner, Bettina, and Alan Kramer, eds. *Welt Der Lager: Zur "Erfolgsgeschichte" einer Institution*. Berlin: DeGruyter, 2013.

Grounds, Adrian, and Ruth Jamieson. "No Sense of an Ending: Researching the Experience of Imprisonment and Release among Republican Ex-Prisoners." *Theoretical Criminology* 7, no. 3 (2003): 347–62.

Hamber, Brandon. "'Blocks to the Future': A Pilot Study of the Long-Term Psychological Impact of the 'No Wash/Blanket' Protest." Derry, Northern Ireland: Action and Research International, 2005.

– "Flying Flags of Fear: The Role of Fear in the Process of Political Transition." *Journal of Human Rights* 5, no. 1 (2006): 127–42.

Hanley, Brian. *The Impact of the Troubles on the Republic of Ireland, 1968–79: Boiling Volcano?* Manchester: Manchester University Press, 2018.

Hennessey, Thomas. *Northern Ireland: The Origins of the Troubles*. Dublin: Gill & Macmillan, 2005.

– *The Evolution of the Troubles, 1970–72*. Dublin: Irish Academic Press, 2007.

– *Hunger Strike: Margaret Thatcher's Battle with the IRA*. Dublin: Irish Academic Press, 2014.

Hepworth, Jack. *"The Age-Old Struggle": Irish Republicanism from the Battle of the Bogside to the Belfast Agreement, 1969–1998*. Liverpool: Liverpool University Press, 2021.

Hoffman, Bruce. "Change and Continuity in Terrorism." *Studies in Conflict and Terrorism* 24, no. 5 (2001): 417–28.

Horgan, John. *Divided We Stand: The Strategy and Psychology of Ireland's Dissident Terrorists*. Oxford: Oxford University Press, 2012.

Hughes, Brendan, and Douglas Dalby. *Up Like a Bird: The Rise and Fall of an IRA Commander*. Castleisland, Republic of Ireland: Time Warp Book, 2021.

Hyslop, Jonathan. "The Invention of the Concentration Camp: Cuba, Southern Africa and the Philippines, 1896–1907." *South African Historical Journal* 63, no. 2 (2011): 251–76.

Irwin, Tracy. "Prison Education in Northern Ireland: Learning from Our Paramilitary Past." *The Howard Journal of Criminal Justice* 42, no. 5 (2003): 471–84.

Jahr, Christoph, and Jens Thiel, eds. *Lager vor Auschwitz: Gewalt und Integration im 20. Jahrhundert*. Berlin: Metropol, 2013.

Jamieson, Ruth, and Adrian Grounds. *No Sense of an Ending: The Effects of Long-Term Imprisonment amongst Republican Prisoners and Their Families*. Monaghan, Republic of Ireland: Seesyum Press, 2002.

Jamieson, Ruth, Peter Shirlow, and Adrian Grounds. "Ageing and Social Exclusion among Former Politically Motivated Prisoners in Northern Ireland." Belfast: Changing Ageing Partnership, 2010.

Kane, Anne, and Dieter Reinisch, eds. *Irish Republican Counterpublic: Armed Struggle and the Construction of a Radical Nationalist Community in Northern Ireland*. London: Routledge, 2023.

Khalil, James. "A Guide to Interviewing Terrorists and Violent Extremists." *Studies in Conflict & Terrorism* 42, no. 4 (2019): 429–43.

Kilcommins, Shane, Ian O'Donnell, Eoin O'Sullivan, and Barry Vaughan. *Crime, Punishment and the Search for Order in Ireland*. Dublin: Institute of Public Administration, 2004.

Lagemann, Ellen Condliffe. *Liberating Minds: The Case for College in Prison*. New York: New Press, 2017.

Laliotou, Ioanna. "On Luisa Passerini: Subjectivity, Europe, Affective Historiography." In *Borders, Conflict Zones, and Memory: Scholarly Engagements with Luisa Passerini*, edited by Donna R. Gabaccia and Franca Iacovetta. London: Routledge, 2018.

Lonergan, John. *The Governor*. Dublin: Penguin, 2010.

Lynn, Brendan. "Tactic or Principle? The Evolution of Republican Thinking on Abstentionism in Ireland, 1970–1998." *Irish Political Studies* 17, no. 2 (2002): 74–94.

MacGiollaChríost, Diarmait. *Jailtacht: The Irish Language, Symbolic Power and Political Violence in Northern Ireland, 1972–2008*. Cardiff: University of Wales Press, 2012.

Maguire, John. *IRA Internments and the Irish Government: Subversives and the State, 1939–1962*. Dublin: Irish Academic Press, 2008.

McCleery, Martin. "Debunking the Myths of Operation Demetrius: The Introduction of Internment in Northern Ireland in 1971." *Irish Political Studies* 27, no. 3 (2012): 411–30.

– *Operation Demetrius and Its Aftermath: A New History of the Use of Internment without Trial in Northern Ireland 1971–75*. Manchester: Manchester University Press, 2015.

McConville, Seán. *Irish Political Prisoners, 1920–1962: Pilgrimage of Desolation*. London: Routledge, 2014.

McEvoy, Kieran. *Paramilitary Imprisonment in Northern Ireland: Resistance, Management, and Release*. Oxford: Oxford University Press, 2001.

– "Elite Interviewing in a Divided Society: Lessons from Northern Ireland." *Politics* 26, no. 3 (2006): 184–91.

– *The Politics of Northern Ireland (Politics Study Guides)*. Edinburgh: Edinburgh University Press, 2008.

McEvoy, Kieran, David O'Mahony, Carol Horner, and Olwen Lyner. "The Home Front: The Families of Politically Motivated Prisoners in Northern Ireland." *British Journal of Criminology* 39, no. 2 (1999): 175–97.

McGlinchey, Marisa. *Unfinished Business: The Politics of "Dissident" Irish Republicanism*. Manchester: Manchester University Press, 2019.

McGuffin, John. *Internment*. Tralee: Anvil Books, 1973.

McKenna, Yvonne. "Sisterhood? Exploring Power Relations in the Collection of Oral History." *Oral History* 31, no. 1 (2003): 65–72.

McKeown, Laurence. *Out of Time: Irish Republican Prisoners, Long Kesh, 1972–2000*. Belfast: Beyond the Pale, 2001.

– "'Casualties of War' or 'Agents of Change': Irish Republican Prisoners, Maze/Long Kesh Prison, 1972–2000." In *Political Ideology in Ireland: From the Enlightenment to the Present*, edited by Olivier Coquelin, Patrick Galliou, and Thierry Robin, 274–83. Newcastle: Cambridge Scholars Publishing, 2009.

McLaughlin, Ciaran. "Memory, Place and Gender: Armagh Stories: Voices from the Gaol." *Memory Studies* 13, no. 4 (2017): 677–90.

McManus, Cathal. "Conceptualising Islamic 'Radicalisation' in Europe through "Othering": Lessons from the Conflict in Northern Ireland." *Terrorism and Political Violence* 32, vol. 2 (2020): 325–44.

Miller, Ian. *A History of Force Feeding: Hunger Strikes, Prisons and Medical Ethics, 1909–1974*. Basingstoke: Palgrave Macmillan, 2016.

Mitchell, Claire. "Behind the Ethnic Marker: Religion and Social Identification in Northern Ireland." *Sociology of Religion* 66, no. 1 (2005): 3–21.

– "The Limits of Legitimacy: Former Loyalist Combatants and Peace Building in Northern Ireland." *Irish Political Studies* 23, no. 1 (2008): 1–19.

Moloney, Ed. *A Secret History of the IRA*. New York: W.W. Norton, 2002.

Morrison, John F. *Origins and Rise of Dissident Irish Republicanism: The Role and Impact of Organizational Splits*. London: Bloomsbury, 2013.

– "A Time to Think, a Time to Talk: Irish Republican Prisoners in the Northern Irish Peace Process." In *Prisons, Terrorism and Extremism: Critical*

Issues in Management, Radicalisation and Reform, edited by Andrew Silke, 75–86. London: Routledge, 2014.

– "Fighting Talk: The Statements of 'the IRA/New IRA.'" *Terrorism and Political Violence* 28, no. 3 (2016): 598–619.

Mulholland, Marc. *Northern Ireland: A Very Short Introduction*. Oxford: Oxford University Press, 2003.

Mulroe, Patrick. *Bombs, Bullets and the Border: Ireland's Frontier: Irish Security Policy, 1969–1978*. Dublin: Irish Academic Press, 2017.

Murphy, William. *Political Imprisonment & the Irish, 1912–1921*. Oxford: Oxford University Press, 2014.

– "Justice and Uncertainty." *Irish Economic and Social History* 47 (2020): 112–21.

Ó Beacháin, Donnacha. "From Revolutionaries to Politicians: Deradicalization and the Irish Experience." *Radical History Review* 85, no. 1 (2003): 114–23.

Ó Brádaigh, Ruairí. *Dílseacht: The Story of Comdt. Gen. Tom Maguire and the Second (All-Ireland) Dáil*. Dublin: Irish Freedom Press, 1997.

O'Brien, Brendan. *The Long War: The IRA and Sinn Féin*. New York: Syracuse University Press, 1999.

Ó Faoleán, Gearóid. *A Broad Church: The Provisional Ira in the Republic of Ireland 1969–1980*. Dublin: Merrion Press, 2019.

OFMDFM. *Recruiting People with Conflict-Related Convictions: Employers' Guidance*. Belfast: OFMDFM, 2007.

Ó hÁdhmaill, Féilim. *Equal Citizenship for a New Society? An Analysis of Training and Employment Opportunities for Republican Ex-Prisoners in Belfast*. Belfast: Coiste na nIarChimí, 2001.

O'Hagan, Des. *Letters from Long Kesh*. Dublin: Citizen Press, 2012.

O'Hearn, Denis. *Nothing but an Unfinished Song: Bobby Sands, the Irish Hunger Striker Who Ignited a Generation*. New York: Nation Books, 2006.

– "Repression and Solidary Cultures of Resistance: Irish Political Prisoners on Protest." *American Journal of Sociology* 115, no. 2 (2009): 491–526.

O'Leary, Brendan. "IRA: Irish Republican Army (Óglaigh Na hÉireann)." In *Terror, Insurgency and the State: Ending Protracted Conflicts*, edited by Marianne Heiberg, Brendan O'Leary, and John Tirman, 189–228. Philadelphia: University of Pennsylvania Press, 2007.

O'Mahony, Sean. *Frongoch: University of Revolution*. Dublin: FDR Teoranta, 1987.

Ó'Mocháin, Deaglán. "Criminalization and the Post Hunger Strike Resistance of IRA Prisoners in the H-Blocks of Long Kesh." PhD diss., Queen's University, 2011.

O'Neill, Paul. *An Loiste Uir: Prisoner/Ex-Prisoners Project*. Belfast: An Loiste Uir, 1998.

O'Rawe, Richard. *Blanketmen: An Untold Story of the H-Block Hunger Strike*. Dublin: New Island, 2005.

O'Sullivan, Eoin, and Ian O'Donnell, eds. *Coercive Confinement in Ireland: Patients, Prisoners and Penitents*. Manchester: Manchester University Press, 2012.

Parr, Connal. *Inventing the Myth: Political Passions and the Ulster Protestant Imagination*. Oxford: Oxford University Press, 2017.

Passerini, Luisa. "'Utopia' and Desire." *Thesis Eleven* 68, no. 1 (2002): 11–30.

– *Memory and Utopia: The Primacy of Inter-Subjectivity*. Critical Histories of Subjectivity and Culture. Edited by Barbara Caine and Glenda Sluga. London: Routledge, 2014.

Pickering, Richard. "Terrorism, Extremists, Radicalisation and the Offender Management System in England and Wales." In *Prisons, Terrorism and Extremism: Critical Issues in Management, Radicalisation and Reform*, edited by Andrew Silke, 159–68. London: Routledge, 2014.

Pitzer, Andrea. *One Long Night: A Global History of Concentration Camps*. Boston: Little, Brown and Company, 2017.

Reinisch, Dieter. "Sport, Resistance, and Irish Republican Identity in Internment Camps and Prisons." In *Sport under Unexpected Circumstances: Violence, Discipline, and Leisure in Penal and Internment Camps*, edited by Gregor Feindt, Anke Hilbrenner, and Dittmar Dahlmann, 245–66. Göttingen: Vandenhoeck & Ruprecht, 2018.

– "Sport, Memory, and Nostalgia: The Lives of Irish Republicans in Internment Camps and Prisons, 1971–2000," *The International Journal of the History of Sport* 36, nos. 13–14 (2019): 1180–96.

– "Prisoners as Leaders of Political Change: Cage 11 and the Peace Process in Northern Ireland." In *Historians on Leadership and Strategy: Case Studies from Antiquity to Modernity*, edited by Martin Gutmann, 55–75. Cham: Springer, 2020a.

– "Teenagers and Young Adults in Dissident Irish Republicanism: A Case Study of Na Fianna Éireann in Dublin." *Critical Studies on Terrorism* 13, no. 4 (2020b): 702–23.

– "Debating Politics during Confinement: Newly Discovered Notebooks of the Sinn Féin Portlaoise Prison Cumann, 1979–1985." *Archives* 56, no. 2 (2021a): 99–122.

– "The Fight for Political Status in Portlaoise Prison, 1973–7: Prologue the H-Blocks Struggle." *War & Society* 40, no. 2 (2021b), 134–54.

– "'Is Austria a Catholic Country?': Trust and Intersubjectivity in Post-Conflict Northern Ireland." *Oral History Review* 48, no. 2 (2021c).

– "Corporeality, Militant Performance, and the Northern Irish Prisons Protests, 1971–1983." In *Performing Memory: Corporeality, Visuality, and Mobility after 1968*, edited by Luisa Passerini and Dieter Reinisch. New York: Berghahn, forthcoming.

Ritchie, Michael. *The Cost of Imprisonment*. Belfast: Tús Nua, 1998.

Rogan, Mary. *Prison Policy in Ireland: Politics, Penal-Welfarism and Political Imprisonment*. London: Routledge, 2011.

Rolston, Bill. *Review of Literature on Republican and Loyalist Ex-Prisoners*. Belfast: OFMDFM, 2011.

Rooney, Kevin. "Education: A Panacea for Our Sectarian Ills?" In *Peace or War? Understanding the Peace Process in Northern Ireland*, edited by Chris Gilligan and Jon Tonge, 119–32. Aldershot: Ashgate, 1997.

Ross, F. Stuart. *Smashing H-Block: The Rise and Fall of the Popular Campaign against Criminalization, 1976–1982*. Liverpool: Liverpool University Press, 2011.

– "The Prisoners' Support Campaign, Sinn Féin and the Hunger Strikes." In *Irish Republican Counterpublic: Armed Struggle and the Construction of a Radical Nationalist Community in Northern Ireland*, edited by Anne Kane and Dieter Reinisch. London: Routledge, forthcoming.

Ryder, Chris. *The Fateful Split: Catholics and the Royal Ulster Constabulary*. London: Methuen, 2004.

Sawicki, Jana. "Feminism, Foucault and 'Subjects' of Power and Freedom." In *The Later Foucault*, edited by Jeremy Moss, 93–107. London: Sage, 1998.

Scheipers, Sibylle. "Introduction: Prisoners in War." In *Prisoners in War*, edited by Sibylle Scheipers, 1–23. Oxford: Oxford University Press, 2010.

Schmid, Alex P. "Radicalisation, De-Radicalisation, Counter-Radicalisation: A Conceptual Discussion and Literature Review." *ICCT Research Paper* 97 (2013).

Shankman, Steven. *Turned inside Out: Reading the Russian Novel in Prison*. Evanston, IL: Northwestern University Press, 2017.

Shirlow, Peter. *The State They Are In: An Independent Evaluation*. Belfast: University of Ulster Social Exclusion Research Unit, 2001.

Shirlow, Peter, and Kieran McEvoy. *Beyond the Wire: Former Prisoners and Conflict Transformation in Northern Ireland*. London: Pluto Press, 2008.

Shirlow, Peter, Jon Tonge, James W. McAuley, and Catherine McGlynn. *Abandoning Historical Conflict? Former Paramilitary Prisoners and Political Reconciliation in Northern Ireland*. Manchester: Manchester University Press, 2010.

Silke, Andrew. "Becoming a Terrorist." In *Terrorists, Victims and Society: Psychological Perspectives on Terrorism and Its Consequences*, edited by Andrew Silke, 29–53. Chichester: Wiley, 2003.

– "The Impact of 9/11 on Research on Terrorism." In *Mapping Terrorism Research: State of the Art, Gaps and Future Directions*, edited by Magnus Ranstorp, 76–93. London: Routledge, 2007.

– "Terrorists, Extremists and Prison: An Introduction to the Critical Issues." In *Prisons, Terrorism and Extremism: Critical Issues in Managment, Radicalisation and Reform*, edited by Andrew Silke, 3–15. London: Routledge, 2014.

Silke, Andrew, and Jennifer Schmidt-Petersen. "The Golden Age? What the 100 Most Cited Articles in Terrorism Studies Tell Us." *Terrorism and Political Violence* 29, no. 4 (2017): 692–712.

Sinai, Joshua. "Developing a Model or Prison Radicalisation." In *Prisons, Terrorism and Extremism: Critical Issues in Management, Radicalisation and Reform*, edited by Andrew Silke, 35–46. London: Routledge, 2014.

Stampnitzky, Lisa. *Disciplining Terror: How Experts Invented "Terrorism."* Cambridge: Cambridge University Press, 2013.

Stone, Dan. *Concentration Camps: A Short History*. Oxford: Oxford University Press, 2017.

Tilly, Charles, Louise Tilly, and Richard Tilly. *The Rebellious Century, 1830–1930*. Cambridge, MA: Harvard University Press, 1975.

Tomlinson, Mike. "Imprisoned Ireland." In *Western European Penal Systems. A Critical Anatomy*, edited by Vincenzo Ruggiero, Mick Ryan, and Joe Sim, 194–227. London: Sage, 1995.

Toolis, Kevin. *Rebel Hearts: Journeys within the IRA's Soul*. London: Picador, 1997.

Townshend, Charles. *Terrorism: A Very Short Introduction*. Oxford: Oxford University Press, 2011.

Voglis, Polymeris. *Becoming a Subject: Political Prisoners during the Greek Civil War*. Oxford: Berghahn Books, 2002.

Wahidin, Azrini. "Menstruation as a Weapon of War: The Politics of the Bleeding Body for Women on Political Protest at Armagh Prison, Northern Ireland." *The Prison Journal* 99, no. 1 (2019): 112–31.

Walker, Clive. "Irish Republican Prisoners: Political Detainees, Prisoners of War or Common Criminals?" *The Irish Jurist* 24 (new series), no. 2 (1984): 189–225.

Wall, Oisín. "'Embarrassing the State': The 'Ordinary' Prisoner Rights Movement in Ireland, 1972–6." *Journal of Contemporary History* 55, no. 2 (2020): 388–410.

Whalen, Lachlan. *Contemporary Irish Republican Prison Writing: Writing and Resistance*. New York: Palgrave Macmillan, 2007.

– "'A Womanish Thing': The Price Sisters and the Gendered Dimensions of Irish Republican Hunger Strikes in England, 1973–74." *New Hibernia Review* 23, no. 2 (2019): 95–113.

White, Robert W. *Provisional Irish Republicans: An Oral and Interpretive History*. Westport, CT: Greenwood Press, 1993.

– "Issues in the Study of Political Violence: Understanding the Motives of Participants in Small Group Political Violence." *Terrorism and Political Violence* 12, no. 1 (2000): 95–108.

– *Out of the Ashes: An Oral History of the Provisional Irish Republican Movement*. Dublin: Merrion Press, 2017.

White, Robert W., and Tijen Demirel-Pegg. "Social Movements and Social Movement Organizations: Recruitment, Ideology, and Splits." In *The Troubles: Northern Ireland and Theories of Social Movements*, edited by Lorenzo Bosi and Gianluca De Fazio, 129–45. Amsterdam: Amsterdam University Press, 2017.

Whiting, Matthew. *Sinn Féin and the IRA: From Revolution to Moderation.* Edinburgh: Edinburgh University Press, 2018.

Whiting, Sophie A. *Spoiling the Peace? The Threat of Dissident Republicans to Peace in Northern Ireland.* Manchester: Manchester University Press, 2015.

Whyte, John. *Interpreting Northern Ireland.* Oxford: Oxford University Press, 1991.

Zimmermann, Doron. "Terrorism Transformed: The 'New Terrorism,' Impact Scalability and the Dynamic of Reciprocal Threat Perception." *Connections* 3, no. 1 (2004): 19–40.

Index

Note: Page numbers in *italics* indicate figures and tables.